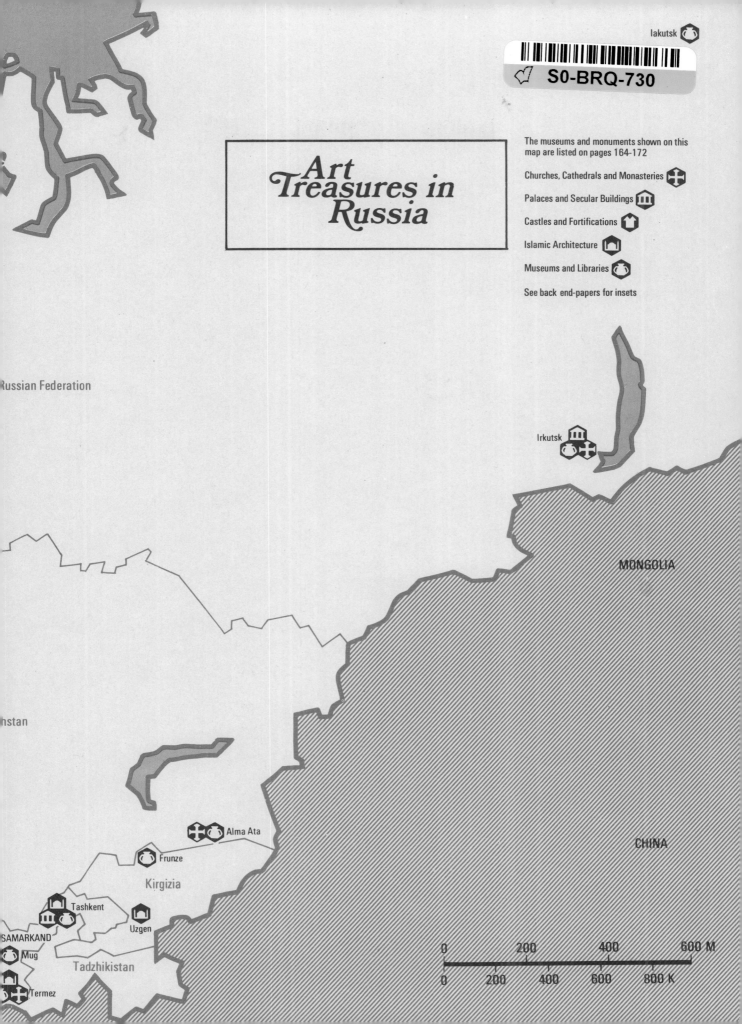

Art Treasures in Russia

The museums and monuments shown on this map are listed on pages 164-172

Churches, Cathedrals and Monasteries

Palaces and Secular Buildings

Castles and Fortifications

Islamic Architecture

Museums and Libraries

See back end-papers for insets

Iakutsk

Russian Federation

Irkutsk

MONGOLIA

CHINA

...hstan

Alma Ata

Frunze

Kirgizia

Tashkent

Uzgen

SAMARKAND

Mug

Tadzhikistan

Termez

0	200	400	600 M

0	200	400	600	800 K

Art Treasures in Russia

Art Treasures in Russia

Monuments, Masterpieces, Commissions and Collections

Introduction by Prince Dimitri Obolensky

Professor of Russian and Balkan History, University of Oxford

McGraw-Hill Book Company

New York Toronto

General Editors
Bernard Myers
New York
Trewin Copplestone
London

half title illustration
Gold chalice,
1664. Armoury Palace,
the Kremlin, Moscow.
frontispiece
Vladimir Borovikovskii
Catherine the Great walking with her Dog
1794.
State Russian Museum, Leningrad.
opposite
Gates painted with the Annunciation
and four saints, early 16th century.
Rublev Museum, Andronikov
Monastery, Moscow.

Library of Congress Catalog Card Number 71–101167
44230
Published jointly by
McGraw-Hill Book Company, New York and Toronto
and The Hamlyn Publishing Company, London and Sydney
Hamlyn House, The Centre, Feltham, Middlesex, England
© The Hamlyn Publishing Group Limited, 1970 All rights reserved
Printed in Italy by Officine Grafiche Arnoldo Mondadori, Verona
Photoset by BAS Printers Limited, Hampshire, England

Contents

Introduction

Since the dawn of recorded history the peoples inhabiting what are now the European regions of the Soviet Union have been in close contact with their neighbours. In ancient and medieval times the Eurasian steppe and its nomadic invaders from Asia impinged on the agricultural communities in the Russian forests and river valleys further north. Across the Black Sea came influences from the Mediterranean world. More recently, and especially since the 17th century, the Russians have borrowed from, and contributed to, the culture of other European nations. Most of the art treasures produced on Russian soil have been shaped by influences stemming from one or several of these cultural areas.

Many of these works were due to a fusion of local and imported traditions. Thus the 'animal style' of the Scythians, the dominant power in the south Russian steppes between the 6th and the 2nd centuries BC,

THE SUMMER PALACE OF ELIZABETH
from 'Plan de la Ville de St Petersburg avec ses principales vues'
1753
Mikhail Makhaev 1716–70
The book of views and maps of St Petersburg, from which this engraving comes, is a valuable source of information about the architecture of the 1750s, in particular about the appearance of buildings, such as the Summer Palace of Elizabeth, which no longer exist. Rastrelli's design reflected Elizabeth's love of pleasure, and this fairy-like palace was her favourite St Petersburg residence.

came into contact with Classical art, brought to this area by Greek settlers on the northern coast of the Black Sea. The world-famous collection of metalwork in the Hermitage Museum in Leningrad shows what could be achieved when Greek goldsmiths adapted their techniques to the taste of their Scythian patrons.

Patronage was of crucial importance in the history of Russian art, not least in the Middle Ages. In the 11th and 12th centuries, and again between 1350 and 1450, architecture and painting embodied the formal principles and mirrored the technical achievements of contemporary Byzantine art. Byzantine masters and their Russian pupils were employed by princes, nobles, prelates, abbots of the great monasteries and, in the late Middle Ages, by rich merchants as well. The more lavish artistic programmes were commissioned, before the Mongol invasion of the 13th century, by the rulers of Kiev and Vladimir, who expressed in the decoration of their churches their personal piety, aspirations to sovereign power, and eagerness to copy the products of Byzantine civilisation.

In medieval Russia, as in other countries of Eastern Europe, local patronage tended to offset in some degree the cosmopolitanism of Byzantine art forms. The Novgorod icons of the 15th century and the work of Andrei Rublev, probably the greatest Russian painter of all times, show how the most refined techniques of Palaeologan art were assimilated and adapted to local tastes. Late medieval Russian painting has no doubt an essence of its own, which can be recognised with experience. Yet it never achieved the coherence or originality of a national school. Until the rise of a recognisably Muscovite tradition of architecture and painting in the 16th century, Byzantine art remained the country's basic international idiom.

The Italian architects imported in the second half of the 15th century to build the cathedrals of the Moscow Kremlin – though in accordance with Byzantine principles of design – were the precursors of the foreign masters – Rastrelli, Quarenghi, Cameron, Rossi – to whose work in and near St Petersburg 'the Palmyra of the north' owes much of its Baroque and Neo-Classical splendour. Russian painting achieved some distinction in the late 18th century, and an international reputation by the turn of the 19th. Portraiture, landscape painting, historical compositions, and especially stage design blossomed in the renaissance of visual arts and poetry which marked the decade between 1900 and 1910. Two factors contributed powerfully to this revival: the growth of museums, where the works of foreign masters acquired earlier by emperors, empresses and European-minded aristocrats were housed, and which helped the public to appreciate both Western art and their own medieval heritage; and the enterprise of a group of wealthy merchants, who purchased in France large collections of Post-Impressionist paintings. The great national collections of Moscow and Leningrad, many of whose masterpieces are reproduced and described in this book, owe a great deal to the discernment and generosity of these pre-Revolutionary patrons of art.

Dimitri Obolensky

The archaeological treasures of the Soviet Union are among the finest and most exciting in the world. They range from ivory votive statuettes to the oldest pile carpet and Persian and Chinese textiles known to us. The area from which these stem is so vast that, in antiquity, people of diverse origins, attainments and backgrounds lived isolated existences in various, widely separated parts of it. Their ethnic and cultural dissimilarities are reflected in the character, styles and nature of the articles which they made for their own use.

The great plain which stretches right across the southern extremity of the country, extending in the east to the borders of China and in the west to Hungary, was inhabited from a very early date. By neolithic times, that is to say by the fourth millennium BC, the two furthest extremities of its Russian section (eastern Siberia and Moldavia) were sparsely inhabited by their first agricultural settlers. The potters of both regions decorated their products with admirably spaced and balanced geometric, circular and corded designs, and they also often enlivened them by the inclusion of animal representations, especially stags, horses and dogs. In addition these gifted craftsmen knew how to depict the human form. Many of their female statuettes were undoubtedly intended to represent divinities. Some of them are primitive in execution; but many of the western figurines of the Tripolie period are spirited and sophisticated, and several are truly elegant and expressive, while the haunting face on a pottery fragment, found in the east at Voznesenovka, must surely have been intended as an exercise in portraiture, for its evocative powers are truly remarkable.

The royal burials of Maikop

The Eneolithic or Copper Age saw in the north of the Caucasus, particularly in the Kuban basin, the rise of great tribal chieftains of immense wealth and power. They must have lived a wholly, or at any rate a largely, nomadic form of life. The royal burials of Maikop reflect something of the splendour to which the mightiest among them had become accustomed. The tomb furnishings included gold, silver and bronze vessels, shaft hole axes and other tools resembling those in use at the time in Mesopotamia, gold, silver and bronze statuettes of lions and bulls, which occasionally also reflect Mesopotamian influence, and costly articles of personal adornment as well as badges of office such as sceptres and diadems. They also contained scores of little stamped and chased gold plaques which had served as dress trimmings. Such plaques remained popular for centuries; the Scythian nomads of the first millennium BC also used vast quantities to trim their clothes.

A silver bowl stands out from among the other impressive finds discovered in the Maikop burials. Its maker adorned it with what may well be one of the world's earliest landscapes. He stamped and chased its surface with representations of a Przevalski horse and a lion, with a bird perching on its back, grazing between two rivers. A bull walks away from each of the rivers, while a bear, a panther and two antelopes stand in a circle below. Mountains, possibly those of the Caucasian range, are outlined on the vessel's neck and provide a background to these scenes.

Greek settlers

The dawn of the Iron Age coincided with the arrival of the Scythian nomads in eastern Europe and the appearance of Greek explorers in the Caucasus and southern Russia. By the 6th century BC the outposts founded by the Greeks on the northern and eastern shores of the Black Sea and the Crimean coast had developed into large, prosperous, self-governing city-states inhabited by Greeks whose outlook and customs remained wholly Greek, as did their art and architecture. These colonials depended

The Ancient Cultures

2500 BC-AD 200

1

STATUETTE OF A WOMAN
2500–2000 BC
clay
height 9·5 in (24 cm)
Institute of History of the Academy of Sciences of Moldavia, Kishinev

The Tripolie culture is remarkable for the high level of taste and sophistication displayed in the decoration of its pottery vessels, decorations which reflect the influence of the Mycenaean world. Though statuettes of female divinities were being made in neolithic and eneolithic times in many areas of the Eurasian plain, few are as elegant as this highly accomplished Tripolie figurine.

for their prosperity upon the trade which they had built up with their homeland, and some of them earned their living as potters, sculptors and metalworkers. These craftsmen not only provided their fellow townsmen with essential goods, but also with luxuries, supplying the wealthiest inhabitants with superb jewellery, sculptures and tableware.

Objects such as these were also coveted by the neighbouring Scythian nomads, and those of them who succeeded in acquiring Greek vases or gold diadems, torques, bangles and earrings valued them so highly that they took them with them to their graves. Scythian chieftains who, while adhering to their native customs, had come nevertheless to appreciate Greek workmanship, must surely have commissioned some of these objects and ordered them to be decorated with scenes of Scythian life. The large electrum vessel in the shape of an amphora, discovered in the burial of Chertomlyk (mid 4th century BC), is perhaps the most spectacular example. Included in its decorations is a frieze showing Scythians dressed in their native clothes engaged in lassoing, breaking in and harnessing their horses. From an artistic point of view, the finest object in the series is perhaps the gold comb from the Solokha burial which dates from the 5th century BC. The high standard of the battle scene which forms its handle has been compared with the Parthenon sculptures.

The Scythians

No two neighbours could have differed more from one another than did the sophisticated, educated and cultured Greek colonials and the Scythians, illiterate and barbarous despite their being among the world's most skilled horsemen. Yet, although the nomadic Scythians were incapable of appreciating the usefulness of money, they were no less proficient than the Greeks at working metals, for they had come to Europe from regions possessing a long tradition in metallurgy.

According to Assyrian records the Scythians reached the northern borders of Assyria in King Sargon's reign (722–705 BC). They came on horseback, and their ability to ride gave them an advantage even over Assyria's highly trained troops, who still fought from horse-drawn chariots. Like all nomads, the Scythians were daring and adventurous. They relied on their successes as warriors and raiders to enrich themselves. The Assyrians were also a martial people and frequently fought neighbours such as the Babylonians, Medes and Urartians. The Scythians seem to have taken part in many of these engagements, sometimes supporting one side, sometimes the other. In the process they gained control of much of north-western Persia during the latter half of the 7th century BC and had soon extended their hold as far as the river Kizil Irmak. They retained their mastery of the area during three or four decades, but were then evicted from Persia by the Medes. Retreating northward, some stayed in the Kuban basin and quickly prospered there, but the majority pushed on till they reached the south Russian plain. The coastal strip to the south was barred to them by the prosperous cities of the Greek colonials. However, the Scythians were able to establish a kingdom in the section of the steppe which lies between the rivers Don and Dnieper.

The Sythians worshipped the elements and believed in a life beyond the grave well nigh identical to that on earth. In the manner of the Egyptians, therefore, they furnished their dead with everything which they had used on earth and were likely to need in the next world, choosing for the purpose the finest articles. Although the construction of the tombs which they made for their chieftains varied slightly according to period and locality, each burial nevertheless reproduced the surroundings to which the dead man had been accustomed in his lifetime. Broadly speaking, the

2

THE CHERTOMLYK AMPHORA
mid 4th century BC
electrum, height 27 in (68·5 cm)
State Hermitage Museum, Leningrad

This vessel was made by a Greek goldsmith living on the northern shores of the Black Sea for a wealthy Scythian patron. The all-over decoration reflects Scythian taste, but the actual motifs and the shape of the amphora are chiefly of Greek origin. The frieze running along the top of the amphora is of particular interest, since it shows Scythian nomads and their horses.

3 *left*
THE MAIKOP BOWL
c. 2300 BC
silver
State Hermitage Museum, Leningrad

The scene on this bowl, found in a royal burial of Maikop, may perhaps be a very early attempt to depict a landscape. It has been suggested that the mountains, which appear around the neck of the vessel, are the Caucasian range and that the two rivers are the Kura and the Terek. The style of the animals displays traces of Meso-potamian influence, yet it is sufficiently distinctive to be accepted as Trans-Caucasian.

4
WOMAN'S FACE
3000 – 2000 BC
pottery
height 5 in (12·5 cm)
Academy of Sciences, Novosibirsk

The type of geometric decorations characteristic of the neolithic period in eastern Siberia, and also found on other vessels from Voznesenovka, are combined on this fragment with a most unusual rendering of a woman's face. The occurrence of the face is remarkable in itself, but it is made still more so by the exceptional degree of feeling with which the potter succeeded in investing it.

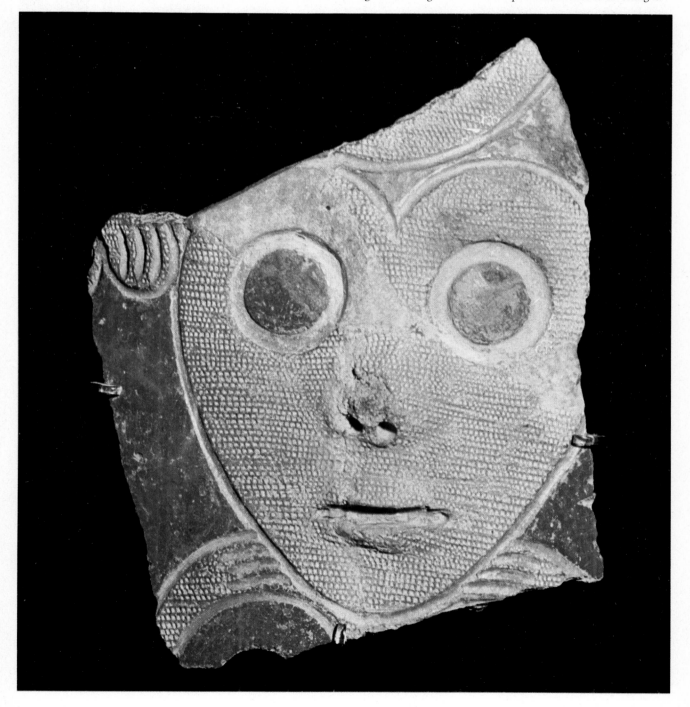

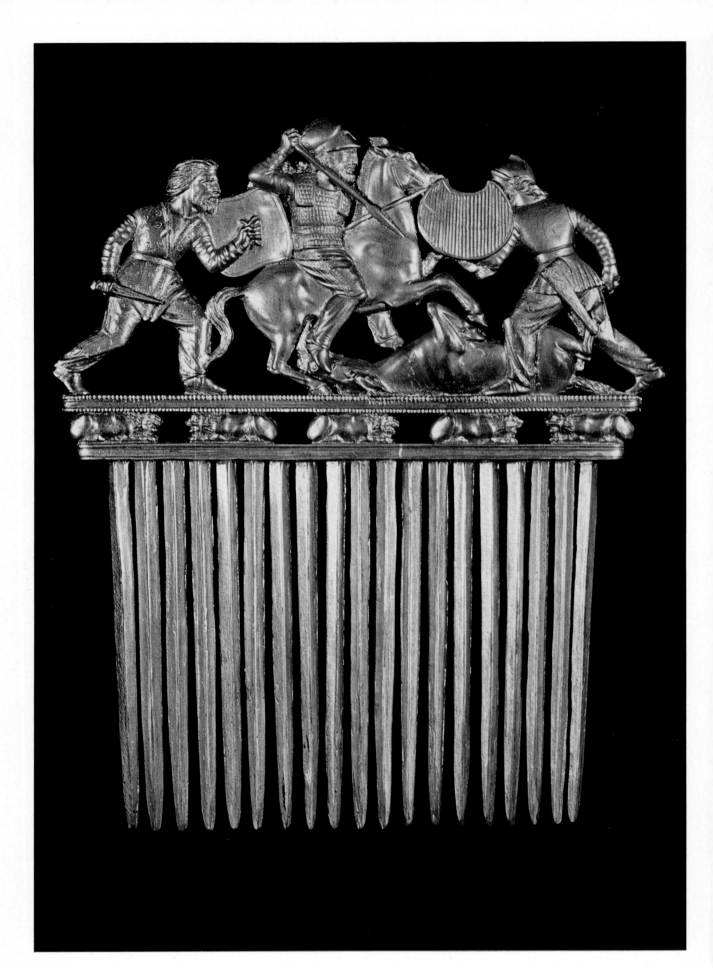

5

THE SOLOKHA COMB
5th – 4th century BC
gold
5 × 4 in (12·3 × 10 cm)
State Hermitage Museum, Leningrad

Though this comb is similar in type to those found in contemporary south Russian burials, it surpasses them in splendour of material and excellence of workmanship. Made by a local Greek for a Scythian patron, it vividly depicts a contest between two mounted nomads and a foot soldier. The horsemen wear their native dress and carry weapons of Scythian origin, but one wears a Corinthian helmet and the other a Macedonian one.

6

THE GREAT GODDESS

5th century BC
appliqué felt on felt
State Hermitage Museum, Leningrad

Among the items preserved in ice in the tombs of the chiefs buried at Pazyryk in the western Altai lay this felt hanging, with a repeat motif of a horseman approaching the great goddess. Each Eurasian tribe had its own way of representing the great goddess which they all worshipped. Here she is shown seated on a throne mounted on turned legs. She wears a straight, close-fitting robe edged either with embroidery, appliqué work or the tiny, stamped gold plaques with which both many Siberian nomads and the Scythians trimmed their garments. She holds the tree of life in one hand and raises the other, perhaps in welcome to the horseman confronting her.

tombs consist either of a single chamber or of a main one with, at most, four subsidiary ones for the companions who were buried with him. In southern Russia and the Kuban the bodies of the dead man's horses were placed outside the chambers, the number of animals varying from very few in a poor burial to almost four hundred at Ulskii. In Siberia, notably in the related frozen Pazyryk burials, a separate chamber was always provided for the horses as an adjunct to the main tomb.

A chieftain's tomb was difficult and costly to build, but the tribe had forty days in which to construct it. While some were doing so, other tribesmen placed the dead man's embalmed body on a cart; they clothed it in his finest garments, laid his most splendid jewellery on it and led it through his territory on a final visit of farewells. On the fortieth day all those concerned assembled at the graveside for the burial. The chieftain's best knife and riding crop were arranged within easy reach of his right hand; his gorytus (a combined bow and quiver case) and his dagger were placed at his left side and his drinking cup, often made of the skull of an enemy mounted in gold, was suspended from his belt. If he had worn armour in battle it was buried with him, together with other greatly prized objects. Changes of clothing were provided; the garments were lavishly trimmed with small, stamped and chased gold plaques and hung **12** on pegs fixed to the wall of the burial chamber. Numerous tools and domestic utensils were included in the furnishings; the ewers, cauldrons and jugs were often of considerable intrinsic value.

According to Herodotus, who devoted a book of his *History of the World* to the Scythians and their neighbouring tribes, exactly a year later fifty stalwart, freeborn Scythians, chosen from the dead man's bodyguard, were killed together with their mounts. Their embalmed bodies were impaled round the mound in order to guard the tomb for evermore. The lives of these warriors were vainly sacrificed, for their sinister presence seldom succeeded in deterring robbers from plundering the mounds. Almost all the tombs which have been excavated were found to have been rifled in antiquity, yet archaeologists have recovered an astonishing number of gold and silver articles from them. The majority take the form of gold casings or solid plaques varying in size from the very small dress **7, 8** trimmings to others measuring a foot in length, which were probably made to adorn the centre of a chieftain's shield. Scythian art is to be seen **13** at its purest and best in the latter.

The animal art of the Scythians

The importance played by animals in the art of many periods is immense. It was, however, the Eurasian nomads of the 1st millennium BC, more particularly Scythians of southern Russia, who transformed animal representations from a feature in art into a distinct form and created an animal art of unusual and compelling beauty, though one which was essentially decorative in purpose and character.

There is nothing surprising about the importance which these pastoral communities attached to the animal world, but the quality and nature of the animal art which the Scythians evolved remain a source of lasting astonishment, admiration and delight. Even a casual glance at their works suffices to convince us that the Scythians, and some of the tribesmen of slightly different stock who shared their culture and way of life (such as those who buried their dead at Pazyryk in the western Altai), possessed **6** remarkable artistic abilities and an unusually keen eye and vivid imagination.

Since nomadism obliges its followers strictly to limit the number of their possessions, they gave expression to their creative impulses by adorning their clothes, weapons, tools, jewellery, furniture, indeed all and each of their few possessions, with an almost overall form of decoration. Because of their love, mastery and dependence on the horse much of their art is related to that animal. They took such immense pride and delight in adorning their mounts that the majority of the objects recovered from their graves consist of harness ornaments. Furthermore, since practically every Scythian burial is also a horse burial the number of harness ornaments is very great, though, surprisingly, the horse itself is seldom represented in Scythian art.

13
15 The gold recumbent stag of the 6th century BC from the Kostromskaia burial, the gold panther of similar date and others of comparable quality are magnificent examples of the metalworker's art. The stag appears more often than any other animal in Scythian art. The Kostromskaia example presents it in the pose which is especially characteristic. It is kneeling with its legs carefully folded over to form a straight line corresponding to that of its body, while the antlers form another straight line along its back. Though appearing to be at rest, its head is raised as if sniffing danger, so that it seems to be on the point of taking flight. The treatment is typical of the style for, although the conception is naturalistic and based on close observation of nature, the rendering is stylised in such a way as to stress the animal's chief characteristics, which in the stag's case are those of speed and grace. Thus, although the pose is a static one, the impression derived from it is one of movement. This is partly achieved by working the metal into slightly inclined planes which, by catching the light, seem to reflect the ripple of the animal's muscles.

Scythian animal representations are intensely vigorous. The animal is frequently shown in a flying gallop, or with its body lithely bent into a
15 circle or contorted so that the hind quarters become inverted. Fighting animals, mythical creatures, such as the griffins which were thought to mount guard over the world's gold supply somewhere in the neighbourhood of Tibet, imaginary cat-like animals, and a series of semi-animal, semi-bird creatures, or a compound of bird and animal with human or animal heads of heraldic and challenging appearance, abound. A large
11 beaked bird was also frequently portrayed.

The Scythian and Pazyryk nomads took such delight in overall decoration and in animal forms, that they sometimes went to the length of
11 filling the empty portions on the body of one creature with representations of other animals and of extending the extremities of one beast, such as its ear, tail, wing or antler, to form a distinctive feature of another. They also often included floral motifs in their art, but the majority of the geometric forms which so frequently occur probably possessed a religious or magical significance. The rosette, for instance, was associated with the sun cult.

The Scythians did not object to the depiction of the human form. Although many of the representations were probably made for religious
6 purposes (for example, the felt hanging from Pazyryk has a repeat motif executed in appliqué work of a female deity granting an audience to a horseman), others clearly were not. Many of the human representations lack the fine quality of the animal designs and are primitive in conception and coarse in execution. Some, however, are more accomplished and possess definite artistic merit.

The ability of the Scythians to assess and appreciate the qualities of Greek art was paralleled by their interest in the art of other of their neighbours. Earlier the Kuban group had already proved capable of doing so and of fusing certain foreign elements with those belonging to their

7
SWORD SHEATH *detail*
6th century BC
wood cased in gold
haft length 6·2 in (15·5 cm) width 2·9 in (7 cm)
State Hermitage Museum, Leningrad

Two of the earliest Scythian burials, those of Kelermes in the Kuban and the so-called Melgunov on the Dnieper, are among the richest so far found. Both contained objects which reflect the influence of Assyria and its satellites, and include two almost identical gold-encased wooden sword sheaths. The decoration of the sheaths includes fantastic monsters each with a lion's tail and feet, a griffin's head and fish-shaped wings. They advance in single file, alternate ones holding drawn bows. The example shown here comes from the Kelermes burial.

8
MIRROR CASING
6th century BC
silver-gilt 6·8 in (17 cm)
State Hermitage Museum, Leningrad

This remarkable mirror comes from the Kelermes burial. The silver-gilt embossed, chased and engraved casing exactly reproduces the decorations executed on the mirror itself. The designs occupy eight triangular-shaped compartments each filled with figures of magical or religious significance. They include the great goddess of Asia, and confronted and superimposed real and imaginary beasts which come from Eastern sources.

9
A GRIFFIN ATTACKING AN ELK
1st century AD
woven material, felt appliqué and silk embroidery, mounted on leather
State Hermitage Museum, Leningrad

own repertory. The gold casing on the sword sheaths and on a mirror from the 6th-century BC Kelermes barrow are adorned with animal decorations stemming from the Orient. Some are shown disposed in single file in the manner which characterises Assyrian and Achaemenid art. The Pazyryk nomads were equally responsive. From China they acquired a superb silk which antedates other known examples by some five hundred years, as well as a carriage which could be dismantled if necessary and reassembled again. Finely woven wool textiles and some knotted wool pile carpets were also brought from Persia to adorn their burial chambers. One dating from the 5th century BC survives virtually entire and shows that, some 2,500 years ago, carpets were being knotted in Persia in the same way as they are today, and that figural motifs figured as prominently in them as the geometric and floral.

7, 8

10

Other nomadic tribes

The culture which is defined as the Scythian survived for many centuries among the nomadic communities which contributed to its formation. In the 1st century AD the Mongoloid Hiung-nu chieftains buried at Noin Ula in Outer Mongolia were provided with graves which in many respects resembled those of the Pazyryk and related Altaian tombs. The seven large mounds which have been excavated at Noin Ula contained long corridors leading to the burial chambers situated in each case some seven metres below ground level. As at Pazyryk, the walls were covered with elaborately worked hangings. Some displayed human forms, but the ceiling of the richest burial chamber was covered with a woven woollen cloth on which splayed-out, double-headed tigers had been worked. Their bodies are formed of black and white stripes; their heads are placed at each extremity; the paws are embroidered.

In all these mounds the dead had been laid in wooden coffins; the one accompanying the tiger hanging had been placed on a superb woven woollen textile mounted on a fine leather lining. Its central design shows a battle between an elk, a griffin, a yak and a beast of prey of Scytho-Altaian character; stylised plants complete the composition. The design is carried out in coloured appliqué feltwork and chain-stitch embroidery. On stylistic grounds alone it would have been difficult to date the textile with any great exactitude, but the presence in the tomb of Chinese silk fabrics and Graeco-Bactrian and Graeco-Parthian woven woollen material would have provided an approximate dating. However, the grave also contained a Chinese lacquer cup inscribed in Chinese with the names of the three craftsmen who had, so it says, made it on 15th September AD 13 for use in the Shahlin Palace.

9

The actual faces of a somewhat similar group of Hunnic people living on the Enisei from about the 2nd century BC to the 4th century AD have been preserved for us in a series of about sixty masks, some of which are actual death masks, while the others are modelled portraits. They are ochre

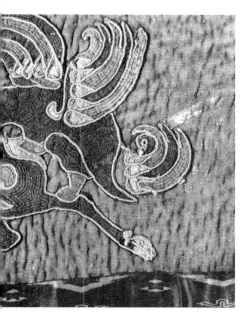

In 1924 the tomb of a Mongol chieftain was excavated at Noin-Ula, some seventy miles north of Urga in northern Mongolia. The finds included a wide variety of objects and textiles, as well as some large carpets made of woven material decorated with silk embroidery and appliqué coloured felts with cord outlines. One carpet of Scytho-Siberian style displays in the centre the characteristic motif of a griffin attacking an elk. Its colours range from brown to purple.

in colour, with the lips and eyelashes indicated by paint. Those of women have painted necklaces, and the vast majority also have on their cheeks and foreheads blue, red or green double-axe and spiral motifs, which perhaps represent tattoos. Some of the men had been buried with the stone scale armour and helms which they had worn in battle; often the helms had designs of real and imaginary animals painted on them, which may have served a magical purpose.

The people depicted on the masks belonged to the Tashtyk culture which was strongly influenced by China. South of Abakan, some four hundred miles south of Krasnoiarsk, archaeologists discovered a large and elaborately designed house built of clay and roofed with tiles. It was heated by a hypocaust system and contained Chinese inscriptions of the 1st century BC.

The survival of Scythian influences

Meanwhile, in southern Russia the Scythians were being superseded by the Sarmatians and were destroyed by them by the 2nd century AD. The region's new rulers were of similar origin to the Scythians; their way of life closely resembled the Scythian, and so did their art, though they made greater use of coloured inlays and gems to obtain the polychrome effects which became one of its chief characteristics. The Goths acquired the Scythian type of animal art from the Sarmatians and retained many of its forms. They made particular use of the large beaked bird popular among the Scythians and helped to transmit it to the Merovingian and Saxon worlds.

It was not until the 6th century AD that the Slavs, who had turned eastward on abandoning their Carpathian homelands, settled in southern and western Russia to serve as the core of the nation which was later to take root there. Though poor and primitive to begin with, by the 8th century some of them were living in settlements which were far from insignificant. Unfortunately very few objects of importance have been recovered from such sites. Their scarcity must be attributed, at any rate in part, to the thoroughness with which the instructions of Vladimir, prince of Kiev, were carried out when in 988 he ordered the destruction of all objects associated with paganism, following his decision to adopt Orthodox Christianity as the official religion of the principality. Only an occasional figure escaped to reveal that the pagan Slavs preferred to place their hopes on a four-faced idol capable of deflecting evil from any of the four major points of the compass. A considerable number of amulets survive, however, many taking the form of a horse's head, the emblem of Apollo's steed, others portraying female divinities. Some show these goddesses with swan attributes, others reflect the influence of certain strongly Hellenistic plaques produced at a late date by the Crimean Scythians. A number of ancient pagan emblems also survive in Russian folk art. The more usual of these consist of solar symbols, such as stars and rosettes, or representations of the great goddess who was worshipped alike throughout the ancient Orient and by the Eurasian nomads of the first millennium BC. Sometimes a design displays an obvious link with a Scythian prototype. When the connection is as marked as it is in an iron weather cock belonging to the Historical Museum in Moscow, dating from the 17th or very early 18th century – when Scythian representations of similar forms were unknown – it becomes difficult to discount the possibility of certain Scythian traditions having survived into the 6th century AD, when the pagan Slavs would have been able to adopt them and extend their life span.

Tamara Talbot Rice

10

THE PAZYRYK CARPET
detail
5th century BC
knotted wool
74·5 × 78·5 in (189 × 200 cm)
State Hermitage Museum, Leningrad

This deep red and yellow carpet was found in one of the Pazyryk barrows; it is the oldest knotted woollen pile carpet in existence. Of the two most important bands, one contains elks arranged in single file, while in the other, riders, advancing in the opposite direction to the elks, alternate with pedestrians leading horses. The centre and intervening borders contain either star shapes or griffins.

11

BEAKED BIRD'S HEAD
5th century BC
bronze
height 10·5 in (27 cm)
State Hermitage Museum, Leningrad

This exceedingly spirited rendering of the head of the large beaked bird, which plays a prominent part in Scythian art, formed the decorative top of a ceremonial or religious standard. The primitive, but typical practice of filling gaps with representations of other animals is used here with a great feeling for balance and form. It comes from the Ulskii barrow.

12 *below*

BELT BUCKLE

4th century BC – 2nd century AD
cast and chased gold
width 4·75 in (12 cm)
State Hermitage Museum, Leningrad

This B-shaped belt buckle represents a
winged and horned lion-griffin attacking
a horse. The composition is distinguished
by its linear rhythm. Characteristic
features are the dot and comma muscle
markings, the ball-shaped terminal of the
griffin's horn, the leaf terminal of its tail (a
Persian element), as well as the horse's
short mane and long, flowing tail. In
particular, the manner in which the hind
quarters of the horse are turned in the
opposite direction from the rest of its body
typifies the animal art of the Scythian and
allied cultures.

13 *right*

THE KOSTROMSKAIA STAG

6th century BC
chased gold
width 17·75 in (20 cm)
State Hermitage Museum, Leningrad

This gold plaque, which originally
decorated the centre of a chieftain's shield,
is among the masterpieces of Scythian art.
The recumbent position of the stag is
typical of the Scythian style. The impression of movement and vitality is
characteristically created by the play of
light on the inclined planes of the metal.
The rendering is both naturalistic and
stylised.

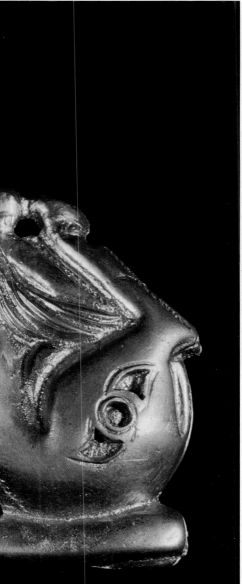

14 *top*

SARMATIAN BOWL

2nd century AD
glass, gold, pearls, cornelians, garnets
height 4 in (10 cm)
State Historical Museum, Moscow

Although the Sarmatians retained many of
the animal forms associated with Scythian
art, they delighted in the polychrome
effects obtained with coloured inlays and
semi-precious stones. They made much
use of tiny gold granules and also of
delicate gold filigree. These elements of
Sarmatian art are employed to advantage
in the gold animal-shaped handles and
bejewelled mount which were fitted to this
glass bowl.

15 *above*

A PANTHER

6th century BC
chased gold
diameter 4·25 in (11 cm)
State Hermitage Museum, Leningrad

This is one of the earliest plaques to combine Scythian and Siberian characteristics.
The panther's body is bent into a circle in
a manner which is typical of the style.
Its ear, eye, nostril and tail originally held
coloured inlays. The metal is worked with
superb skill, and, despite its unnatural
position, the animal has a reality which is
almost natural. This plaque was one of the
first collected by Peter the Great.

For far too long the great civilisations which flourished in the ancient Orient and in Greece have diverted attention from the vigorous and distinctive cultures which were evolving at the time in Transcaucasia. In the 9th century BC, while the Assyrians were trying to subjugate their neighbours, and the Medes were striving to become a nation, some Hurrian tribes settled on the shores of Lake Van, in what is now eastern Turkey, and the region in the Soviet Union to the north of it. Their boldness and enterprise enabled them to form themselves rapidly into the kingdom known as Urartu. It entered its period of greatness in the 8th century when the Urartians, led by their king, Argishti I, expanded their territory as far as Lake Urmiia. Under Argishti's son, Sarduri I, they proceded to harass the borders of Assyria, even though their ties with that country had been so close in the past that their forebears had adopted certain features of Assyria's art and culture to serve as the basis of their own. Semiramis, the legendary founder of their capital of Toprak Kale, a flourishing city situated on the outskirts of Van, was reputed to have brought twelve thousand labourers and six hundred master masons from Assyria to build it for her.

The kingdom of Urartu

Urartu appears to have been one of the earliest, large slave-owning societies in the area known to history. The system enabled it to become wealthy and to acquire such vast stocks of valuable metals as to arouse the envy of the Assyrians, who frequently took up arms in the hope of seizing some of the Urartians's gold, silver, copper, and bronze supplies, as well as their iron which was just as valuable at that time. Argishti I built a series of forts and defences to protect his territory. One fort, that of Argishihinili, situated to the west of Erevan, was excavated recently and found to contain an inscription assigning it to his reign (c. 778–50 BC). The wars of 743 and 714 appear to have been fought with particular ferocity; ties of vassalship were imposed on the Urartians as a result, but they do not seem to have been of a crippling nature.

In recent years two very important Urartian sites have been excavated in Armenia. One, identified as the town of Irepuni, lies on the southern outskirts of Erevan and dates from the 8th century BC. Though Irepuni contained a handsome palace and much else of outstanding interest, the excavations of Teishebaini proved even more rewarding. There the citadel occupied the summit of the hill of Karmir-Blur, which is also situated on the outskirts of Erevan, overlooking the river Razdan. It was built by King Rusa, Argishti's son, in the latter half of the 8th century to serve as the headquarters of a governor and the Urartian kings must at times have stayed there; it also contained a shrine. An inscription on a bronze door bolt found on the site reads 'Of Rusa, son of Argishti, this town of Teishebaini'.

The ruins of Karmir-Blur extend over ten acres. The citadel took the form of a single structure. Its walls were built of sun-dried bricks mixed with straw laid on a foundation of large stones, with battlemented towers set at their corners. The Scythians besieged Karmir-Blur as they retreated northward from Persia's borders and managed to break into and loot it, but they left behind much of value and interest for the archaeologists to recover from the ruins. These exciting objects are to be seen admirably displayed in the Historical Museum of Armenia at Erevan. They include some bronze belts, recalling the rather earlier ones associated with Georgia, as well as twenty helms and fourteen shields of Assyrian shapes. Some two hundred of the objects are thought to have been made especially for the Urartian kings and their courtiers. Many bear Assyrian inscriptions which enable them to be dated precisely. The helms include one inscribed

The Civilisations of the South West

800 BC–AD 1600

16
TWO PENDANTS
from the Akhalgorsk hoard
5th century BC
gold
State Museum of Georgia, Tbilisi
The goldsmith who made these superb gold pendants was influenced by the contemporary art of neighbouring Persia, but he infused his work with a wholly Georgian vitality. His artistry expressed itself with particular felicity in the rendering of the horses; nevertheless, their style and trappings remain essentially Achaemenid. Rosettes and disks figure frequently in the arts of the Perso-Caucasian and southern Russian areas, where they often served as symbols of the sun cult.

with the name of Argishti I and three with that of Sarduri II, while the inscriptions on the shields refer either to Argishti I, Sarduri II or Rusa I and therefore cover a century and a half—a passage of time which brought no changes to the style of decoration. The animal motifs, like all those which figure in Urartian art, derive from Assyrian prototypes; they are static yet heraldic in pose, staid rather than forbidding. Their appearance had not markedly changed by the latter part of the 7th century, when the Medes put an end to the Urartian kingdom, which had been too much weakened by the Scythian onslaught to be able to defend itself effectively from these new invaders.

Ancient Armenia

The people of Hai were to replace the Urartians in Transcaucasia. Their original homeland was probably situated in the district of Ersincan, in eastern Turkey, but they slowly moved northward from it, gaining in strength and importance as they did so. By the 4th century BC they must already have been a force to be reckoned with, since Darius included their name in the inscription which was cut at his orders on the face of the great rock of Bisitun in Persia. The Hai gradually took possession of the territory which had a century or two earlier formed the Urartian kingdom, absorbing as they did so the few remaining pockets of Urartian and Scythian inhabitants. Their kingdom became known to the Persians as that of Armena. Though small, it soon acquired immense strategic importance for the Persians on the one hand and, first for the Romans, then for the Byzantines, on the other. Sometimes one of these great powers, sometimes the other, reduced the Armenians (the Ararat people of the Bible) to the status of members of a satellite country; at other times they divided them into two subject zones. Throughout, most of the Armenians lived by means of agriculture, though their kings encouraged the growth of craftsmanship and trade in the towns.

Armenia's greatness dawned with the reign of Tigranes II (95 – 56 BC). Until about the 5th century AD first he, then his followers, used the citadel of Garni as their summer palace and military headquarters. Its fortifications still rise above the rivers Azad and Gegard to enclose among its splendid ruins the remains of a fine Classical temple. In the 7th century AD the Arabs conquered Armenia and established their capital in the thriving town of Dvin. Founded in the 4th century AD, it had by then developed into a prosperous industrial and commercial centre, the full importance of which has been revealed by recent excavations on the site.

Armenia regained its independence two and a half centuries later, and its ruler marked the change by transferring the capital from Dvin to Ani, a town which he had founded for the purpose. It now lies just within Turkey's boundaries, a ruined and deserted site of immense beauty and architectural interest. Indeed, present-day Armenia remains rich in build-
17 ings of comparable importance. The ruins of the castle of Anberd, once the stronghold of a local chieftain, are among the most romantic of these. This magnificent example of domestic architecture remained in use into the 12th century, and its walls contain remains of several important domestic and religious buildings of various dates.

Christian Armenia

Armenia has the distinction of being the first country to adopt Christianity as its official religion. Though King Tiridates III may have been baptised as early as c. 280, the country's conversion did not occur till 301, when it was brought about as a result of the missionary activities undertaken there by the Armenian prince known to Christendom as St Gregory the Illuminator. It was Gregory who established the Church's head-

17
THE CASTLE OF ANBERD
12th century
In addition to these powerful walls, the castle of Anberd was afforded further protection by its position on a promontory between the confluence of two rivers. The local chieftain who built it clearly needed to take strong precautions to ensure his safety from the invaders who throughout the Middle Ages frequently raided Armenia.

18
THE CATHEDRAL OF ECHMIADZIN
5th – 7th century
The Monastery of Echmiadzin lies fifteen kilometres west of Erevan where, in the 6th century BC, Erevard I founded a town. The square walls of the monastery enclose Armenia's mother-church and cathedral, founded in the 5th century, but often altered. The exterior of the cathedral is adorned with sculptured decorations. Its main turret is pencil shaped and twelve sharply pointed triangular sections emphasise its line. Within, the throne of Armenia's archbishop stands on the spot where, according to tradition, Christ appeared before St Gregory.

35 quarters at Echmiadzin, near Erevan, where they remain to this day. A
church, in the form of a small basilica, was built there in 303. In 483 it was
18 superseded by a more elaborate cathedral, which was in its turn replaced
in the 8th century by one in the fully developed national style.

A number of Armenia's churches survive from the 5th century and they
are some of the earliest known to us. They are built of blocks of carefully
dressed and skilfully laid stone, so that the masonry forms one of their chief
glories. Though the earliest churches were basilican in shape, others were
among the first to be roofed with a tall drum surmounted by a high,
, 243 slender, pencil-tipped turret of distinctive shape. From a slightly later date
their outer walls were often broken up by pilasters, blind arcading and
similar features, and adorned with elaborate sculptures. These generally
consist of biblical scenes executed in rather low relief, though they sometimes include a portrait of the church's founder. Mural paintings played a
very important role in the decoration of the interiors, but today the skill of
9, 33 Armenia's artists is even more evident in the numerous illuminations with
which they adorned their religious books. Though these follow the
Byzantine iconographic tradition and generally reflect Syrian influence,
their style is an entirely distinct one. Masterpieces such as the 9th-century
Lazarev Gospel or the 10th-century Echmiadzin Gospel can now be seen
at their best in the superb Martanadoran Library recently built at Erevan
to contain them.

Trialeti and Koban cultures of Georgia

Georgia, situated to the north of Armenia, has an even longer and no less
impressive artistic history than Armenia. Metallurgy developed there
early and was well established in several areas by the start of the Bronze
Age. The Trialeti necropolis situated in the foothills of the Caucasian
range, about 120 kilometres to the west of Tbilisi, is of exceptional richness. It came into use in about 1800 bc, when the cremated bodies of the
dead were buried there in four-wheeled wooden carts placed in individual
grave chambers. These had been furnished with painted pottery vessels,
tools and weapons which sometimes included silver daggers and arrows
with flint heads. Objects of high intrinsic value, such as gold or silver
vessels, were found in the richer burials, and two cups are especially
29 interesting. One is of heavy gold studded with semi-precious stones, such
as agates and turquoises, set amidst exquisitely worked filigree, a technique in which the Georgians were later to excel. Lying beside the cup
was an elegant little silver bucket fitted with a gold handle and decorated
30 with a hunting scene. The other cup is of silver, adorned with two bands
of elaborate chased and embossed decorations; the upper one contains a
procession of twenty-three animal-headed human beings carrying offerings to a seated deity, and in the lower one stags advance in single file. The
bronze belts found at Trialeti are often decorated with hunting scenes set
within borders, which look as if they have been derived from textiles.

From about 1200 bc to ad 500 metalworkers living in the foothills of
western Georgia, in the area known to the ancients as Colchis, created a
culture which has been given the name of Koban after the first village in
which their products were discovered. These craftsmen adorned their
wares with animal designs, but between about 1200 and 1000 bc they
produced a series of ceremonial axes of unusual shape which they decorated
with geometric and astral motifs as well as with stylised animal forms,
particularly stags.

Georgia was as much coveted by the Persians and the Romans as
Armenia, but at an even earlier date Greek explorers penetrated to the
coastal strip known to them as Iberia. The legend of Jason's search for the

19
TWO EVANGELISTS
from a gospel, MS no. 2877
first half of 12th century
manuscript
Martanadoran Library, Erevan

The Armenians adorned the interiors of
their churches with murals and their
religious books with illuminations. Though
their paintings conformed with Byzantine
iconography, they often reflect Syrian
influence in addition to native traits. In this
miniature the native tradition was responsible for the strongly individualised
character of the faces, the rhythmical
nature of the draperies and the choice of
deep colours.

20 *above*
ST GEORGE
first half of 11th century
silver
16·25 × 11·5 in (41·5 × 29 cm)
Historico-Ethnological Museum, Kutaisi

From at least as early as the 6th century
the Georgians were producing silver icons,
gospel covers and plaques with many of
the qualities of sculpture. Until well
into the 18th century the workmanship
was generally of the finest order; the
repoussé plaques were carefully chased,
while delicate filigree work provided the
intricate background decorations. On this
11th-century example a spirited St George
is depicted attacking the Roman emperor
Diocletian, persecutor of the Christians.

Golden Fleece may be derived from the region's mineral wealth. The influence which the Greek adventurers succeeded in exercising over the
local craftsmen is reflected, alongside that of the Scythians, in the bronze
and iron belt buckles which were produced by the Koban metalworkers **28**
from about the 5th century BC onwards. However, Achaemenid elements often prevail in the gold jewellery and in the silver vessels made
elsewhere in Georgia at a similar and slightly later date; these are well to
the fore in objects such as those belonging to the Akhalgorsk hoard. **16**

Christian Georgia

The Georgians became converted to Christianity very soon after the
Armenians. Like the Armenians they had abundant supplies of good
building stone and were such excellent masons that some of the churches
which they built in the 4th century survive, though ruined, today. The
earliest were small, but by the 5th century many spacious basilicas were
being erected. The Sion at Bolnisi shows the style at its best, and the

21 *far left*

DZHVARI CHURCH

586/7–604
stone

At their conversion the Georgians placed a wooden cross on the summit of a hill overlooking the meeting point of the Kura and Aragva rivers. Early in the 6th century they erected beside it a chapel (now a ruin), and later they built Dzhvari Church nearby. Portraits of the royal founder of the church and two of his relatives are carved on the façade, and the tympanum above the south door is filled with a sculpture of two angels raising a cross.

22 *above left*

THE CASTLE OF ANANURI

16th–17th century

The stronghold of Ananuri, a chieftain's residence, lies to the north of Tbilisi, commanding the Georgian Military Highway. The older of its two churches is a single-aisled building of the 16th century, roofed with a pencil-shaped dome. Ananuri reached the height of its prosperity in the 17th century, and the larger church dates from 1689.

23 *left*

METEKHI CHURCH

13th century
Tbilisi

Built of dressed stone in the 13th century on the site of an earlier basilica, Metekhi belongs to the group of cruciform-shaped single-domed Imeretian churches which is best represented by the Church of the Virgin's Birth, Gelati. However, in contrast to other east Georgian examples of the type, Metekhi and the Sion Cathedral in Tbilisi are the only ones in which semi-circular apses project at the east end.

inscription which assigns the building to the years 493/494 is the oldest known example of Georgian epigraphy. The church is one of the first to have a protruding apse, while its dome served as a model for churches such as those at Dzhvari and at Mtskheta. **21**

It was in the 4th century BC that some Georgians settled on the summit of the hill situated close to Samtavro, overlooking the Kura river. Calling their settlement Armazi, they fortified it and used it as their capital till the 2nd century BC, when they abandoned it in favour of Mtskheta. In the 6th century AD Tbilisi became Georgia's capital, but Mtskheta retained **23** its religious significance, for it continued to serve as its ecclesiastical see. The burial ground of Samtavro testifies to the antiquity of the region, for it came into use in prehistoric times and continued until the rise of Tbilisi. Though a stone church was built at Mtskheta early in the 4th century, the cruciform church that replaced it in the 7th century holds a special place in the history of the country's architecture, for it is one of the first, possibly even the first, to have been built in Georgia on that plan.

Many monastic complexes of great splendour occupy beautiful sites in various parts of the country, the quality of the architecture helping to **22** enhance the beauty of the setting. Among the finest of these is the monastery which King Bagrat III founded in the 10th century at Gelati, near Kutaisi. Domestic and defensive architecture also attained a high standard from an early date, and sculpture, painting and the minor arts kept pace with building developments.

Georgian churches are rich in fine sculptures which are often of early date. The majority are in low relief and appear on pilasters and blind arcading as well as on decorative panels, arches, window and door surrounds. Animal, floral and geometric motifs are numerous, so are biblical scenes and even portraits of donors.

Inside the churches sculptured capitals and altar screens make a special contribution to the building's beauty; in these Byzantine influence often predominates, but at times the impact made on Georgia by Sassanian Persia, even by central Asia, is also noticeable. The Georgians liked to cover the floors of their churches with glazed tiles or stone and marble mosaic pavements, to adorn their walls with magnificent religious mural paintings and to place icons in the body of the church. The paintings are often of the highest quality, but it is in metalwork that the national genius **20** is perhaps to be seen at is finest.

From at least as early as the 6th century, and possibly even before that date, the Georgians were producing large numbers of repoussé and chased silver plaques depicting saints and biblical scenes, which are the **20** equal of their sculpture. Their jewellers also excelled in making the gold cloisonné enamels – among the most difficult techniques which a medieval goldsmith was called upon to master – which figure so prominently in Byzantine art. Georgian enamels differ in colour from the Byzantine. Both schools are represented in the most precious of all Georgia's treasures, the 10th-century triptych known as the Khakuli Triptych, a **32** masterpiece which owes much of its quality to the delicacy of the gold filigree work covering its surface.

Fergana, Sogdiana and Khorezm

While these developments were taking place in Transcaucasia, very different trends were making themselves felt in what is now Soviet Central Asia, but then constituted the small states of Fergana, Sogdiana and Khorezm, which acted as lively cultural outposts. As all three had access to the waters of the Amu Dar'ia, agriculture had at first provided the basis for their economy, but greater understanding of irrigation had encouraged the growth of towns. Urbanisation was stimulated afresh by the economic policies evolved for the area by Alexander the Great and the Seleucid rulers who assumed control following his death in 323 BC. The multiplication of towns raised the standard of craftsmanship and stimulated its growth throughout western Turkestan, with the textile industry flourishing especially in Sogdiana. The nobility became wealthy in all three states, and as a result many of its members were able to build large castles and hunting lodges in districts which were being reclaimed from the desert.

In Achaemenid times Persian influence predominated in the towns of western Turkestan, as those of Sassanian Persia were to do later. However, Alexander the Great's conquests in central Asia brought a new element to the area by drawing Greek artists to it in the wake of the victorious armies. The artistic traditions which the Greeks had introduced had scarcely had time to establish themselves before Roman traders started to arrive in the neighbouring Baktrian areas of Afghanistan in search of supplies of silk. Under their guidance the Greek styles which the local artists assimilated were not the pure ones of Classical Greece, but rather Hellenistic versions which had been evolved by the Romans and by the Parthians, who had replaced the Seleucids in western Turkestan and northern Persia.

The Parthians established their first capital at Nisa, a site situated some twenty-eight kilometres from Ashkhabad in Tadzhikistan, using it as such till c. AD 10, when they abandoned it in favour of Dara in Damgan. At Nisa Parthia's rulers and noblemen continued to wear clothes of nomadic cut, even though they were living in great urban splendour. Excavations carried out on the site in recent years led to the discovery of one of their temples and a necropolis. The great hall in the palace must have been spectacular; it had a flat roof supported by four piers or pillars, between each of which stood baked clay statues of men and women over life-size. The finds included a remarkable series of ivory rhytons (drinking horns) mounted in silver or gold and embellished with carved human figures and heads of Hellenistic style. These rhytons often terminated in an animal's head, and jewels and polychrome glass inlays adorned the finest. Statuettes of deities such as Athene were also found there, as well as figures of sphinxes and other imaginary animals, bronze and iron weapons, painted pottery and fluted glass vessels.

The tradition of representational art was kept alive in western Turkestan, particularly in Sogdiana, by the Tokharians or Kushans, who replaced the Greeks as masters of Baktria late in the 2nd century BC, but it flourished with especial vigour after the Sassanian conquests of 558 in central Asia. Sassanian influence is clearly evident in the fine, though fragmentary, painted shield discovered in the castle of Mug, situated some two hundred kilometres to the east of Samarkand. The castle belonged to a prince of Sogdiana who, in 722, rebelled against the Arab invaders of his country and died as a result. His magnificent castle was abandoned after his death, the desert sands swept over it, and it lay hidden and forgotten for some 1200 years, until a shepherd came across a basket lying in the sand which contained documents in Sogdianian, Arabic, Turkish and Chinese dating from 717–19. Excavations followed, and in the course of them a fine painted shield was discovered.

The first large figural paintings were found between 1947–53 at Varaksha, the capital of a vanished fief in the Bukhara oasis, which had been abandoned in the 9th century. The palace of its chieftains had been adorned 26, 27 in the 8th century with stucco statues and mural paintings of hunting scenes, in which elephants, and both mythical and real animals play a

24

A MUSICIAN FROM AIRTAM

1st century AD
stone
State Hermitage Museum, Leningrad

This head is part of a frieze of musicians and garland bearers found in a building that was probably a monastery in the Buddhist settlement of Airtam. It is thought that the sculptor was of local Baktrian origin, but the style clearly shows Indo-Hellenistic influences.

prominent part. These works contain elements which possess certain affinities both with Persian and nomado-Scythian art. The style of the 6th- to 7th-century mural paintings decorating a temple excavated at Balalyk Tepe, a site in southern Uzbekistan close to the Afghan border, not only reveals especially close links with Sassanian Persia, but also with the inhabitants of the oasis towns of the Tarim basin in eastern Turkestan. One of the compositions here includes some fifty men and women whose clothes closely resemble those depicted in the frescoes of Kizil in eastern Turkestan, though they sit cross-legged in the Sassanian manner and hold vessels of Sassanian shapes.

The sculptures and paintings found in Piandzhikent, some thirty-five kilometres from Bukhara, are even more important, and the sculptured caryatids are the earliest yet discovered in the region. Although some of the statuettes display Indian influences and certain wall paintings (such as a lute player) reflect those of China, Sassanian generally prevail. An important cycle illustrates the Sogdianian burial rite and another episode from Persia's greatest epic, the Shah-nama.

The sculptures which were found in the fortified Khorezmian town of Toprak Kale are better preserved and point to the existence of contacts with the Indo-Hellenistic world of the Kushans and the more markedly Hellenistic one of Baktria. Indo-Hellenistic elements are also apparent in a remarkable sculptured limestone frieze of the 1st century AD from the fortified Buddhist settlement recently discovered at Airtam, eighteen kilometres to the north-west of Termez. Yet, even though Indo-Hellenistic elements were felt so far to the west of their places of origin, they could not compete with the influence which Sassanian Persia established over the inhabitants of western Turkestan, Transcaucasia and, to judge from the number of silver Sassanian vessels discovered in the district of Perm' and neighbouring regions, of eastern Russia also.

Sassanian Persia's artistic conventions became so firmly rooted both in western Turkestan and in Transcaucasia that they survived in certain localities either until the Arabs or the Mongols had put an end to representational art there, or the Mongols had made it impossible for local notables to sponsor the production of works of art.

Caucasian Albania

The traditions stemming on the one hand from Achaemenid and Sassanian Persia, on the other from the Eurasian nomads who formed part of the Scythian world, survived longest in the remote, virtually impregnable little kingdom of Caucasian Albania, a small state situated to the west of Georgian Kakhetiia and bounded on the north by the Derbent range, on the east by the Caspian Sea and on the south by the river Kubachi. Its history begins in the 4th century BC, its first rulers belonging to the Persian house of the Arsacids. Persian influence over Albania, which was established virtually from its inception as a state, persisted even after Gregory the Illuminator had introduced Christianity into the country, and continued to make itself felt in Albania's art for centuries. Even in the 13th century Albania's extremely gifted sculptors and metalworkers were still introducing motifs both of Sassanian and nomadic origin into the decorations with which they adorned their stone panels, and also their bronze cauldrons and vessels. However, by the 16th century these influences had run their course, and Kubachi potters were responding with warmth to contemporary Persian trends, producing under their impact such lovely floral and stylistic decorations that these wares can hold their own beside those of the better known schools of Islamic pottery.

Tamara Talbot Rice

25

STATUE FROM TOPRAK KALE
*3rd – 4th century AD
painted clay
State Hermitage Museum, Leningrad*

The remains of several large houses, an extensive bazaar, three temples and a fine palace indicate that Toprak Kale was a highly prosperous city. It was founded in the 1st century AD, flourished as the capital of Khorezm until the 8th century, and continued to be important until its destruction by the Arabs in the 7th century. In one of the large halls of the palace were found several over-life-size statues of members of the royal house; this example may have represented a wife of one of the kings.

28 *above right*

KOBAN BELT BUCKLE

5th century BC
bronze
State Museum of Georgia, Tbilisi

From the 6th century BC the skilled metalworkers of Colchis were quick to blend
Scythian, Greek and, more especially,
Ionian elements with their native style.
Their belt buckles continued to reflect
these trends even when the Hellenistic
horse replaced the stag as a favourite
central motif. Scythian influence prompted
the retention of roundels on their bodies
and the inclusion of smaller animals in the
spaces available above and beneath the
main composition.

26 *top*

A MOUNTAIN RAM

5th – 6th century AD
alabaster
height 20 in (50 cm)
Historical Museum, Tashkent

Prior to the Arab invasion Sogdia's
chieftains lived at Varaksha. Excavations
undertaken on the sites of its citadel and
palace in 1939 and after the war revealed
the existence of a vital and fascinating
culture in which sculpture played an
important role. Animal motifs and scenes
of Perso-Scythian origins were as popular
there as the equally ancient geometric and
floral compositions. This mountain ram
originally formed part of a hunting scene.

27

HEAD OF A WOMAN

5th – 6th century AD
alabaster
height 3·3 in (8 cm)
Historical Museum, Tashkent

Figural art was highly developed at
Varaksha in the Bukhara oasis where the
finer rooms were often decorated with
large and complex murals and stucco or
alabaster sculptures. Many of the large-
scale stucco statues must be classed as
portraits, but the smaller figural works,
whether architectural adornments
or statuettes, can hardly be regarded as
such. This small alabaster head of a woman,
a fragment of a frieze, nevertheless,
remains full of character, force and vitality.

29 *right*

GOLD TRIALETI CUP

mid 2nd millennium BC
gold and semi-precious stones
State Museum of Georgia, Tbilisi

The restrained decoration of this admirably
proportioned gold cup creates a sumptuous
effect by the use of bands of filigree
studded with round semi-precious stones
around the edge of its rim and base. In the
intervening space similar bands form spiral
designs which must be among the earliest
to figure in metalwork. The base of the cup
is also edged with filigree and has a
triangular-shaped gem set at each of its
quarters.

SILVER TRIALETI CUP

mid 2nd millennium BC
silver
height 4·5 in (11 cm)
State Museum of Georgia, Tbilisi

This silver goblet is perhaps the most
remarkable of the many important objects
recovered from the Trialeti burials, on
account of the scene in the upper of its two
decorated bands. It contains a procession
of twenty-two animal-headed and tailed
beings bringing offerings to a seated
animal-headed deity wearing garments of
Hittite style and holding a vessel. Below
them stags advance in single file in reverse
direction.

31 *above*

WINGED BULL

8th–7th century BC
bronze with traces of gold leaf
State Hermitage Museum, Leningrad

This is one of a pair of winged bulls made in Urartu to serve as
throne terminals. Its legs are folded in the manner of the
recumbent stags of Scythian art. Its head is turned outwards, but
the inset face, probably made of white stone, is missing, as are
the coloured inlays which filled the rectangular incisions on its
wings. It was held in place by the knob at the base.

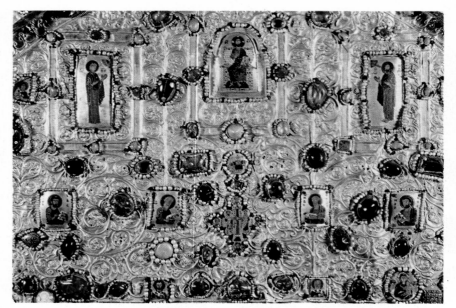

32 *left*

DETAIL OF
THE KHAKULI TRIPTYCH

1125–34
gold, cloisonné enamels,
semi-precious stones
overall 58 × 80 in (145 × 200 cm)
Georgian Museum of Fine Art, Tbilisi

This superb triptych shows the skill of
Georgia's goldsmiths at its finest. It was
designed and made by three jewellers in
the workshops of Gelati Monastery, and
holds the deeply revered 10th-century
Georgian cloisonné enamel of the Virgin,
of which only the face and hands remain.
Its surface is covered with exquisitely
delicate filigree scrolls of Eastern inspiration, which serve as a setting for ninety-
four Byzantine and Georgian gold
cloisonné enamels of various dates as well
as for many gems.

33 *left*

JONAH AND THE WHALE

1288, illumination
attributed to T'oros Roslin
Martanadoran Library, Erevan

Little Armenia in Cilicia, where this
painting was done, became the centre of
Armenian culture following the Mongol
conquest of Armenia. Here the now
elderly painter continued to adhere to the
Syrian style when rendering faces, but
used the precious colour blue lavishly and
also responded to Chinese influence. This
is evident in his treatment of the sea – for
the waves resemble the swirling clouds
seen in Chinese paintings – and in the
tiger-like appearance of his whale.

34 *left*

KUBACHI DISH WITH A LOTUS DESIGN

16th century
pottery
State Hermitage Museum, Leningrad

The contribution of Persian potters to Islamic art is of a high order. Their artistry was so compelling that potters in neighbouring countries found inspiration in their works and often adapted Persian elements to suit their own needs and taste. In the 16th century Caucasian Albanians of the Kubachi district excelled at presenting Eastern floral and leaf motifs in an ordered, yet rhythmical and lively manner. They offset the deep pastel shades of the pattern by means of a near white background.

35

CHURCH OF ST RIPSIME

618
Echmiadzin

The little Church of St Ripsime at Echmiadzin was built by the Catholicos Comitas in 618, but extensively restored in 1892. The plan, a cruciform one with a central dome which in Armenia takes the form of a turret of pencil shape, was popular in Transcaucasia in early Christian times, and is to be found in Georgia, for example at Dzhvari. In Armenia it was often combined with a more complex roof-line.

Of all the regions where architecture was developed under Islamic patronage that of Transcaspia is certainly the least well known. The area, all of it today within the confines of the USSR, has never been easily accessible; before the Revolution only a few very enterprising travellers had visited it, and few scholars had paid serious attention to its monuments; between the two wars it was even more difficult to get there. Even now, when the two most important cities of the area, Bukhara and Samarkand, have become centres of tourism, other less well known places like Uzgen or Urgench are still not easy to visit, though they contain important monuments, while really out-of-the-way places have up to now hardly been investigated even by Russian scholars.

Though the region became particularly important when Tamerlane chose Samarkand as his capital, it is not only the architecture of the Timurid period that is represented; some extremely important buildings survive from earlier times, and excavations, in such places as Termez, have begun to produce finds of very great interest. There are even a few buildings of the 10th century still standing, and monuments of the 11th and 12th are quite numerous in spite of the devastations wrought by the Mongol conquests of the early 13th century. The years around 1300 were those of greatest glory, under the patronage of Tamerlane, who preferred Samarkand to any other place. Thereafter, in spite of wars and conquests, work continued with little interruption, and fine and impressive buildings were even built in the 16th and 17th centuries.

The inhabitants of the area are, and have always been in the main, Turkish speakers. Though the area has sometimes been called Turan, to distinguish it from the Aryan Iran to the south, it has throughout most of its history been closely linked with Persia, and has suffered the same conquests and the same vicissitudes; more often than not the whole area has been controlled by the same rulers.

The early period

In the 10th century, when the story of architecture in Transcaspia begins, both Turan and northern Iran were ruled by the Samanid dynasty, which had been founded by Shah Ismail, a Persian from Balkh. He chose Bukhara as his capital. Among the remains of several buildings of this period, the most interesting of them is a curious structure known as the mausoleum of Shah Ismail. The plan is conservative, but the construction is highly original, for it is built of well baked, buff-coloured bricks which are set three together, alternately horizontally and vertically, so that they produce the effect of a simple over-and-under woven pattern. Inside, however, the setting of the bricks is more varied, and it is one of the earliest examples of the use of bricks as a sort of sculptural ornament.

The Samanids were overthrown by the Karakhan Turks, and a somewhat unsettled period ensued until the arrival of another Turkish group, the Seljuks, under Malik Shah, who conquered Bukhara and Samarkand in 1089. The whole area thereafter enjoyed great prosperity and much building was done. The earliest example that survives is the minaret of Jar Kurgan at Termez, dated 1108–09, which is an impressive structure in spite of the fact that the top section is missing. It is one of a series of fine minarets; the most famous of them is the Kalyan Minaret at Bukhara, which is often called the tower of death, for the later rulers of Bukhara used to execute prisoners by throwing them from the top. There are similar minarets at Dahistan and at Vabkent, and another existed at Uzgen, though what is to be seen today is a 20th-century reconstruction.

The Uzgen minaret is associated with two 12th-century mausoleums, and there is a larger mausoleum of 1157 at Merv which was noted by the

36
VIEW OF THE CHOR-BAKR
Bukhara
Ceramic tilework was used with very great effect in Persian architecture and some of the finest examples are to be found in the buildings of Bukhara and Samarkand. In later times the designs were painted below glaze on large square tiles; earlier they were produced by cutting up monochrome tiles and piecing them together like a mosaic; that is the technique employed here. The predominating colours are black and brilliant blue.

traveller Yakut because it could be seen from two days' journey away (this was not surprising, as the country is flat and the dome is thirty-five metres high). It survived the destruction of the city by the Mongols in 1221, as did a mausoleum at Urgench. There is another mausoleum at Urgench in the name of Tekesh, a ruler of the early 13th century, and a better known one of much the same date at Merv.

Tamerlane and Ulugh Beg

This period of activity was brought to an end in 1219 when the Mongols under Genghis Khan attacked and burnt first Bukhara and then Samarkand. The Mongols were still pagans, and Genghis himself desecrated the great mosque at Bukhara. It was more than a century before the country recovered, and the next dated building of any consequence is the mausoleum of Bayan Kuli Khan at Bukhara, dating from 1359; its portal is adorned with glazed ceramic tiles, here used in Turan for the first time. There are several buildings of these years elsewhere, notably at Urgench and Termez, but the real glories of Turanian architecture belong to the last quarter of the century, when Tamerlane had established his capital at Samarkand. He was born at Kesh, known today as Shakhrisyabz, and he favoured this town also. A palace, with extensive gardens, and a fine mosque, are mentioned by the Spanish traveller Clavijo. The palace gate, known as the Ak Saray, and part of the mosque, which was used as a mausoleum for Tamerlane's eldest son Gahangir, survive.

It was Samarkand that Tamerlane loved the most, and he embellished it with numerous buildings. One of the most striking must have been the Registan, a great square rather like that at Isfahan, surrounded by impressive buildings; the Madrasah (school) of Ulugh Beg, built in 1420, still stands; the others were replaced in the 17th century by the madrasahs of Shir Dar and Tila Kari. Equally magnificent was the great congregational mosque, the Bibi Khanum, the building of which began in 1399. The mosque was built very quickly, and today much of it is in ruins, but enough survives to attest to the great beauty of the original conception.

In spite of the originality of these structures, it is the mausoleums that today constitute Samarkand's greatest glory. They were mostly grouped 41 together to form what is known as the Shah-i-Zind complex, a sort of street, with the mausoleums disposed along it on either side. The earliest of them, that of Khoja Ahmed, dates from 1360–61, and building continued thereafter till about 1430. In fact the street became virtually a necropolis, like that formed by the tombs of the Mamluks at Cairo. It is now impossible to associate all the tombs with individuals, but some of the more important can be identified, notably those of Tuglu Tekin, Turkhan Aga, Shirin Bika Aga and Emir Zadak, which stand opposite each other in pairs. The mausoleum of Tuman Aga, Tamerlane's wife, was built in 1405, and a fine entrance to the street was added by Ulugh Beg, Tamerlane's grandson, in 1434–35. These buildings are small, but they are all adorned with turquoise blue tiles, and the effect is one of great peace and beauty, hardly surpassed elsewhere in the Islamic world.

Tamerlane himself was buried in a separate mausoleum known as the 38 Gur-i-Mir, which was begun in 1404 for one of his grandsons; it was conceived as part of a larger complex, comprising mosque, college and monastery. Its two minarets collapsed, one in 1860 and the other in 1903, but it is hard to believe that when complete it can have been more beautiful than it is today. The proportions of the dome, with its tall drum, multiple lobes and brilliant tiles, are perfect; it is without doubt one of the finest products of Islamic architecture.

At Tamerlane's death his eldest son, Shah Rukh, preferred to stay in

37 *above*

DETAIL OF THE BRICKWORK

Mausoleum of the Samanids (or Shah Ismail)
9th or early 10th century
Bukhara

The mausoleum has been associated with the name of Shah Ismail (848–917), but it was more probably intended for members of the Samanid family. It is square below, with a dome above, but there are openings on all four sides, which suggest a derivation from a fire temple of the Sassanian period. It is the earliest surviving mausoleum in the Persian area; and the way that the bricks are set to form a decorative pattern started a fashion which was later to become universal in Persian architecture.

38 *above right*

THE GUR-I-MIR

1405
brick and glazed tiles
Samarkand

This domed mausoleum was set up in 1405 by Tamerlane who was buried here. The fine portico was added by Muhammad of Isfahan in 1434. The beautiful, tall dome is covered with tile mosaic of the finest quality, and the dazzling blue colour serves to accentuate the superb proportions of the building. The lobed form of dome became particularly popular in eastern Persia in the 15th century.

Herat, and it was there and in Shiraz that the patronage of painting, especially miniature painting, was centred. However, Shah Rukh's son, Ulugh Beg, became governor of Samarkand, and during his life-time the importance of the city in no way declined; indeed its importance as a centre of science and learning even increased, and this was really the city's golden age. Ulugh Beg was buried in 1448 in a magnificent mausoleum which had been begun some twenty years earlier. It is somewhat more reticent in style than many of the buildings of around 1400, and areas of plain brick alternate with glazed tiles on its façade with great effect. It is the last of the great 15th-century buildings in the city.

40 *above*
THE KALYAN MINARET
1121/22
brick
Bukhara

The form of this minaret, tapering upwards and adorned with bands of decorative brickwork, is characteristic of the region north of the Oxus. There are closely similar minarets at Uzgen and elsewhere. The Bukhara minaret is known as the Tower of Death, for the later rulers of the city executed their prisoners by throwing them from its summit. The minaret is free standing, but forms a part of the mosque which was built by Arslan Khan in 1121/22 to replace an earlier structure. It was restored in the 15th century.

39 *right*
CAULDRON

c. 1397
bronze
diameter 96·5 in (245 cm)
State Hermitage Museum, Leningrad

This enormous bronze cauldron was made for the Mausoleum of Chasret Achmed Yassivi in the city of Turkestan. It bears the name of Tamerlane, who gave a similar cauldron to the mosque at Herat. Though Tamerlane is primarily known to the Western world as a ruthless conqueror, he was also an ardent patron of the arts and was responsible for building and beautifying mosques, colleges and other structures throughout Turkestan.

35

The 16th and 17th centuries

Though Transcaspia was to be the scene of more or less continuous strife between various claimants to power during the next two centuries, daily life never seems to have been very seriously interrupted, and fine buildings were set up in most of the cities of the region, especially in the later 16th and the 17th centuries. The Barak Khan Madrasah at Tashkent and the Shir Dar Madrasah and the Tila Kari Madrasah at Samarkand may be noted; they are impressive even if the style is less individual than was that of the earlier structures. It was at Bukhara that the best work of this later age was done. The Kalyan Mosque, though built on an older core, mostly dates from 1514; its great portal, with dome behind it, is extremely impressive. It is adorned with rather formal and severe tile mosaics which suggest a rather earlier date though the columns at the sides are covered not with tile mosaic, but with large square tiles on which the decoration was painted under the glaze. The Mir-i-Arab Madrasah still has tile mosaics, but new colours like pink, yellow and bright green play an important part. Even more elaborate tiles appear in the interior of the Khoja Zaineddin Mosque, which dates from the middle of the century. The Namasgah Mosque, founded in the 12th century, was entirely refurbished in 1586, and the Barland Mosque is of much the same date, and some quite impressive buildings were set up as late as the 17th century, in a rather conservative style. They perhaps contribute little to the history of architecture, but they are well proportioned and fine. New ideas did however penetrate, and the interior of the Abdul Aziz Khan Mosque (1652) is painted in the Baroque style which was fashionable in Turkey at the time.

Azerbaidzhan

Though Islam was adopted as the faith of the region as early as the 8th century, the country for long remained very much on the side lines so far as art and architecture were concerned, and it was not really till Asia Minor fell to the Seljuks after their victory over the Byzantines at Manzikert in 1071 that Azerbaidzhan began to develop as a centre of building. Thereafter quite a lot of work was done but, with one or two exceptions, very little is known in the west about this architecture. Possible exceptions are the minaret of the mosque of Sinik Kala at Baku and two 12th-century tomb-towers or gumbats—a characteristic Seljuk form—at Nakhichevan, that of Yusuf ibn-Kuseyir and that of Mumineh Khatun, both the creations of the same architect, Ajem. Unlike similar structures in Asia Minor they are both built of bricks, those on the former being set in a pattern reminiscent of woven textiles, similar to that used in the Shah Ismail Mausoleum at Bukhara, while those of the latter are disposed in geometric patterns or formal inscriptions.

Early in the 13th century the country was overrun by the Mongols and little building was done till the 14th century. A mausoleum at Barda of 1322 represents the revival, but it stands rather alone, for the region was never favoured by the same rich patronage as Transcaspia, and despite the rise of Baku to a considerable degree of economic prosperity in the later 14th century, the region saw little change. The most impressive structure is a mosque at Karabaglar with a fine lobed portal and rather ornate tile work.

As studies progress, the role of this rather out-of-the-way area may prove to be more important than has hitherto been realised, because of its proximity to Armenia and Georgia, where important architectural styles were developed from an early date. At the moment however it is of local rather than international interest.
David Talbot Rice

41
THE SHAH-I-ZIND
late 14th and early 15th centuries
brick and glazed tile
Samarkand

The Shah-i-Zind complex consists of a street, about seventy metres long, of a number of mausoleums, the earliest of which dates from 1324/25 and the most recent from 1434, though the majority of them were set up for members of Tamerlane's family. The buildings on the left of the photograph are the mausoleums of Oldshah Aim and Bibi Sineb, while in front are those of the Emir Hassan and Shirin Bika Aga. The complex is one of the greatest glories of all Islamic architecture.

42 *below right*
TILE MOSAIC
from the arch leading from the Shah-i-Zind to the Mausoleum of Ulugh Beg
c. 1400
Samarkand

The tiles form an elaborate geometric pattern, with an inscription above. All the mausoleums of the Shah-i-Zind complex are adorned with mosaics such as this, and the brilliant blue of the tiles, combined with the intricate patterns of their designs, makes them astonishingly beautiful. In addition to the abstract designs, script was frequently used for decorative purposes and with great effect; usually its form is geometric and austere, here it is more flowing in form.

43 *far right*
MAUSOLEUM OF SULTAN SANJAR
c. 1157
brick
Merv

The plan of this mausoleum represents an elaboration of that of the earlier Mausoleum of the Samanids at Bukhara. The old square form is retained, but there is only one entrance instead of four, and the dome is set on a high drum, supported on squinches. The external façade is plain, but the inside is adorned with fine stucco panels, and the squinches are of the type known as stalactite, the first instance of its use in the architecture of Turkestan.

Vladimir I, prince of Kiev, was baptised at some time between the years 987 and 989. Whether his baptism preceded, or resulted from, his successful Crimean campaign in the early summer of 989, it is evident that he returned later that year to his pagan capital as a Christian, bringing with him relics and sacred vessels, Byzantine icons and crosses. To make way for these unfamiliar symbols of his new faith he ordered the destruction of the idols of Kiev, many of which he had himself been instrumental in setting up only a few years earlier. According to the *Russian Primary Chronicle*, the wooden idol of Perun was subjected to particular indignities: it was tied to a horse's tail, dragged through the city, beaten and eventually thrown into the river Dnieper. On the following day the people of Kiev were ordered down to the river which had yesterday disposed of their disgraced idol to be baptised into the faith that was to remain theirs throughout the succeeding centuries.

The destruction of the wooden idols which preceded the baptism may be seen as a symbolic overture to Russian medieval art, in which sculpture in the round was destined to play an extremely minor role. Moreover, pagan or secular art was to be little in evidence, and the paganism of which it was the expression was itself gradually to fade from the scene. Furthermore, art of non-Byzantine origin (as we must presume the idols were) was not to be of great significance in the Russian Middle Ages. The art of medieval Russia was to be Christian in content and essentially Byzantine in form, and its major achievements were to be in the field of two-dimensional mural or panel painting.

Kiev's Byzantine heritage

Vladimir's acceptance of Orthodox Christianity and his marriage to the sister of the Byzantine emperor associated the Russian principality formally and irrevocably with the Byzantine world, its religion, its thought and its art. It would be a mistake, however, to ignore the non-Byzantine currents in Russia's medieval culture. While it is difficult to assess the contribution made by the Slav tribes of the Russian realm (or to assess the extent to which they, in their turn, were influenced either by the Scythians, their precursors, or by their Scandinavian neighbours and eventual rulers), it is possible to speak with greater confidence of the contribution made by the West or by the cultures of Georgia, Armenia and Persia that lay at the further end of Russia's Volga trade route. Nonetheless, almost invariably only the nuances or the exceptional features, rather than the fundamental pattern, of Russian medieval art were affected by these currents from the non-Byzantine world.

Byzantine art and religion were each other's servants. It is interesting that the *Russian Primary Chronicle* assigns an important role to art in the very conversion of Vladimir and his people. According to this source, the first missionary to give Vladimir a detailed exposition of the Orthodox faith appears to have impressed him more by an embroidered image of the Last Judgment than by his lengthy discourse.

Vladimir reacted to it (and to various economic and political pressures of which the chronicle says little) by initiating a survey of the religions of his monotheistic neighbours, among whom, by this time, Russia was exceptional in her polytheism. The chronicler relates that Vladimir was anxious for his representatives to supplement their abstract knowledge by experiencing their neighbours' worship. The Russian envoys rejected the religions of the Moslem Bulgars and the German Christians ('We saw no beauty there whatever', was their comment on the latter). But in Constantinople they were overwhelmed by a service in the Cathedral of St Sophia, which was specially celebrated for them by the patriarch at the

Icons & Architecture in a Byzantine World

900–1460

44

THE VLADIMIR MOTHER OF GOD

early 12th century
tempera on wood
39·5 × 27·5 in (100 × 70 cm)
Tret'iakov Gallery, Moscow

This is the most venerated of Russia's icons, and one of the masterpieces of Byzantine art. Of the original little has survived apart from the two heads. The remainder of the icon conveys some idea of the 12th-century composition, though its subtleties are lost. Particularly haunting is the Virgin's carefully modulated face. Three features stand out against the rich olive background: the brilliant touches of vermilion at the lips, the delicately highlighted nose, and the large and sorrowful eyes, which look calmly past the Child to the outside world, as if to communicate his Mother's apprehension of the sufferings which await him.

emperor's request 'so that the Russians should see the glory of our God'. Their report to Vladimir is often, and deservedly, quoted: 'We came to the land of the Greeks, and they brought us in to where they hold services to their God, and we did not know whether we were in heaven or on earth. For on earth there is no sight or beauty to equal this, and we are at a loss to describe it. We know only that God abides there with his people, and that their service is superior to that of any other country. We cannot forget that beauty.'

It is not necessary to accept this as an accurate report of the actual events of the year 987 in order to discern in it the authentic voice of early Russian Christianity. The beauty of a church service and of its setting was considered to be expressive of the glory of God: thus it could initiate one into the Christian faith. Moreover, the medieval Russian Christian was keenly aware that liturgy and art involved not only statements about God: in some degree they were held to involve his presence. According to the same chronicle, Vladimir's first catechistic instruction included a quotation from St Basil to the effect that 'veneration of an icon is transferred to its prototype'. The Russian medieval artist, whether lay or clerical, freelance or attached to a monastic or princely workshop, was to work in the awareness that the icon he painted had such a connection with its prototype, and that, similarly, the church he built (in the words of St Germanos, 8th-century patriarch of Constantinople) was 'heaven on earth, where God, who is himself higher than the heavens, abides and dwells'. The solemnity and beauty of Russian medieval art results in a large measure from this awareness.

As the form of the liturgy was prescribed, so was the form of an icon. The iconographer was responsible to the Church, whose teachings he expressed in paint, metal or mosaic. Thus, the absence of shadows in an icon suggested that the light of God is all-pervasive, or the use of reverse perspective reminded the spectator that he was not the most prominent person involved in the picture-person relationship: in an icon, space tended to recede towards him, and to reduce his significance by comparison to that of the figures depicted, while they, by contrast, partook of a world of absolutes in which there was no vanishing point. Russia inherited from the Byzantine world a complex and mature iconographic tradition, to which each generation made its contribution, but from which radical deviations were not considered either tolerable or desirable. The way in which an Annunciation was depicted, or the way in which it was related to other imagery, to the building in which it was placed and to the liturgy performed in it – all this was regulated by tradition.

The size, as well as the disposition of certain images, might also be carefully regulated to conform to the demands of a particular church. Thus, it is no accident that the original nave of the Dormition Cathedral in Vladimir (31 metres long), the principal icons of its 1405 icon screen (3·13–3·17 metres high), and the halo of this screen's central figure (·31 metres in radius) echo each other's proportions. Such a building formed a coherent unit in its structure, in its decoration and its theology. When a church has such well integrated icons removed from it, or when it is no longer used for its original purpose, its coherence and its impact are inevitably reduced.

It would be a mistake to suppose that early Russian church buildings were erected exclusively to the greater glory of God. The local prince, bishop or merchant also sought to achieve personal glory by his constructions (Prince Andrei of Suzdal' 'built this church to commemorate himself' wrote one chronicler about a church at Bogoliubovo). The building

45

THE VIRGIN ORANS
1043–46
Byzantine masters, mosaic
Cathedral of St Sophia, Kiev

Above the sanctuary in the central nave of St Sophia is poised the monumental Virgin Orans. In the register below is represented the Eucharist, with an altar table at the centre, attended by two angels, on either side of which stands the figure of Christ. The apostles approach to receive communion: they receive the Bread at one side, the Wine at the other. This scene would correspond to that in the sanctuary itself, where, beneath the mosaic, the officiating bishop would offer communion in a similar manner to his clergy.

46

AN APOSTLE

detail of the Eucharist composition
1043 – 46
Byzantine master
mosaic
Cathedral of St Sophia, Kiev

This detail shows one of the apostles who is
approaching Christ to receive the holy
Bread. A photograph such as this reveals
the contrast between the detailed mosaic
work on the face and that in the vestments:
many more, and smaller, cubes are used in
the former – about four hundred cubes per
square decimetre. By contrast, the gold
background in the conch of the apse, where
less subtlety is required, contains no more
than 150 cubes for the same area.

47

CHRIST PANTOKRATOR

1043 – 46
Byzantine master
mosaic
Cathedral of St Sophia, Kiev

The Christ Pantokrator in the central dome
of St Sophia is framed in light from the
windows below him. He blesses the wor-
shippers with his right hand, while in his
left he holds the book of the Gospels,
richly bound in gold. His stern features are
presented almost symmetrically, and he
gazes straight down. He is surrounded by
four archangels, one of which survives
from the mid 11th century, while the
remainder (as well as much of the Pantokrator's beard) were skilfully restored in
oils by the painter Vrubel' in 1884.

programme carried out in Kiev by Vladimir and, more particularly, by
his successor Iaroslav, was intended not only to establish the new faith and
to embellish the capital, but also to render the latter worthy of comparison
even with Constantinople. Certainly, if such a comparison was sought, it
was provided by such contemporary writers as Adam of Bremen, in
whose estimation Kiev was '*aemula sceptri Constantinopolitani, clarissimum
decus Graeciae*' ('The rival of Constantinople's realm, the brightest ornament of the Greek Orthodox world'). On his coins, Vladimir was depicted with the regalia of the Byzantine emperor; and his immediate
successor was dignified – if only exceptionally and unofficially – by the
title tsar, as is demonstrated by a recently discovered graffito of 1054 in the
Cathedral of St Sophia at Kiev. The dream to equal Constantinople absorbed Russians of many generations. After the fall of Constantinople in
1453 it was to find its classic expression in the concept of Moscow as the
third Rome.

Not only was distant Constantinople to be rivalled: there was also
rivalry between various Russian principalities as the power of the grand
prince of Kiev waned progressively in the late 11th and 12th centuries. A
city like Vladimir-on-Kliaz'ma or Moscow demonstrated its superiority
to a large extent in stone, metalwork and paint, and the possession of a
celebrated icon could have a marked effect on its status. As the city of
Vladimir took precedence over Kiev, or as Moscow eventually superseded
Vladimir, so *The Vladimir Mother of God* was translated from one to the **44**
other, as if to confirm the transfer of authority.

The art of Kiev

Neither the palaces nor the earliest churches of Kiev have survived. Knowledge of their existence is derived partly from literary and, more, from
archaeological evidence. Thus we know that the most spectacular of the
early churches of Kiev was the Church of the Tithe, for the building of
which Vladimir invited Greek architects to his city. Like all the distinguished (and all the surviving) churches of early Russia, it was built of
stone – a material that was new to Russian builders. It had a typically
Byzantine plan, that of a Greek cross inscribed in a rectangle, and it was
crowned with one central and a number of subsidiary domes. Originally
it had three naves; these were later augmented to five.

Unlike the Tithe Church, the Cathedral of St Sophia (begun 1037) has
survived, if not entirely in its original form. The exterior, in particular,
gives no idea of the original (though it is an imposing example of 17th- and
18th-century Ukrainian Baroque). The interior, fortunately, has been less
transformed, and as the result of recent restorations the 11th-century frescoes and mosaics are again revealed. From the beginning the cathedral was
planned as a much more complex building than the Tithe Church. It had
five naves and – unprecedented in the Byzantine world – thirteen domes,
grouped on three levels to form a pyramidal outline. Twelve were distributed, like apostles, around the central dome, which was the symbol of
Christ: his image was displayed within it, and his cross (as is now evident)
surmounted this dome alone. As is now not obvious (except at the west
end), St Sophia was built of brick and pink cement, alternating horizontal
stripes of which decorated the exterior. In addition, a good proportion of
natural stone was used in the lower reaches of the walls; this was necessary
support, since brick was not yet being produced of sufficiently dependable
quality in Russia. Later it became possible for buildings to depend entirely
on brick.

Within, the building is more complex than the majority of later Russian
churches. Particularly impressive is the dramatic use made of daylight,

which illumines the central area at the expense of the more mysterious side aisles. The mosaics are deliberately concentrated in this central area: in the dome, for instance, where the stern Pantocrator, framed in light, is **47** supported by four archangels; in the conch of the apse, which houses the monumental, if somewhat ungainly Mother of God; and in the sanctuary, **45** which the celebrated Eucharist composition appropriate to this setting shares with a row of saints in holy orders. There is no doubt that the **46** majority (if not all) of the approximately eight masters at work on the mosaic were Greeks. At the same time it is probable that they used Russian assistants, and a Russian school of mosaicists may well have been founded in connection with this enterprise. Later in the same century we know of at least two local workshops producing the raw materials for mosaic.

The tesserae used in St Sophia are subtle and wide ranging in their colours. Among the 177 tints, for instance, 34 varieties of green alone have been detected. In the finest compositions the masterly use of this rich arsenal of small tesserae (whose density is varied according to the demands of the composition) results in some impressive portraits. However, though **46** the larger compositions convey a sense of strength and stability, they do this at the expense of flexibility; there is a certain heaviness, even monotony in the distribution of the figures.

The frescoes of St Sophia, most of which were completed by the 1060s, have suffered from time. In their present state, despite their profusion, they cannot rival the mosaics in artistic interest, though some, like the portrait group of Prince Iaroslav's family, and the later (early 12th-century) frescoes in the towers at the west end are of considerable interest to the historian. Unusual, even (as far as is known) unprecedented in the Byzantine world, is the juxtaposition of mosaic and fresco within the walls of one building. Fresco was to survive in Russian practice, whereas mosaic – more demanding and expensive – was soon to be abandoned.

Only one other monument (in which the two media were again used in combination) survives as evidence of Russia's early interest in mosaic. Unfortunately, it survives only in part. The mosaics in question adorned the walls of the Kievan Church of St Michael (1109–13), and this was gratuitously demolished in 1934–35. With one exception (in the Tret'iakov **48** Gallery), the few mosaics that had survived until then and which were hastily, but successfully, removed from the walls are now displayed in one of the galleries of St Sophia; however, they may no longer be seen at the distance and in the light for which they were intended. The general plan of the mosaics must have corresponded to that of St Sophia, but only a remarkable Eucharist ensemble survives, together with some additional full-length figures of saints. Unlike the Sophian type of composition, however, the figures are alive corporately and differentiated individually. Their varied movements suggest that they are participating in a solemn, sacred dance. While fewer colours are used than in the Sophian mosaic (the range of tones is reduced by perhaps thirty to fifty per cent), the overall effect is one of controlled brilliance. The mosaic cubes are larger and more freely applied than those at St Sophia; a rich and varied texture is the result. Some of the finest figures are certainly the work of a Greek master. Precisely how much of the work is to be ascribed to Russian assistants remains uncertain, but there can be no doubt that they contributed immeasurably more to this mosaic ensemble than they were in a position to contribute seventy years earlier to the work in St Sophia. In view of the level of Kievan achievement in this medium there is good cause to regret the fact that no more mosaics were to be executed on Russian soil until the 18th century. **188**

48

ST DIMITRII OF SALONIKA

c. 1109–13
master of the St Michael mosaics
mosaic
87·5 × 50·75 in (222 × 129 cm)
Tret'iakov Gallery, Moscow

This mosaic of St Dimitrii adorned one of the cruciform pillars in the Church of St Michael, Kiev, until 1934–35, when the church was demolished. It was placed so as to be clearly visible from the gallery, where the prince (the church's founder) stood during the service. St Dimitrii was the patron of the founder's father, and, probably in the awareness of the family connection with the saint, the mosaicist turned St Dimitrii's eyes to the right, in the direction of the gallery.

49
THE POKROV CHURCH ON THE NERL'

1158–65
Bogoliubovo

The Pokrov Church was built on the orders of Prince Andrei of Suzdal', within sight of his new palace at Bogoliubovo. It has suffered considerably through the centuries from restoration and demolition: its roof-line has changed, its galleries have been removed, and the platform of white stone on which it was once elevated and protected from the flood waters has disappeared beneath the earth. Yet it remains one of the most gracious and captivating of Russian churches, as delightful in its proportions as in its site.

50
THE CROSS OF SVIATOSLAV

1230–34
master of the Crucifixion, sometimes identified as Prince Sviatoslav of Iur'ev-Pol'skoi
stone
Cathedral of St George, Iur'ev-Pol'skoi

The iconography of this relief has certain features reminiscent of the Romanesque, rather than the Byzantine tradition. The composition is remarkable both for its subtle asymmetry and for its psychological insight. The face of Christ is particularly moving, though the sculptor could hardly have expected its refinements to be visible at the height for which the work was intended: the relief once dominated the upper part of the northern façade of the original cathedral at Iur'ev-Pol'skoi, which was almost twice the height of the present structure.

51 *right*
ST DIMITRII OF SALONIKA

late 12th–early 13th century
school of Vladimir-Suzdal'
tempera on cloth and wood
61·5 × 42·5 in (156 × 108 cm)
Tret'iakov Gallery, Moscow

When this icon was restored in the 1920s
it was discovered that while the most
significant sections of the original painting
had survived (in particular, the head and
torso, the right arm and sword), much of
the remainder had been replaced by over-
painting of later centuries, especially the
16th. The majestic head is turned slightly
to one side; accordingly, the eyes are
carefully differentiated, and the serene face
is brought to life.

52
OUR LADY OF THE SIGN

early 12th century
ascribed to the school of Iaroslavl'
tempera on cloth and wood
76·5 × 47·25 in (194 × 120 cm)
Tret'iakov Gallery, Moscow

The symmetry of this noble Virgin's head
is counteracted only by the accentuation of
the highlights on the left of her face. She
stands in the *orans* position. Her upper
garment falls in even folds from her
outstretched arms, and above her waist it
seems as if her stance is a frontal one. By
contrast, the flow of her lower garment is
asymmetrical and suggests that her body
is turned to the spectator's right.

53 *far right*
THE SAVIOUR
NOT MADE BY HANDS

13th century
school of Rostov-Suzdal'
tempera on cloth and wood
39·5 × 29·25 in (100 × 74 cm)
Tret'iakov Gallery, Moscow

The imprint of Christ's face is depicted on
the cloth which, according to a legend that
antedates that of St Veronica's kerchief,
Christ sent to a certain Abgar, king
of Edessa. Both legends may perhaps be
related to the mysterious shroud of Turin
(venerated in Constantinople until 1204,
when Crusaders removed it to the West).
The icon's remarkably fresh colours have
been revealed only with its recent
restoration.

54 *right*
THE MOTHER OF GOD OF
TOLGA

late 13th century
school of Iaroslavl'
tempera on cloth and wood
55·25 × 36·25 in (140 × 92 cm)
Tret'iakov Gallery, Moscow

It is tempting to wonder whether the
femininity and refinement of this icon were
perhaps particularly favoured in an age of
anguish and destruction, since the painting
dates from the period of Russia's subjuga-
tion, less than a century after the Mongol
conquest. The artist displays almost as
much interest in the carefully deployed
vestments as in the enthroned Mother and
Child.

55 *right*
THE HELMET OF PRINCE IAROSLAV VSEVOLODOVICH

early 13th century
silver-gilt repoussé on iron
diameter 8 in (20 cm)
Armoury Palace, the Kremlin, Moscow

The helmet belonged to the father of
Aleksandr Nevskii: the owner's name is
engraved in niello around the figure of the
angel in the central panel. Around the
apex of the helmet are grouped repoussé
panels on which are represented Christ,
St George, St Basil and St Theodore
Stratilates. That the helmet was not
intended merely for ceremonial use is
indicated by the fact that it was discovered
(in 1808) on the site of the Battle of Lipitsa,
a battle in which its owner took part.

56 *left*
GOBLET

12th century
silver-gilt
height 4·75 in (11·7 cm)
State Hermitage Museum, Leningrad

The goblet is elaborately decorated at all levels. The rim, for
practical purposes left flat, is decorated with a frieze of running
animals, engraved on a stippled ground. The base is adorned by
hares and peacocks, while the body is enriched with bosses
(worked partly in repoussé), whose sphinxes, sirens, dancing
women and animals speak of an exotic and, to the medieval
Russian, utterly foreign world. It is not known when the goblet
was brought to Russia from central Asia, where it was made.

57
SPEARHEAD OF
PRINCE BORIS OF TVER'

early 15th century
Damascus steel, overlaid with silver-leaf
length 18 in (46 cm)
Armoury Palace, the Kremlin, Moscow

The spear belonged to one of the last rulers of the independent principality of Tver', who was its prince 1425–61. An elegant inscription at the base of the spearhead states the owner's name. The hollow shaft is decorated with eight engraved scenes. Some are taken from domestic life, some from hunting. One of the engravings indicates that the spear was probably used for boar hunting.

58
MEDALLIONS FROM
THE RIAZAN' TREASURE

c. 1170–1240
gold and cloisonné enamel
Armoury Palace, the Kremlin, Moscow

The treasure hoard, of which these medallions formed a part, was discovered in June 1822 by a peasant ploughing. No doubt it was originally buried to preserve it from plunder by the Mongols. The majority of old Russian hoards contain material that may be dated, like this necklace, to the half century preceding the Mongol conquest. On the medallions are represented the Mother of God, flanked by St Irina and St Barbara.

The frescoes and mosaics of pre-Mongol Kiev are all the more precious, since no undisputably Kievan panel paintings appear to have survived from this period. For these, and for some of the most impressive Russian achievements of the 12th and early 13th centuries, we need to turn elsewhere–to the growing centres of central north-east Russia, and to Novgorod.

The rise of Vladimir–Suzdal'

Kiev was unable to maintain her hegemony for long in what had become, before the end of the 11th century, a loose federation of Russian states plagued by internecine strife. The development of trade routes other than that 'from the Varangians to the Greeks' reduced the prosperity and the prestige of Kiev to a marked degree. By the middle of the 12th century the city of Suzdal' was no longer paying taxes to Kiev, and when Prince Andrei of Suzdal' conquered and sacked the old capital in March 1169 he did not even deign to use it as his seat. Instead, he returned to his own principality, there to embark on an ambitious building programme appropriate to a new pan-Russian centre. As if in anticipation of its establishment and acceptance, and in order to ensure both, *The Vladimir Mother of God* **44** had been transferred by him in 1155 from the Kievan suburb of Vyshgorod to the recently founded fortress city of Vladimir, a city which was due soon to outshine the slightly more mature splendour of its neighbour Suzdal'. This icon–one of the masterpieces of Byzantine art–was to become the guardian of the Russian people, and until the Revolution it was to be venerated in the principal cathedrals of the land.

The area to which Prince Andrei brought the icon was about to enter into the period of its greatest flowering. Vladimir Monomakh had already built a stone cathedral in Suzdal' in the first years of the 12th century, but its replacement by another building in 1222–25, and its subsequent reconstruction in 1531, leave as the oldest surviving harbinger of the imminent glory of Vladimir-Suzdal' the humble Church of St Boris and St Gleb, built in 1152 in the village of Kideksha, near Suzdal', on the banks of the river Nerl'. This charmingly sited church is significant less for itself, than for the pattern of church building which it typifies, and which, in this area, it is now the earliest to reveal. Like so many of the stone churches of Vladimir-Suzdal' (and of contemporary Novgorod), it had three naves, ending in semicircular apses, four supporting pillars, and a single central drum, originally crowned with an essentially semi-circular cupola.

More sophisticated and impressive is the Pokrov Church on the Nerl', **49** built on the orders of Prince Andrei within sight of the palace which he erected at Bogoliubovo. As it now stands, reflected in the waters of the Nerl' and surrounded by greenery and quiet, one is almost persuaded to evaluate it in terms of 18th-century English landscape gardening, but recent archaeological research has demonstrated that neither the touching simplicity of the building, nor the bucolic nature of its immediate setting are primitive. The hill on which the church is placed was artificially raised above flood level and was once enclosed in white stone; the building was thus apparently elevated and cut off firmly from the vegetation immediately surrounding it. Moreover, it was flanked and expanded on three sides, as it now is not, by a stone arcade. The pilasters on the lower half of the walls (which end somewhat inconclusively above the level of the doorways) may once have merged with the arcade roof. Now, with the disappearance of the arcade, the building has an ever greater upward movement, a movement that is accentuated by the lightly tapered full-length pilasters which break up the surface of the outer walls. In addition to these, stone reliefs form a restrained decoration on the external walls. By the end of the century such carvings were to proliferate and to leave undecorated few areas on the external walls of Vladimir-Suzdal' churches. The Pokrov Church stood above waters by which many a merchant sailed as he entered the principality, duly impressed, en route for Vladimir. Even more imposing buildings awaited him there.

60 In the city itself, the Dormition Cathedral was begun by Prince Andrei in the same year as the Pokrov Church. It was completed after two years. Originally it was a church with three naves, six pillars and a single, gilded cupola raised on a sparsely decorated drum. Few medieval Russian buildings can rival the drama of its position on the heights overlooking the river Kliaz'ma and the forests which spread out beyond.

Happily, the cathedral still dominates the landscape, and the glint of its cupola may still be seen six or seven miles away. However, the gilded central cupola is now one of five, and the cathedral has been widened by two naves, as well as lengthened considerably beyond the limits of the original structure. After a fire in 1184, the opportunity was taken to extend as well as to restore the building, with the result that the second cathedral was made to enclose the first, whose outside walls were pierced in the process to form arches and pillars. The cathedral gained in complexity and in dignity appropriate to its eventual role as metropolitan cathedral of all Russia (for the metropolitan of Kiev was to transfer his residence to Vladimir in 1299, before eventually moving on to Moscow). Unfortunately, the interior simultaneously lost much of its original radiance as the result of the withdrawal outwards of the external windows. The addition in 1774–75 of the grandiose icon screen, which cuts off the sanctuary and its windows almost entirely from the nave, served further to darken the interior. It is important to remember that the original icon screen must have been only a low stone balustrade, and that even its superlative replacement of 1408 did not have this effect.

The 12th-century visitor, on his way to venerate the Vladimir icon, as he proceeded to the cathedral through the new Golden Gates of the city (the width of which echoed the width of the cathedral's principal nave), could not fail to sense that the cathedral confirmed, enhanced and sanctified Vladimir's ascendancy.

Within about five years the architects of Prince Andrei's successor were once more at work on the heights overlooking the Kliaz'ma, this time on

61 the construction of an entirely new church dedicated to St Dimitrii, a few hundred yards eastward from the expanded cathedral. It was intended as the chapel of the prince's palace, which has long since vanished. Stately and coherent, the church has a single dome (with its original gilded cross), three naves and four pillars. The evenly lit interior is now stripped to its white stonework, and there is no longer even an icon screen to impede one's apprehension of this pure ensemble. However, a modest area of the original fresco has survived in the large and small vaults under the gallery, the work of a Greek master and his Russian assistants. The master's Last Judgment, with its easy brushwork and its psychological insight, is of exceptional interest.

Unlike the now virtually unadorned walls within, the exterior walls are

81 richly decorated by stone reliefs. Though the local chronicles speak of artists coming from all over the world, and parallels for these reliefs may be found as far apart as France and Georgia, it may be that the motifs arrived in prosperous Vladimir by way of imported metalwork or embroidery, rather than through live carriers. Be that as it may, the quality of the reliefs, as well as their number, ensures them a prominent place in the history of Russian art. Their symbolism, which the more culti-

59
THE DEISIS: THE SAVIOUR, ATTENDED BY THE MOTHER OF GOD AND ST JOHN THE BAPTIST
late 12th century
attributed to the school of Vladimir-Suzdal'
tempera on wood
24 × 57·5 in (61 × 146 cm)
Tret'iakov Gallery, Moscow

This icon is remarkable for its aristocratic sobriety and serenity. The classic Deisis composition is reduced to a minimum, and only the inclination of their heads suggests that the Virgin and St John are suppliants before Christ. The group is skilfully coordinated and brought to life by the rendering of the eyes. Christ looks slightly to his left, across the path of the Baptist's downward gaze; the Mother of God has her eyes focused on the spectator.

vated visitors to the prince's church were better placed to read than the simpler pilgrims to the nearby Dormition Cathedral, remains unclear to the contemporary scholar.

In 1230–34, on the eve of the Mongol invasion, a church dedicated to St George was built at Iur'ev-Pol'skoi. Like the St Dimitrii Cathedral, its external walls were richly decorated with stone carvings in relief. It was to be the last example of such work in the Vladimir-Suzdal' area and, indeed, in Russia as a whole. The church was reconstructed two centuries later, and at this time the carvings were redistributed in a somewhat arbitrary fashion over the new (and reduced) wall surfaces. Consequently, the carvings cannot be evaluated as an ensemble. Nevertheless, they merit careful attention, whether as fragments of the whole, or as individual compositions. Under the guidance of a master-mason (possibly named Bakun), whose evident knowledge of Romanesque work may have been

60 *right*

CATHEDRAL OF THE DORMITION, VLADIMIR

east end
1158–60 and 1185–89

Few medieval Russian buildings can rival the drama of the position of this great cathedral on the heights overlooking the river Kliaz'ma and the forests which spread out beyond. After a fire in 1184, the opportunity was taken to extend, as well as to restore, the original building of 1158–60; the second cathedral encloses the first, whose outside walls were pierced to form arches and pillars. The great belfry dates from 1810, and the extension of the cathedral to the north from 1862.

61 *left*

THE CATHEDRAL OF ST DIMITRII, VLADIMIR

1194–97

This stately and coherent building was erected as the chapel for the prince's palace. The palace has long since disappeared, as have some other structures which adjoined the church from the time of its construction to 1837–39. However, since these were appendages to the church rather than expansions of its form, their demolition is perhaps to be regretted more for archaeological than for aesthetic reasons. The walls and drum of the cathedral are richly ornamented in carved stone relief. The dome is crowned by the original gilded cross and by a copper weather vane in the form of a dove.

gained in Galicia, the sculptors produced works which, at their best, unlike the comparatively staid reliefs at St Dimitrii, are dynamic and moving. Among the most memorable are the figure of St George himself, and–perhaps finest of all–a Crucifixion group, known as the Cross of Sviatoslav.

The surviving panel paintings of Vladimir and of its neighbours (Suzdal' and Iaroslavl') are few but remarkable. Two icons of particular solemnity (both in the Tret'iakov Gallery) deserve mention: the icon of St Dimitrii of the Vladimir-Suzdal' school (late 12th or early 13th century), and the monumental *Our Lady of the Sign* (*Znamenie*), usually assigned to Iaroslavl' and to the same period. In the latter the brilliance of the colour, the rich decoration of the Virgin's veil and cuffs, and the dramatic gesture of the Christ-Emmanuel before her in blessing with arms extended beyond the limits of the golden medallion which encloses him (a departure from

50

59

51

52

Byzantine practice) are features which speak of a fresh, Russian contribution to received tradition.

The decorative arrangement of this Virgin's vestments is paralleled in another icon of the Iaroslavl' school, *The Mother of God of Tolga*. In other **54** ways, however, the two icons have little in common. The emotional restraint of the earlier *Our Lady of the Sign* is countered here by warmth and femininity; the frozen stillness of the one is far removed from the graceful swaying movement of the other. *The Mother of God of Tolga* is exceptionally refined, even mannered in its composition and its colour scheme.

By the time it was painted Russia was desolated. The Mongols had suddenly appeared on the horizon and as suddenly disappeared in 1223. By the end of the following decade, however, they had captured and sacked Riazan', Vladimir and, on 6th December 1240, Kiev itself. St Sophia of **58** Kiev lay in ruins, the symbol of the universal destruction worked by the invaders. 'All this happened because of our sins,' wrote one of the citizens of Riazan' in retrospect, several decades later. 'There was a city of Riazan', and a province of Riazan', but her wealth has vanished, her glory has passed, and it is impossible to recognise in her any of her assets – all that remains is smoke, earth and ashes . . . . Neither songs nor bells are now to be heard. Ceaseless weeping has displaced joy.' 'Villages are overgrown with weeds', wrote the bishop of Vladimir towards the end of the century, 'We are brought low in our greatness, our beauty has perished'.

A slow and painful process of recovery awaited central and southern Russia, and it was not until the century after the Mongol onslaught that cities like Moscow and Tver' began to show signs of vigour once more. Only the far north-west of Russia, comparatively safe behind treacherous expanses of marshland, maintained its independence of the Mongols. The powerful principality of Novgorod experienced neither destruction nor degradation at the hands of the invader.

The art of Novgorod and Pskov

Novgorod, a prosperous mercantile community, was one of the ancient centres of the Russian realm, and it was to retain its importance and its independence long after the eclipse of Kiev and Vladimir. Only in 1478 did it succumb to the forces of Moscow. Until this time its social, economic, political and artistic development distinguished it from other Russian principalities. Here, more than in any other Russian city, democratic and republican forces were at work. Although an oligarchy tended to control the administration, a city assembly involved most of the male population in its deliberations and fostered popular self-confidence. In the 14th and 15th centuries the same self-confidence made Novgorod the breeding ground for at least two major heresies. The independent citizens of Novgorod insisted on electing their own bishops and on dismissing their own princes. Eventually the prince's role was virtually reduced to that of a hired minister of defence, and from 1136 he was no longer permitted to purchase land in the principality. Architects and artists looked to a different type of patron for their commissions than did their counterparts elsewhere: their work reflects their patrons' energy and their unsophisticated bluntness.

The 12th century in the south had seen a move towards even greater simplicity in architecture. This was to be paralleled in Novgorod. Admittedly, the great, stone Cathedral of St Sophia is still a complex, **82** spacious and imposing structure with five naves, flanked by galleries, and supported by something like a dozen cruciform pillars. It is nevertheless a markedly less complex and less dynamic building than its Kievan prototype.

62

ST GEORGE

12th century
school of Novgorod
tempera on wood
Cathedral of the Dormition,
the Kremlin, Moscow

It is possible that this icon was located originally in the Church of St George in the Iur'ev Monastery, Novgorod – a princely foundation, where such a work, with its marked Byzantine characteristics, would have found favour. St George is depicted as a warrior; his rich red cloak reveals a shirt of armour; his right hand holds a spear, his left, a sword. The near-illusionistic rendering of the left hand is exceptional.

63 *above*

FOUR SAINTS *detail*

14th century
school of Pskov
tempera on cloth and wood
58 × 52·75 in (147 × 134 cm)
Tret'iakov Gallery, Moscow

The hieratic and geometrical character of
the male saints' vestments provides a vivid
contrast to the more freely painted faces,
with their subtly indicated sobriety and
intensity. The freedom with which the
highlights have been applied on the faces
has given grounds for speculation about
the influence of Feofan Grek on the painters
of Pskov. The outer figures (St Basil the
Great and St Paraskeva) look across in
front of the two saints in the centre (St
Gregory Nazianzen and St John
Chrysostom) and St Paraskeva is placed at
an oblique angle; this modifies the severity
of the saints' frontal poses, and suggests
the existence of a bond between them.

64

THE MOTHER OF GOD'S
ASSEMBLY

c. 1350–1400
school of Pskov
tempera on cloth and wood
31·75 × 24 in (81 × 61 cm)
Tret'iakov Gallery, Moscow

The vitality of the earth's response to the
Incarnation is dynamically conveyed in the
rhythms of these dark green hills, against
the background of which the Mother of
God is calmly enthroned. She is surrounded
by figures that acclaim her Son's advent
and dance in honour of it. The spiral of the
Virgin's throne is reflected in the swiftly
indicated highlighting of the hills around
her. The intense green and the orange-red
are peculiar to Pskov.

THE ANNUNCIATION
OF USTIUG
c. 1119–30
school of Novgorod
tempera on cloth and wood
93·75 × 66 in (238 × 168 cm)
Tret'iakov Gallery, Moscow

This still and monumental icon is unusual
in depicting the mysterious presence of the
Christ Child at the moment of the Annunciation. The firm gesture of the archangel,
echoed in the Virgin's right hand, links the
upright and otherwise only tentatively
related figures. Particularly memorable is
the contemplative gaze of the Virgin. The
Almighty is depicted above in a somewhat
freer style than is prevalent elsewhere in
the icon. Gabriel's wings may have been
added only in the 16th century.

Originally only five semi-circular domes arose from a somewhat mono-
lithic exterior to dominate the city. Within, the lighting was distributed
much more mechanically than in the Kievan Sophia, there was no
mosaic to highlight the central areas, and the decorative detail was also
comparatively simple. Later buildings in Novgorod were to be simpler **89**
still (to heat, as well as to apprehend), and only one other five-cupola
church was to be built – also, like the cathedral, under princely patronage.

The most significant of the early princely foundations apart from these,
the St George Cathedral of the Iur'ev Monastery, of 1119, has three un-
evenly distributed cupolas, three naves and six pillars. Its exterior is
modelled with restraint, and the whole conveys an impression of clarity,
solidity and dignity, rather than of grace. It was not only the increasing
modesty of the princes' resources and prestige, but also the local architectural tradition which determined that the last princely church at Nereditsa
near Novgorod (built in 1198) should be a single-cupola structure, with a
mere three naves and four rectangular pillars. This unpretentious building
(destroyed during the Second World War, but reconstructed since) was
renowned for its frescoes and its site, rather than for its architectural
subtleties. Yet its very homeliness and clumsiness endeared this type of
cubic building to the Novgorodians, as may be seen in the numerous ana-
logous structures of the province. The ground plan and interior of Novgorod churches, reduced in most cases to a single nave, was to remain
little changed throughout the centuries of Novgorod's independence. The
most notable developments were in the roof line, which acquired more
flexible and rhythmic contours in the course of the 14th century and
prevented the solid Novgorodian churches from being too earthbound.

Two outstanding churches of the late 14th century are those dedicated
to St Theodore Stratilates and to the Transfiguration. By contrast to the **89**
sparse exterior decoration of most Novgorod churches, the exterior walls
of these elegant buildings were enlivened by the use of crosses in relief and
decorative niches, though the essential features of the structures were left
unaffected. These churches failed to entice the Novgorodians away from
their modest tastes. Later buildings followed their pattern only occasionally. Indeed, in the 15th century a tendency to reflect earlier and less
ornate models manifests itself. The business-like patrons and builders of
Novgorod favoured churches that were functional, unspectacular and
familiar; they were content with roughly hewn contours and uneven wall
surfaces; sophistication and complexity made them feel ill at ease.

The builders of nearby Pskov were like-minded, and nowhere is the
Novgorodian taste for honesty and simplicity taken to further extremes.
The low, somewhat stolid churches of Pskov, also the products of a demo- **87**
cratic milieu, may owe at least something of their forthright character to
Pskov's position as a western frontier city; its architects were accustomed
to building solidly for reasons of defence. By the 15th century the compact
churches of Pskov were able to dispense even with the minimal four
internal pillars, and their cubic interior was thus transformed into a single,
unencumbered unit.

Two of Pskov's churches contained fresco cycles of great interest,
though of widely differing styles: the Transfiguration Cathedral of the
Mirozhskii Monastery (1157–58) and the Church of the Nativity of the
Mother of God in the Snetogorsk Monastery (1313). The first is decorated
in the Byzantine manner, though the feeling which modifies the severity
of its linear style suggests that the artist or artists may have drawn also on
Georgian, Serbian or Sicilian models. Much more typical of Pskov are the
Snetogorsk frescoes which, with their free use of highlights and their

colour range, anticipate Novgorodian developments in the time of Feofan Grek.

The panel icons of Pskov echo the sturdy simplicity of the city's churches, though at their best they surpass them in dignity and refinement. Perhaps the most outstanding are two icons in the Tret'iakov Gallery that survive from the 14th and the 15th centuries: *The Mother of God's Assembly* and *Four Saints*. In the latter, the hieratic and geometrical character of the male saints' vestments provides a vivid contrast to the more freely painted faces, with their subtly indicated sobriety and intensity. In the former the free manner of painting predominates. The intense green and the orange-red used in this and other local icons is peculiar to Pskov.

Pskov became independent of Novgorod only in 1348, but her earlier political dependence did not bring about identity between the artistic traditions of the two centres. At the same time neither did Pskov's ultimate independence provoke any radical divergence between them. Nevertheless, partly because of Novgorod's superior status and greater prosperity, partly because more of her monuments have survived, the history of Novgorod icon painting is more complex than that of her sister republic.

There is hardly any evidence of Novgorod icon painting from the 11th century, but the surviving monuments suggest the existence by the end of the 12th century of an established painterly tradition with well defined local features. Unfortunately, only fragments of one of the most important monuments of this period survived the Second World War. The frescoes at Nereditsa, of 1199, once covered the interior walls, and the stern, impassive figures of its saints looked down to the worshipper from all around him. The surviving frescoes at the Church of St George at Staraia Ladoga of *c.* 1167 – more Greek-orientated than those at Nereditsa – represent the achievements of this period in their own way.

From the 12th century a number of first-class panel paintings have survived, among them *The Veneration of the Cross* on the obverse of *The Saviour not made by Hands*, *The Head of an Archangel* and the monumental *Annunciation of Ustiug*. Such icons provide evidence of a cultivated taste for the Greek style in certain, possibly princely, circles, though (like several other important icons of this period) they are not yet typically Novgorodian works.

The familiar characteristics of Novgorod painting may already be discerned in works of the late 13th century, but before this style came fully into its own in the late 14th and the early 15th centuries, the city's art was to pass through a period during which her linear tradition (which she ultimately favoured) was displaced by the dramatic and painterly work associated with the name of Feofan Grek.

Feofan is one of the few painters of the Russian Middle Ages about whose personal character and career we have some precise information. Even so, much of his work is lost, and we have to assess his contribution by reference to a disappointingly narrow range of monuments. Feofan, an immigrant from Constantinople, received his formation in the early Palaeologian renaissance, whose spirit he helped to introduce to Novgorod. However, Feofan undoubtedly gained from, as well as contributed to, his new milieu. His extraordinary frescoes (1378), which survive only in the Church of the Transfiguration, clearly owe at least something to the local style, as represented in the Snetogorsk Monastery and in the St Michael Church of the Skovorodka Monastery near Novgorod. The latter was destroyed in the Second World War, as was another important church of this period, the Church of the Dormition in Volotovo field near

Margin references: 64, 63, 71, 88, 66, 67, 71, 65, 85, 86, 72, 73, 90, 93, 94, 68

66

MICAH

c. 1167, fresco
Church of St George, Staraia Ladoga

The frescoes in the cupola and drum of the restored church at Staraia Ladoga are the best preserved of this ensemble. The prophet Micah is typical of these frescoes in his severity, and in the linear character of the treatment. The two fresco painters who worked here were evidently strongly influenced by the Byzantine tradition, though it is thought that they were themselves Novgorodians.

67

THE SAVIOUR
NOT MADE BY HANDS

late 12th – early 13th century
school of Novgorod
tempera on cloth and wood
30·25 × 28 in (77 × 71 cm)
Tret'iakov Gallery, Moscow

This icon has on its reverse an equally remarkable painting of the Veneration of the Cross. Stylistically the two sides have little in common, and, although they belong to the same period, they are clearly the work of different painters. The Saviour is painted with great restraint; the subtle modelling of the face contrasts effectively with the stylised hair.

68

MELCHISEDEC *detail*

1378
Feofan Grek, c. 1340 – c. 1410
fresco
Church of the Transfiguration, Novgorod

Only a small proportion of Feofan's creations have survived, and among them only one fresco ensemble. In it, his dynamism, which so fascinated his Russian contemporaries, finds its full expression. Feofan is less concerned with detail in his frescoes than with overall, dramatic effect. Of particular interest is the freedom with which he highlights the face and hair.

69

CATHEDRAL OF THE TRINITY

1422
Monastery of the Trinity and St Sergii, Zagorsk

This church, one of the few surviving examples of early Muscovite architecture, was originally built to house, as it still does, the relics of St Sergii of Radonezh. Its original roofline was restored in 1966. The church contains an icon screen by Rublev and his assistants. To one side stands the chapel erected in 1548 over the tomb of St Nikon, Sergii successor as abbot.

Novgorod. Happily, the murals of the Church of St Theodore Stratilates (*c.* 1380) have survived as additional material evidence of Feofan's influence in the north-west.

In his frescoes Feofan is concerned less with detail than with overall, dramatic effect. Much of this is attained by the daring highlighting of his saints, particularly of their faces and beards. Against backgrounds of brown or light blue (Feofan's range of colours is deliberately restricted) his freely rendered highlights – white, grey, light blue and (occasionally) red – stand out sometimes as virtually the only element that defines the features of his saints. The freedom with which the paint is applied renders Feofan's figures dynamic, and effectively counteracts the comparative stillness of their poses and the calm sobriety of their features.

Whether or not it is possible to attribute to Feofan (or to the Master of Volotovo?) the double-sided icon with *The Virgin of the Don* on one side **94** and *The Dormition* on the other, this superlative work unquestionably **93** owes a great deal to Feofan's influence. This is specially evident in the modelling of the apostles' expressive heads in *The Dormition*, a work whose unassuming delicacy of composition, sensitivity to mood, dogmatic precision and remarkable combination of colours single it out as one of the most impressive icons of the Russian Middle Ages.

The typical Novgorodian painter of the succeeding period favoured clear, bright colours, dramatically juxtaposed against light or vermilion **72, 73** backgrounds. His brilliant colours provide variety, tension and movement, qualities that are less evident in the restrained outlines of his composition. The resolute, clearly defined silhouettes of his saints rather than their somewhat generalised, though never effeminate, countenances convey his message. Unlike the Feofan of the frescoes, he generally prefers direct, linear, somewhat hieratic patterns to painterly modelling, though he is generous in his use of facial highlights. One has the impression that here, as in architecture, the citizens of Novgorod preferred to commission works in which sturdiness, clarity of form and directness of colour predominate over psychological, theological or visual refinement.

Novgorod's days, however, were numbered, and an unusual icon, *The Battle between the People of Novgorod and Suzdal'*, reminded Novgorodians **74** of their cherished independence on the eve of their artistic and political incorporation into the Muscovite state.

Moscow succeeds Vladimir

At the time of the Mongol invasion, Moscow was an insignificant township with not a single stone building to hint at its future prominence. In the course of the 14th century, however, it became increasingly evident that Moscow, despite the rivalry of Tver', was likely to become a major centre of power. Its territory, traversed by profitable waterways, was expanding, and its gifted dynasty of princes knew how to deal profitably with the Mongols at the time of their ascendancy as well as how to combat them when an opportune moment appeared to have arrived. By the end of the 15th century, the Muscovite prince, to whom most of the central and northern principalities of Russia had submitted or were about to submit, was encouraged to consider his capital as the successor to Constantinople. It was to be the third (and ultimate) Rome, the unique Christian capital, 'shining throughout the entire universe like the sun in its Orthodox faith'. In due course its grand prince was to be crowned tsar of all Russia, and its metropolitan raised to patriarchal status.

We know of the comparatively ambitious embellishment of the Moscow Kremlin, as well as of other 14th-century building programmes, but the earliest surviving Muscovite buildings are of the early 15th

70

THE MOTHER OF GOD

1405, Feofan Grek, c. 1340 – c. 1410
tempera on wood
63 × 32·75 in (160 × 58 cm)
Cathedral of the Annunciation, the Kremlin,
Moscow

When the Annunciation Cathedral was rebuilt in 1484–89 the icon screen of the earlier building was retained. It had been painted in 1405 under the aegis of Feofan Grek, with the assistance of Andrei Rublev and Prokhor of Gorodets, and the quality of its Deisis and Festival registers remains virtually unrivalled. Seven icons of the Festival register are usually attributed to Rublev. The Mother of God forms part of the central Deisis composition, for which Feofan himself was responsible.

71

HEAD OF AN ARCHANGEL

late 12th century
school of Novgorod
tempera on wood
19·25 × 15·25 in (49 × 38·7 cm)
State Russian Museum, Leningrad

Originally, the head of this archangel probably formed part of an extended Deisis composition. However, its present isolation permits its individual qualities to be appreciated. The archangel is closely related to the Gabriel of *The Annunciation of Ustiug* (**65**); yet the two archangels are distinct in mood. The Gabriel of the Annunciation is alert and outward-looking; this archangel is pensive, melancholy and withdrawn.

century. Four churches of the first quarter of the 15th century (three of them princely foundations) indicate that the taste and essential techniques of ancient Vladimir were inherited by the builders of Moscow: two Zvenigorod churches of about 1400 and 1405, the Trinity Cathedral of the Trinity Monastery at Zagorsk, of 1422, and the Saviour's Cathedral of **69** the Andronikov Monastery in Moscow, of 1425–27 (now part of the Rublev Museum). These are all churches with three naves, four supporting pillars, a single drum and cupola. But unlike the later churches of Vladimir, with their generously embellished walls, the walls of early Moscow churches were left chaste except for narrow bands of ornamental carving. Relief work was replaced by structural embellishments, and the recent restoration of both the Trinity and the Saviour's cathedrals once more reveals the manner in which this was done. At first two, then (as in the Saviour's Cathedral) multiple levels of onion-shaped gables (*kokoshniki*) were introduced: these encircled the building, echoed the outline of the cupola and, most important, suggested an upward movement. That an upward movement was of interest to the architects of the time is indicated also by such devices as are used at the Trinity Cathedral to accentuate the height of the interior: the walls are constructed to incline imperceptibly inwards (up to forty-five centimetres from the vertical), and the pillars are similarly adjusted, though only on the inner side, where the adjustment is unlikely to be noticed. Later Muscovite architecture was to show its predilection for height with less reticence, and the modest cubic outline of earlier churches was to be superseded by the pyramidal upward thrust of such a building as the 16th-century Ascension Church at Kolomenskoe, **131** on the outskirts of Moscow.

Significant as these developments were for the future, Moscow's outstanding achievements were in the sphere of painting. Again, the Vladimir-Suzdal' school is the background against which the early Muscovite school presumably developed; an icon like the superlative *St Boris and St* **76** *Gleb* of the early 14th century could have been the product of either school, and may act as a symbol of their interdependence. Unfortunately, the early history of the Moscow school can only be described tentatively for lack of monuments. Greek influences appear to have competed with the less marked influence of immigrant, south Slav masters; the local painters tended to produce work which, by comparison with imported models, was unsophisticated, and there was little to suggest that such a painter as Andrei Rublev, the greatest painter of the Russian Middle Ages (arguably, Russia's most significant painter, regardless of period) was to develop on these foundations.

The age of Rublev

Rublev is first mentioned in the chronicles as an associate of Feofan Grek. Feofan was in Moscow by 1395, and in 1405 we hear of Feofan and Prokhor from Gorodets at work in the Annunciation Cathedral of the Kremlin together with Rublev, at least seven of whose un-Feofan-like icons are **70** located there. Of Feofan's work in Moscow nothing appears to have survived apart from his icons for this church, though his influence (if not his actual hand) may be detected without difficulty in one of the most powerful icons of this period, *The Transfiguration* from Pereiaslavl'-Zalesskii. **90**

In the Annunciation Cathedral (the private chapel of the grand prince) Feofan created not only individual icons of distinction: it seems that he was instrumental, together with his colleagues, in devising a more complex and extensive type of icon screen than had hitherto been the norm in the Orthodox world. Its acceptance by his contemporaries and immediate successors ensured its distribution in subsequent centuries throughout

72 *below*

ELIJAH

late 14th–early 15th century
school of Novgorod
tempera on wood
17·75 × 13·75 in (45 × 35 cm)
Tret'iakov Gallery, Moscow

This dedicated prophet was painted at the turn of the 14th century, at a time when some of the finest and most typical Novgorodian icons were being produced. The red background is particularly interesting; the colour is peculiar to Novgorod. A comparable and contemporary Novgorodian Elijah, also in the Tret'iakov Gallery, has the same background, as do many other icons of the province.

73 *left*

PATERNITY

second half of 14th century
school of Novgorod
tempera on cloth and wood
44·5 × 34·5 in (113 × 88 cm)
Tret'iakov Gallery, Moscow

This icon – a typical product of its school –
depicts the Holy Trinity in a form which
was far less widespread in Russia than that
of the Old Testament Trinity where
Abraham's three mysterious visitors are
represented (**98**). At the side of the throne,
on which are shown the Father, Son and
Holy Spirit, stand an apostle and two
stylites, Daniel and Simeon. These were
probably the patron's family saints.

74 *below*

THE BATTLE BETWEEN
THE PEOPLE OF NOVGOROD
AND SUZDAL'

c. 1460, school of Novgorod
tempera on wood
67·25 × 49·25 in (171 × 125·5 cm)
Museum of History and Art, Novgorod

The icon is divided into three zones, and is
to be read from top to bottom. It tells the
story of the miraculous Novgorodian
victory over the prince of Suzdal' and his
allies in 1169, but it probably had a contemporary significance in the second half of
the 15th century, when Muscovite en-
croachments on Novgorod were being res-
isted. This would help to explain why no
icons of this type appeared before the 1460s.

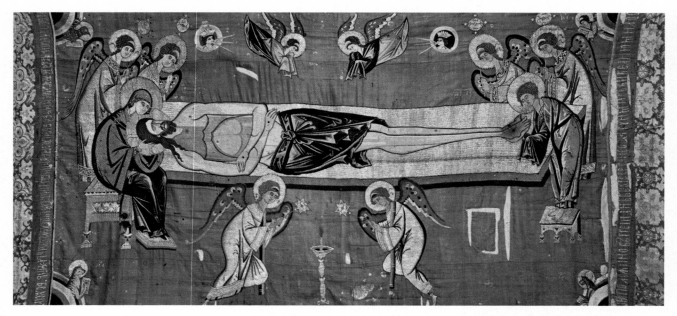

75 *above*

THE SHROUD OF PUCHEZH

1441
silk, gold and silver threads
69 × 100·25 in (175 × 255 cm)
Armoury Palace, the Kremlin, Moscow

The shroud was commissioned by Evfimii,
archbishop of Novgorod. It depicts the
burial of Christ. The Virgin and St John
are supported by mourning angels. The
sun and moon (shown as crowned heads)
shed their light upon the scene. The four
evangelists are represented by their
symbols. Joseph of Arimathaea, however,
is curiously absent from this and from
several other Novgorodian shrouds,
though he is mentioned in the hymn for
Holy Saturday which forms part of the
inscription round the border.

76

ST BORIS AND ST GLEB

early 14th century
school of Vladimir-Suzdal'
tempera on wood
56·25 × 37·5 in (143 × 95 cm)
State Russian Museum, Leningrad

Boris and Gleb, the first Russian saints to
be canonised, were originally depicted as
martyrs with crosses in their hands; later
they were shown as healers, holding the
churches where their relics had effected
cures. Neither of these iconographic types
survived the destruction of their church
and the loss of their relics at the time of the
Mongol invasion. Subsequently, they were
represented as princely warriors, almost
invariably together, whether on horseback
or (as here) on foot.

77
ST SERGII OF RADONEZH
c. 1422–24
school of Moscow
silk embroidery
77·5 × 32·25 in (197 × 82 cm)
Museum of History and Art, Zagorsk

Sergii of Radonezh (1314–92) is venerated as one of the greatest of Russian saints. This embroidery was probably prepared for his tomb at the time of his canonisation, and it is thought to have been a princely donation. The personal character of the representation suggests that it may have been worked by someone who remembered the saint. The portrait is particularly effective since the threads themselves have been made to follow the facial contours. St Sergii is vested in his monastic mantle and his priestly stole.

Russia and beyond its frontiers. This was a development that gave the icon painter new responsibilities, though at the expense, iconographically, of the mural artist and, liturgically, of the lay worshipper, for whom the actions of the clergy in the sanctuary behind the screen were almost invariably rendered invisible by it.

In 1408 Rublev was sent with his colleague and life-long friend Daniil Chernyi to the Dormition Cathedral in Vladimir. The frescoes with which they redecorated the entire cathedral have survived only in part; the sur- **92** viving sections of their great icon screen are preserved elsewhere. Never-theless it is possible to see that this must have been one of the most remarkable ensembles of the Russian Middle Ages.

In the icon screen, one of the Festival panels (*The Ascension*) and possibly three of the Deisis register are currently attributed to Rublev. In the frescoes at least two masters may be distinguished, each outstanding in his own manner. While Rublev must have been responsible for such com-positions as the enthroned Apostles with Angels, Daniil may be credited with the equally remarkable composition in which St Peter and St Paul **92** lead the elect into Paradise.

All the surviving frescoes form part of a Last Judgment composition. In Rublev's interpretation of the scene (and this is typical of him) there pre-vails an atmosphere of quiet and confident expectation, in keeping with which his trumpeting angels summon the assembled figures with deli-cate instruments, to which they only lightly press their lips. Though Rublev was prepared on some occasions to depict a stern Saviour in Glory, as in the superlative miniature icon of about 1411 in the Tret'iakov Gallery, the Christ who presides over this Last Judgment is a gentle figure. **78** He finds his counterpart in the compassionate Saviour of the Zvenigorod **97** Deisis, an icon that was found, together with its peers St Michael and St **95** Paul, in the autumn of 1918 under a pile of firewood, apparently ready for destruction. Five-sixths of its paintwork has vanished: yet the bare wood around the miraculously preserved and resolute face of Christ is somehow not incongruous, consonant as it is both with Christ's kenosis, and with the modern history of the Russian Church.

The three icons from Zvenigorod were painted in Rublev's maturity, at about the same time that he produced his materpiece, *The Trinity*. It was **98** commissioned by the abbot of the Trinity Monastery in honour of its founder, St Sergii of Radonezh, and was painted probably for the wooden **77** Trinity Church, erected in 1411 over the saint's grave. A decade later, after Sergii's canonisation, it was incorporated into the icon screen of the stone Trinity Cathedral, where it remained until after the Revolution. From the beginning it was placed (as the rest of the icon screen still is placed) only a few feet away from Sergii's relics—a significant juxtaposi-tion, since the work of Rublev (who was a monk of Sergii's monastery and who probably knew the founder himself) could be described as the visual expression of Sergii's teaching. Both the saint's kenotic and his visionary experience find their reflection in such an icon as *The Trinity*. **98**

The three figures of this Trinity represent the angels who appeared to Abraham. They are in silent communion with each other, seated around an altar table on which a chalice indicates that the subject of their contem-plation is self-sacrifice. The table, which echoes the form of the chalice, also echoes its implications—it contains a niche for the deposit of martyrs' (and other saints') relics.

The central figure behind the table (most probably God the Son), though he is further back than his companions (God the Father on the left, the Holy Spirit on the right), is brought forward into their midst by the daring use of brilliant lapis lazuli in his upper garment. The same colour has its subdued reflection in the robes of the angels on either side–subdued, since (to borrow the words of Saint John Damascene, 676–749), 'The persons (of the Trinity) are not made one so as to commingle, but so as to cleave to each other, and they have their being in each other without any coalescence or commingling'. The angels are further linked to each other, and their equality is confirmed, by the unobtrusive circle which contains them, and which introduces the symbol of eternity into the composition. Possibly there were literary sources for Rublev's use of the circle (he may have had access to the recently imported 1371 Bulgarian translation of Pseudo-Dionysius, in whose work God is associated with circular movement). There were formal reasons also, which prompted Rublev to favour the circle: circular forms clearly attracted him because of the calm they conveyed. Rublev placed his figures at an angle rather than frontally; this reduces the width of their shoulders and renders their outline more fluid. At the same time, he carefully used verticals and sharp angles, both to counteract the curves and to accentuate the symbolism. Thus, the angular folds of the lapis lazuli garment lead the eye inexorably to the chalice, as well as providing visual drama. Despite its intensity, the lapis lazuli is absorbed in Rublev's unique and radiant colour scheme, whose rich yellows, golds, oranges, chestnut-browns, dull light greens, pink-mauves, maroons and whites are reminiscent of the Russian landscape in the early summer, the season of the Trinity (Pentecost) festival.

Only by comparison to such a work ('perfect and most beautiful, it answers all questions, it satisfies all desires', in one critic's view) are the remaining panels in the Trinity Cathedral icon screen of lesser interest. If one is to ignore the icons attributed to the elderly Rublev (perhaps three in all), one is still left with a rich collection of the most diverse works, whose diversity is explained by the need to complete the commission at some speed, and by the consequent involvement of numerous painters, not all of whom were attuned to Rublev's manner. Generally, Rublev's was not to be the only, or even the dominant influence in Muscovite painting during the first half of the 15th century.

In some of these icons his influence is minimal. The most outstanding of the non-Rublevian (and by comparison to Rublev, somewhat archaic) **80** icons is the dynamic *Last Supper*. In some respects closer to Rublev, though still independent of him, is an icon which may also have been painted originally for this church, though in the second quarter of the century, the **96** magnificent *Enthroned Mother of God and Child, together with St Michael and St Sergii* in the Historical Museum, Moscow.

Other paintings in the Trinity screen are almost indistinguishable from Rublev's work, or (like *The Presentation in the Temple*) very close to it. **79** Later icons, such as the newly uncovered *St John the Baptist* were also to follow closely in the master's footsteps.

Finally, there are several icons in the Trinity screen which, while basing themselves on Rublev's work, develop it in a new direction and act as signposts to the future. The elegant forms of *The Appearance of the Angel to* **126** *the Women at the Tomb* anticipate the refined work of Dionisii in the second half of the century. They promise a new graciousness, though at the expense of virile sobriety. They foreshadow a new sophistication on the formal plane, while simultaneously they threaten the Rublevian synthesis, a synthesis in which harmony of form was essentially the outward and visible sign of an inward and spiritual grace.

Sergei Hackel

78 *below*
THE SAVIOUR IN GLORY
c. 1411
Andrei Rublev 1370–1430
tempera on wood
7 × 6·25 in (18 × 16 cm)
Tret'iakov Gallery, Moscow

This superlative miniature icon was probably painted when Rublev's powers were at their height. It shows Christ enthroned in glory (Revelation IV); he is surrounded by seraphim and by the symbols of the four evangelists, 'who rest not day and night, saying, Holy, holy, holy, Lord God Almighty, which was, and is, and is to come'. The Gospels are open at the words, 'Come unto me, all ye that labour and are heavy laden'.

THE LAST SUPPER

1425–27
unknown master of the Moscow school
tempera on wood
15 × 26.5 in (38 × 67 cm)
Cathedral of the Trinity, Monastery of
the Trinity and St Sergii, Zagorsk

This is one of the outstanding icons of the Trinity Cathedral icon screen. It has perhaps less in common with the work of Rublev and his school than with the more Grecophile and comparatively archaic tendencies of a painter like Prokhor of Gorodets, whose earlier scheme for the Last Supper in the Annunciation Cathedral of the Moscow Kremlin is followed here. Tentative attempts have been made to associate this icon with the name of Rublev's life-long companion Daniil Chernyi. The dramatic pose of Judas is effectively echoed in the arch behind him, and the apostles are carefully differentiated.

79 *left*
ST JOHN THE BAPTIST

c. 1425–40
follower of Andrei Rublev
tempera on wood
41.25 × 33.5 in (105 × 85 cm)
Tret'iakov Gallery, Moscow

It is tempting to attribute this recently uncovered icon (restored in 1960) to Rublev himself, or at least to one of his immediate followers. It is certainly an outstanding work. Originally St John was shown full length: the icon was sawn in half some centuries ago. The supplicatory pose suggests that it formed part of a Deisis composition, the remainder of which is now lost. This Baptist is not a fierce ascetic: with his pensive, somewhat sorrowful countenance, he has the appearance of a cultivated spiritual guide.

81

STONE RELIEF CARVINGS

detail of the north façade
1194−97
Cathedral of St Dimitrii, Vladimir

The three main façades of the cathedral are richly decorated with
carved stone relief; and the pilasters and other architectural
features are no less decorated than the wall surfaces which they
define. Animal and vegetable images predominate, but their
symbolism remains obscure. The presence of King David at the
apex of three façades suggests that much of the imagery may have
been derived from the Psalms.

82 *far right*

CATHEDRAL OF ST SOPHIA,
NOVGOROD

east end
1045−50

This northern St Sophia has preserved more of its original outline
than its southern counterpart in Kiev. Though the ground-plan of
the Kievan Sophia was used as a prototype, its complexity was
modified in accordance with the Novgorodian preference for
simplicity. There were originally five cupolas, and the exterior
was at first unplastered. The cathedral dominated the city, of
which it was the symbol.

83 *above* **84** *right*

THE KORSUN DOORS

1152—56
Masters Requinus and Weismut of
Magdeburg and Avram of Novgorod
bronze, mounted on oak
Cathedral of St Sophia, Novgorod

No Russian city had as much contact with
Western Europe in the post-Kievan period
as Novgorod. As if to symbolise these
contacts, the west doors of its St Sophia
Cathedral are of German workmanship.
They were originally commissioned by a
German bishop, Wichman of Magdeburg
for the cathedral of Plozk; it is not known
under what circumstances they reached
Novgorod. There they were reassembled,
probably in the 13th century, by a Russian,
Avram, who added a self-portrait (**83**).

86

ST GEORGE

late 14th century
school of Novgorod
tempera on cloth and wood
23 × 16·25 in (58·3 × 41·5 cm)
State Russian Museum, Leningrad

This St George is an outstanding example
of the mature Novgorodian style. Against
a magnificent background of Novgorod
red, St George, with his leaping horse, is
barely contained by the borders of this
icon: his hand, his halo and his cloak,
together with one of the horse's hooves,
project beyond the picture plane. The
upward curve of the dragon's belly is
matched exactly by the downward curve
of the saint's saddle – a reminder of the
artist's obvious interest in formal
equilibrium and tension.

87 *right*

CHURCH OF ST BASIL THE GREAT 'ON THE MOUND'

1413
Pskov

The sturdy simplicity of the Church of
St Basil is typical of Pskov. The decoration
of the drum, for which parallels may be
found in Novgorod, is of the type that
was to find favour with the builders of
Pskov over the succeeding century and a
half. This church retains the usual four
internal pillars to support the roof and
drum. Later in the 15th century Pskovian
churches were to dispense with these
altogether, and their modest interiors were
thus transformed into single,
unencumbered units.

85 *above*
ST CLEMENT *detail*

14th century
school of Novgorod
tempera on wood
State Russian Museum, Leningrad

The intensity of St Clement's face is
accentuated by the heavy furrows on the
brow, by the painterly treatment of his
cheeks and by the skilful application of
highlights. His hair, while congruent with
the rest of the painting, was probably
remodelled at a slightly later date.
Clement, as pope of Rome, wears the
episcopal omophorium over his shoulders.
The cult of St Clement was established in
Russia by Prince Vladimir, who brought
the saint's relics to Kiev from Kherson in
989 when he was about to embark on the
Christianisation of his subjects.

88 *below*

ST NICHOLAS

late 12th–early 13th century
school of Novgorod
tempera on cloth and wood
57 × 37 in (145 × 94 cm)
Tret'iakov Gallery, Moscow

The figure of St Nicholas, with high
forehead and tapering fingers, is elongated
as if to indicate his spiritual character. The
alert thoughtfulness of his countenance is
emphasised by the curious drawing of the
eyebrows. The delicate highlighting of his
moustache and chin is particularly
effective. The sober browns and reds in
which St Nicholas is painted stand out
against a silver background. The saints in
the margins were added somewhat later
in a more popular and more typically
Novgorodian style.

89 *left*

CHURCH OF THE
TRANSFIGURATION

1374
Novgorod

This impressive church was commissioned
by a member of the local gentry, together
with the residents of the street in which it
was erected. In many ways it follows in the
pattern set by its near-contemporary, the
Church of St Theodore Stratilates.
However, the curiously asymmetrical
distribution of windows, crosses and
decorative niches and the uneven division
of the walls is highly idiosyncratic and
provides a striking contrast to the logic,
simplicity and restraint of most
Novgorodian buildings. The drum,
recently restored, is in a more traditional
style.

90 *right*

THE TRANSFIGURATION

c. 1403
school of Feofan Grek
tempera on cloth and wood
72·5 × 52·75 in (184 × 134 cm)
Tret'iakov Gallery, Moscow

The nature of the uncreated light of the Transfiguration had been debated in the Councils of Constantinople of 1341 and 1351, and in the writings of St Gregory Palamas (died 1359). In the later 14th century widespread interest in the question may well have invigorated the iconography of the feast. This icon, if not by Feofan himself, is by someone who was intimately acquainted with his work. As is evident from the way in which he occasionally almost overdiluted his paint or left sections of his preparatory drawing uncovered, he was a daring and impulsive painter.

91 *above*

THE SYMBOL OF ST MATTHEW

from the Khitrovo Gospels
late 14th – early 15th century
possibly school of Feofan Grek
tempera on parchment
Lenin Library, Moscow

The magnificent Khitrovo Gospels take their name from their 17th-century owner, who donated the manuscript to the Monastery of the Trinity and St Sergii, Zagorsk, in 1677. Earlier that year he had received it as a gift from the tsar. The authorship of the illuminations is disputed. While attempts have been made to link at least some sections of it (like this dynamic angel) with the name of Rublev, the best authorities ascribe the manuscript to the school of Feofan Grek. The mauve and blue of the angel's garment contrast vividly with the red of the Gospels in his hand.

92 *right*

THE PROCESSION OF SAINTS INTO PARADISE

1408
Daniil Chernyi
fresco
Cathedral of the Dormition, Vladimir

This complex fresco is usually attributed to Daniil Chernyi, and must be accounted his masterpiece. It is part of a Last Judgment ensemble, and it shows St Paul leading the apostles and other groups of saints into Paradise. Particularly striking is the grouping of three heads immediately below St Paul. The fresco is carefully accommodated to the cathedral's contours: the heads and torsos of St Paul and of the figures in the upper register are distributed along the overhanging curve of a vault to bring them closer to the spectator.

93

THE DORMITION

late 14th century
attributed to Feofan Grek, c. 1340–c. 1410
tempera on cloth and wood
34 × 26·75 in (86 × 68 cm)
Tret'iakov Gallery, Moscow

In this Dormition, painted on the reverse
of *The Virgin of the Don* (**94**), the artist has
carefully limited the number of figures
present and has avoided the overcrowding
to which icons on this theme are sometimes
prone. Its calm coherence, its sensitivity to
mood, its dogmatic precision and its
remarkable combination of colours single
it out as one of the most memorable of
Russian icons.

94

THE VIRGIN OF THE DON

late 14th century
attributed to Feofan Grek, c. 1340–c. 1410
tempera on cloth and wood
34 × 26·75 in (86 × 68 cm)
Tret'iakov Gallery, Moscow

The icon is one of a remarkable pair: on its
reverse the same artist, possibly Feofan or
one of his immediate entourage, painted a
superlative Dormition (**93**). It is remarkable for its delicate, yet utterly unsenti-
mental lyricism. The vivid blue is rare in
14th-century Russian painting. The icon
invites comparison with the *Vladimir
Mother of God* (**44**), and like the latter it
played a prominent part in Russian history.
The Don Monastery in Moscow is named
in its honour.

95
ST MICHAEL

c. 1410–15, Andrei Rublev 1370–1430
tempera on cloth and wood
62·25 × 42·5 in (158 × 108 cm)
Tret'iakov Gallery, Moscow

This icon of St Michael forms part of the
Zvenigorod Deisis, together with *The
Saviour* (**97**) and *St Paul*. The four
remaining icons of the series have
disappeared. Unlike the icon of the
Saviour, this St Michael has suffered
comparatively little from time. The light
blue of the angel's hair band and of his
under-garment is effectively contrasted
with the coral pink of his outer robe. The
angels of Rublev's *The Trinity* (**98**) are
comparable in features and in mood.

96 *right*
ENTHRONED MOTHER OF GOD
WITH ST MICHAEL
AND ST SERGII

c. 1425–50, tempera on wood
63 × 44·25 in (160 × 112·5 cm)
State Historical Museum, Moscow

This unusual icon, painted soon after
Rublev's death, may have been intended
for the original shrine of St Sergii of
Radonezh, whose humble figure is to be
seen in the lower left-hand corner.
According to the life of St Sergii, he
received a visitation from the Mother of
God, to which there is some reference in
this composition. Of particular interest is
the calm, slightly melancholy expression
of the Virgin's face.

97 *below left* THE SAVIOUR

c.1410–1415, Andrei Rublev 1370–1430, tempera on cloth and wood
62·25 × 41·75 in (158 × 106 cm), Tret'iakov Gallery, Moscow

In 1918 this icon, together with two others from the same
Zvenigorod Deisis (**95**), was found under a pile of firewood,
apparently ready for destruction. The icon of the Saviour has
suffered more than its companions, and the head and shoulders of
Christ stand out against a stark background of lime wood. The
head is turned slightly towards the spectator, who is confronted
by a compassionate Saviour, 'meek and lowly in heart'.

98 THE TRINITY

c.1411, Andrei Rublev 1370–1430, tempera on cloth and wood
55 × 45 in (142 × 114 cm), Tret'iakov Gallery, Moscow

This icon, Rublev's masterpiece, is unsurpassed in Russian
medieval art either in its aesthetic or in its theological refinement.
Abraham's three visitors in Genesis XVII are used to represent the
persons of the Holy Trinity. The central figure is probably God
the Son, with God the Father on the left and the Holy Spirit on the
right. An unobtrusive circle contains the three figures and
introduces the symbol of eternity into the composition.

The rise of Muscovite power was favoured by military, economic and ideological factors, but more important than any of these was the fruitful alliance of monarchy and Church. By transferring his see from Vladimir to Moscow in 1328, the metropolitan greatly enhanced Muscovite prestige, approved the grand prince's policy of uniting all the Russian lands, and made possible the realisation of that medieval ideal—a harmony of Church and State. From then on Muscovite expansion developed into a crusade for the defence of Orthodox Christianity and national independence.

Historical events increased the prestige of the Muscovite grand prince as the defender of Orthodox Christian culture. The first of these events was provided by the spectacular decline of the Mongol empire. Seizing his chances as they presented themselves, Ivan III (1462–1505) secured his virtual independence from Mongol overlordship, to the point of being able to style himself Autocrat or Self-upholder. It was, in fact, his grandson, Ivan IV, the Terrible (1533–84) who reaped the full benefit of his grandfather's successful diplomacy by incorporating the Mongol khanates of Kazan' and Astrakhan' into his patrimony. The elimination of the Mongol threat was a major victory for Muscovite culture.

In 1453 Constantinople fell to the infidel Turk. The news of the dramatic capture seemed to invest Muscovy with a special destiny as the only surviving Orthodox state. Ivan III's marriage to Sophia Palaeologa, niece of the last Byzantine emperor, could only increase the feeling that Moscow was now the legitimate heir of Constantinople. It now devolved upon the city of Moscow to reign as the third Rome. This glittering assessment of Moscow's mission influenced the evolution of Muscovite art forms. Large-scale building operations, such as the reconstruction of the Kremlin under Ivan III at the end of the 15th century, were intended to express Moscow's new civic and religious dignity. Icon painting now became much more self-conscious and, apart from a small category of decorative folk-art items and silver vessels, all predominant art forms in 16th-century Muscovy continued to owe their existence to the spiritual stimulus of Orthodox religious consciousness.

The influence of Byzantine culture on Russian civilisation continued to be as powerful in the 16th century as it had been during the Kiev period. Direct contact with the Greeks and southern Slavs kept up the continual flow of Byzantine cultural ascendancy, and the Byzantine liturgy, translated into the Slavonic language, was a potent vehicle for the assimilation of Byzantine culture.

During the Muscovite period the Kremlin was the centre of the nation's life—artistic, no less than spiritual. Icon painters, metalworkers, architects and writers were summoned there to work for the grand prince (after 1547 called tsar) or metropolitan (after 1589 called patriarch). In this way, artists from many local centres and foreign lands worked together under the vigilant eye of the authorities. In the course of the 16th century a uniform Muscovite style of painting and architecture emerged, and was then disseminated from Moscow throughout Russia, replacing the local schools which had existed previously.

The patronage of the monarchy

The greatest art patron was always the tsar. His leadership on questions of aesthetics was an essential part of his royal duties and, undoubtedly, he took this duty seriously. His patronage was bound up with events in the life of the dynasty or the nation. The recapture of the Russian city of Smolensk from Poland was immediately followed by the founding of the Novodevichii Monastery to honour a vow made by the grand prince

The Flowering of Moscow
1460–1700

99
THE CATHEDRAL
OF THE DORMITION
1475–79
Aristotle Fioravanti
The Kremlin, Moscow

The coronation Cathedral of the Dormition is the central church of the Kremlin, and was the first to be rebuilt by Ivan III on a more imposing scale. As the Mongol domination had reduced native skill to a low level, Ivan was forced to seek help from abroad. The Italian architect was, however, obliged to adhere to the traditional plan evolved to suit the requirements of the Byzantine liturgy. Fioravanti, therefore, took the Cathedral of the Dormition in Vladimir (**60**) as his model.

Vasilii III. D'iakovo Church (one of the first of a new type of church known as a tent church) was built by Vasilii III as a votive offering for the birth of an heir. As soon as a son, the future Ivan the Terrible, was born, Vasilii marked the occasion by covering the tombs of the metropolitans Peter and Alexis in the Dormition Cathedral with repoussé work in silver and gold. The most revolutionary building of the period of Ivan the Terrible – the Church of St Basil – was built as a token of thanksgiving for victory over the Mongols. The grandiose superstructure of the Ivan the Great belfry, which towers over the Kremlin, was completed in 1600 by Boris Godunov both as a supplication for deliverance from a devastating famine and as a monument to lend prestige to his newly founded dynasty.

Art as sponsored by the tsar, apart from being commemorative, was also frequently didactic. A fresco in the apartments of Ivan the Terrible, executed immediately after the great fire of 1547, was used to express the theory of government. The fresco was obviously designed for the practical purpose of acting as a positive influence on those who saw it, and was in this case intended for the personal edification of the tsar, who is represented as a Christian judge and military leader. He distributes alms to the poor and sanctifies the people with water flowing from his hands. Inconspicuously included in the fresco is a wise old hermit acting as the tsar's mentor. It has been suggested that this may in fact be a portrait of the priest Sylvester, who filled just such a role between 1547 and 1561, and who may possibly have been instrumental in commissioning this fresco.

Our ignorance as to whether this work was undertaken primarily at the instigation of the tsar or the Church applies also to more important monuments. It seems clear that the tsar relied on the clergy for more than mere advice; sometimes indeed they even planned and supervised whole projects. There are grounds for believing that Metropolitan Makarii was no less responsible for the Church of St Basil than his imperial master, Ivan the Terrible. Makarii, himself a painter and encyclopaedist, played a crucial part in cultural life. It was he who summoned artists from Novgorod and Pskov to repair the damage done to Moscow's churches by the devastating fire of 1547. He was also to establish the first permanent workshop for icon painters in the Kremlin.

The most direct symbols of the tsar's dignity and prestige were his regalia. Crowns, orbs, sceptres and thrones of precious metals were made for the tsar in his personal workshops in the Kremlin or sent as presents by foreign powers or trading organisations. A number of thrones are among the treasures that have been preserved. The wooden Tsar's Throne in the Dormition Cathedral was made for Ivan the Terrible by Russian craftsmen. Boris Godunov received a throne of fairytale appearance from the Persian Shah Abbas in 1604. Overlaid with a thin sheet of beaten gold, it is studded with scintillating stones. Also in existence are the high-backed throne of Mikhail Romanov, inset with massive smoky topazes, and the 17th-century Oriental Turquoise Throne given to Mikhail's son Alexis by an Armenian trading company operating in Persia in the mid 17th century.

Apart from more precious objects, the tsars collected fine silver. Silversmiths from Greece, Georgia, Persia, Turkey and the West are all recorded at various times as having been in the tsar's service. Ivan the Terrible employed a number of German silversmiths captured during the Livonian War; later he encouraged English silversmiths to settle in Moscow. Tsar Alexis was especially fond of niello work (finely engraved silver with lead inlay) at which the artists of Persia excelled. The chronicler attests that the tsar's son Fedor, who had a preference for German silver, would while away whole evenings admiring the finer pieces in his possession. This col-

136

102, 110

100

114

124, 246

100

THE TSAR'S THRONE

1551
wood
Cathedral of the Dormition, the Kremlin, Moscow

The relief carvings on the waist-high sides of the throne depict the arrival of the royal regalia, which were reputed to have been a gift from the Byzantine emperor to Vladimir Monomakh. The canopy on four pillars, made by Russian craftsmen, shows their skill in handling wood at a time when their only tool was the axe.

101

MONASTERY OF VOLOKOLAMSK

mainly 17th century

The Monastery of Volokolamsk was founded by St Iosif of Volokolamsk, who died in 1515. Just as monastic ideals dominated the culture of Muscovite Russia, so the picturesque towers of her monasteries stood vigil over the vast expanses of her countryside. The panorama of gilt and brightly painted domes – squat, bulbous, pear-shaped or tapered like a burning candle – recall for us today the Muscovite vision of a heavenly Jerusalem.

102

THE CROWN OF KAZAN'

mid 16th century
gold
height 10·5 in (26·5 cm)
Armoury Palace, the Kremlin, Moscow

The golden crown of Kazan' was made in Moscow for Ivan the Terrible. Its Eastern workmanship suggests that it may have been designed by jewellers brought to Moscow from the captured Mongol stronghold of Kazan'. On the other hand tradition links it with the Mongol prince Sain, who adopted the Christian faith in 1574, and was created Prince of Tver' by Ivan. The crown has also been ascribed to Ediger Makhmet, last independent ruler of Kazan', who was christened in 1553.

lection continued to grow as the tsars amassed gifts from foreign courts and trading companies. Although Muscovy was a poor country, the Muscovites endeavoured to disguise the fact by putting on display a staggering amount of gold and silver and presenting an array of finely clad attendants.

These royal and ambassadorial gifts, preserved to this day in the Armoury Palace of the Kremlin, consist of silver and gold plate, drinking **124** cups, enamel work, elaborate vessels in the form of birds and wild **111, 123** animals, fine weapons, armour, horse trappings and even carriages. Gifts **115** arrived from Turkey, Persia and the East as well as from Holland, the German principalities, Poland and Great Britain. The Kremlin collection of English Elizabethan and Stuart silver is the finest and most complete in **132-5** existence.

Monastic patronage

The patronage of the monasteries ranks next in importance to that of the tsar. Havens of learning and wealth, the monasteries were also instruments of government and training centres for the higher clergy, many of whom presided over the aesthetic taste of their time.

During the great period of monastic expansion (1340–1550) the search for God had driven many monks to settle in remote areas. These distant outposts slowly led to the colonisation of the hinterland. By the late 15th century once-primitive settlements had accumulated sufficient wealth to

be remodelled, and during the course of the 16th and 17th centuries most monasteries were rebuilt on a more grandiose scale. The Volokolamsk Monastery stood as a distant outpost on the western approach to Moscow, **101** but its founder St Iosif was an energetic church leader and upholder of the close ties with the monarchy. He was also the champion of monastic land ownership against the conception of monastic poverty preached by his contemporary, St Nil Sorskii. The ritualistic developments of the 16th century, and the resplendent embellishments of monasteries and churches, are the direct result of the victory of St Iosif's followers.

The monasteries were not only cultural centres, they also played an essential part in the defence of the realm. Moscow itself is surrounded by a belt of fortress-monasteries. In 1591, when the city was besieged by the khan of Crimea, the Danilov, Novospasskii, Novodevichii and Simonov **117** monasteries were armed with artillery for the city's defence. Muscovite victory was ascribed to the icon, *The Virgin of the Don*, in whose honour **94** Tsar Fedor began the construction of the monastery of the Don in the following year. Perhaps the most famous Russian monastery is that of the Trinity and St Sergii to the north-east of Moscow at Zagorsk. It too was **69** associated with defence, for in 1608 it was the seat of early resistance to the Polish conquerors which turned the tide in Russia's favour. Endowed with numerous gifts from the tsars, it is rich in painting, architecture and silverwork.

The great cathedrals of Moscow

The reconstruction of Moscow's Kremlin undertaken by Ivan III at the end of the 15th century was not only a sign of growing economic prosperity, it was also a conscious symbol of Moscow's new prestige. Ivan III's first concern was naturally for the coronation Cathedral of the Dormition. When Muscovite architects failed him, he entrusted the construction to architects summoned from the vassal city of Pskov. However, the collapse of the new structure as soon as it reached the vaults is a sad indication of the depth to which Russia had been reduced by Mongol domination. Ivan was obliged to seek help elsewhere, so Muscovite agents abroad secured the services of the Italian, Aristotle Fioravanti, official engineer and architect of the city of Bologna, who had also been in the service of the Sforza family in Milan. Although the entire process of reconstruction was undertaken by Italian architects, Ivan allowed them little scope to carry out their own ideas. Fioravanti and his assistants realised that their services were primarily required to instruct the Russians in the technicalities of building and to teach them how to span a roof and how to use hoists. As experts familiar with the up-to-date siege-resistant devices, they were entrusted with the designing of the Kremlin walls and towers (the upper part of these towers were added during the 17th century), but when it came to planning the Kremlin cathedrals, the Italians were required to adhere to Byzantine principles of design. Fioravanti was actually obliged to go to Vladimir in order to study the 12th-century Cathedral of the Dormition.

In the Dormition Cathedral Fioravanti fulfilled all the stipulations required of him. By reproducing the salient features of Vladimir-Suzdal' architecture, the architect provided a symbol of the continuity of the Russian tradition of architecture, as well as of the continuity of the power of the ruling princes of Moscow, handed down to them by their Vladimir-Suzdal' predecessors. The five-domed cathedral, the repository of Moscow's holiest relics and a symbol of her might and glory, became a prototype of ecclesiastical architecture. It was the inspiration and model for church building over the next two centuries. The Novodevichii Monastery and Nikon's Church of the Twelve Apostles both follow essentially the same pattern.

The next cathedral church of the Kremlin to be reconstructed was the Chapel Royal of the Annunciation, where members of the tsar's family were baptised and married. The building was designed by Pskov mastermasons as a small and intimate chapel, with easy access to the royal palace.

After the completion of the florid St Basil's Cathedral in 1560, the Annunciation Cathedral appeared too simple for contemporary taste and was therefore remodelled by Ivan the Terrible. The raised platform, which already connected the building with the palace, was extended on three sides and topped at the four corners by miniature chapels, each marked by a single golden dome. On the south side of the edifice a covered staircase was constructed to permit the tsar to follow divine service when, after his uncanonical fourth marriage, he was forbidden to enter the church itself. The interior of the cathedral has preserved much of its original character. The icon screen, although it incorporates several panels painted for the earlier structure by Feofan Grek and Rublev, dates from the period after the great fire of 1547. The icon screens commissioned by Ivan the Terrible for his four miniature chapels are superlative examples of the art of that period. The frescoes of the main church were

103 *above*
CATHEDRAL OF
THE ANNUNCIATION
1484–89
The Kremlin, Moscow
The Cathedral of the Annunciation was completed for Ivan III by master masons from Pskov in 1489. The double row of receding gables spanning the roof is a device borrowed from wooden architecture, and this is one of the earliest examples of its adaptation to masonry. Originally conceived as a simple cube surmounted by three cupolas, the building was remodelled by Ivan the Terrible.

104

ST DIMITRII OF SALONIKA
AND ST GEORGE

1508
Feodosii
fresco
Cathedral of the Annunciation,
The Kremlin, Moscow

In these frescoes which he painted for
Vasilii III, Feodosii carefully adhered to
the tradition of his father Dionisii. The
elegant drawing and the clear, cheerful
colours recall the frescoes at Ferapont
Monastery executed jointly by Dionisii
and his two sons in 1502.

105

CHURCH OF THE
TRANSFIGURATION

c. 1550
Ostrovo

In attempting to render the basic character
of Byzantine architecture in wood, Russian
craftsmen evolved a style both national
and original. Reworked in stone during
the 16th century, the tradition resulted in
such masterpieces as this church. The bank
of gables ranged one behind the other was
a common device in the 16th century; a
hundred years later they were to be over-
lapped as in the Church of the Georgian
Mother of God (**107**).

commissioned by Vasilii III in 1508, and are reminiscent of the wall-paintings of the Ferapont Monastery executed by Dionisii. The 16th-century stone door frames, carved in low relief with swirling decoration and picked out in blue and gold – the work of Italian masons – initiated the Russians into Renaissance decorative motifs. These designs were to be frequently re-interpreted by Russian builders during the next century. **104**

The gem-like Chapel of the Deposition of the Garments is also the creation of the master-masons of Pskov. Unlike the Annunciation Cathedral, it has not suffered from later additions, and its delicate proportions and single cupola distinguish it as a masterpiece of 15th-century architecture. **118**

The most famous of all the great churches of the tsars, St Basil's Cathedral, was influenced by a long tradition of popular architecture. Wood, which is plentiful in north and central Russia, provided the Russian artist-craftsman with a material which he learnt to handle with skill and self-assurance. He was able to reproduce in wood all the basic features of Byzantine architecture. At their simplest, wooden churches are rectangular structures with a pitched roof and cupola. The more elaborate examples have octagonal towers (which enclosed the maximum area with the minimum material) capped with a lantern and cupola. Because of the climate the place of worship was on the first floor with access from enclosed galleries and covered staircases. The outline of these churches was devised to appeal to the visual senses of the traveller, and for the same reason they were often picturesquely sited on the edge of a forest or close to a river or lake. **136**

Between 1532 and 1640, a number of stone churches were built which were directly inspired by the tent-shaped silhouette of wooden architecture. The first of these was built in 1532 by Vasilii III at his summer palace at Kolomenskoe near Moscow. Variations on this theme are provided by the churches of St John the Baptist at D'iakovo, the Transfiguration at Ostrovo and St Basil's Cathedral outside the Moscow Kremlin. **131** **105**

The Pokrov Church, properly known as St Basil's Cathedral in memory of the 'fool for Christ's sake', who in life dared to defy Ivan the Terrible and now lies buried there, has become a symbol of 16th-century Muscovite culture. It has always exercised a powerful fascination over the minds of foreign travellers who have been misled into believing, owing to its exotic character, that Russian architecture was beholden to that of Persia and India. St Basil's consists of eight miniature chapels, each dedicated to a victory over the Mongols, which reproduce various features of wooden architecture. They cluster round a central, tent-shaped tower, to which each chapel is linked by means of a covered passage. If it is treated as a series of distinct chapels, rather than as a single, grossly over-burdened unit, it strikes a less discordant note. However, as the building stands today, the proportions have suffered by the addition of an external gallery which has the effect of making the whole heavier. The original, whitewash finish was also replaced in the 18th century by over-ornate, polychrome decoration. **136**

The activity of the artist Dionisii is contemporary with the construction of the great dynastic churches of the Kremlin. His art, unsurpassed in late 15th-century painting, was a worthy ornament of the Muscovite court. Two large panels preserved in the Moscow Dormition Cathedral, considered to be early works, show full-length figures of the metropolitans Peter and Alexis, vested with the imposing hieratic insignia, and surrounded by a border of miniature paintings illustrating incidents taken from their lives. By these paintings, Dionisii lauded the sainted metro- **126** politans as men of God and architects of Muscovite unity. Far more directly than Rublev, Dionisii succeeded in founding a school or tradition of painting. His spirit, his love of elegance and the graceful self-assurance of his figures pervaded the art of his followers for at least a century.

The Stroganovs

The name of the Stroganov family was linked with art patronage from the late 16th century. The founder of the family fortune was Anika Stroganov (1498–1570), a merchant of Novgorod extraction who colonised the north-eastern frontier forest regions. Subsequently, family settlements were developed at Perm', Velikii Ustiug and Sol'vychegodsk where the family bondsmen were engaged in fur-trapping and worked the salt mines. The Stroganovs became so phenomenally wealthy that even the tsars resorted to them for financial assistance.

A family of such wealth could not fail to leave its mark on the history of Russian art, and apart from having churches built and founding monasteries, they made generous gifts of gold, silver and fine embroideries to icon shrines. But where, as patrons, they outscored all their rivals, was by lending their name to a school of icon painting. A number of exquisite panels painted between 1580–1620 is evidence of this unique distinction. Contrary to common usage, both the name of the artist and the name of the member of the Stroganov family who had commissioned the painting, were inscribed on the reverse side of each icon. Altogether too sophisticated to be the work of local craftsmen, icons of the Stroganov school were painted by artists in the tsar's Kremlin workshop who had received special assignments to execute them for members of the family. These panels then served as models in the various local workshops of the family settlements. In some instances, artists from the Kremlin went to Sol'vychegodsk to undertake commissions, and it may well be that some went to settle in the north following the disruption caused in the capital by the Polish occupation.

The Stroganovs followed the work they commissioned with keen interest; they did not merely stipulate the theme for the icon assignments, but gave guidance on style, composition and, above all, on colour. The colour-tones of Stroganov icons are not only pure, they are brighter and more pleasing to the eye than those of other Muscovite paintings of the period.

The conflict between West and East

Stroganov painting marks a period of transition in the history of Russian taste and art patronage. Although still objects of worship, these icons show for the first time a dominance of aesthetic requirements over religious ones. Exclusive and ultra refined, they are also a foretaste of what Russia was to expect following the period of Peter the Great's Westernisation. From now on the nature of art was increasingly determined by the personal taste or whim of the aristocrat, and the popular basis of art was accordingly superseded by a rarefied salon atmosphere. Thus, Stroganov painting seriously challenged Byzantine achievement, causing a rift in the impressive cultural and ideological harmony of old Russia.

In the early 17th century the danger threatening Muscovite culture was very great, for Russia was unable to revitalise her art. Moscow was caught between reproducing and elaborating upon motifs from her own past, or, alternatively, turning for inspiration to the brilliant West. The latter course meant not only technical advancement, but also, ultimately, secularisation and distortion of the wholeness and clarity of the Byzantine vision. The former course meant stagnation by the repetition of worn-out forms.

106
THE CHURCH OF THE TWELVE APOSTLES AND THE PATRIARCH'S PALACE
1656
The Kremlin, Moscow

Patriarch Nikon exercised a prodigious influence on the architectural and artistic development of the mid 17th century. His own grandiose palace, built on a scale never previously encountered in a secular building, was meant to serve as a model for future generations of architects. The adjoining Church of the Twelve Apostles also served a purpose. It boldly reasserted the pre-eminence of the traditional Russo-Byzantine five-domed building over the popular tent-shaped towers which Nikon had banned.

138

107

THE CHURCH OF THE GEORGIAN
MOTHER OF GOD
'IN NIKITINKA'

1635–53
Moscow

Despite the vivid poetic emotion that went
into creating the medieval cultural tradition, 17th-century art failed to revitalise
itself with new principles. Pre-Petrine
culture was eroded by the relentless
pressure of copying and proliferating
themes of the previous century. The
Church of the Georgian Mother of God
illustrates this tendency. It is the sad and
beautiful swan song before Peter's fierce
onslaught against Russo-Byzantine culture.

The dynasty which had ruled Russia for eight hundred years came to an
abrupt end with the murder by Ivan the Terrible of his own son, in a fit of
uncontrollable rage. After this horrifying episode, Muscovy suffered a
harsh occupation by the soldiers of Poland and Sweden. It is possible to
speculate that during this time of troubles (1605–13), Russian Orthodox
civilisation might well have been completely annihilated, and Muscovy
incorporated within the framework of the Germano-Latin West. This,
however, did not happen. The country rallied dramatically, and the invaders were expelled. Finally, a new wave of religious and national fervour
followed upon the election to the throne of the Romanov dynasty in 1613.

The seeds of decay, though unobserved by contemporaries, were, nonetheless, present. National feeling, however intense, is not in itself sufficient
to stimulate the growth of new art-forms. Nevertheless, 17th-century
Russian art is rich and beautiful; it is invested with the imagination and
charm of a folk-legend and seems just as unreal. Clarity, harmony and
perception were replaced by fantasy and by an ever-increasing tendency to
confuse, complicate the essentials and overload. Every motif of the 16th
century was reworked; every possible method of embellishment adopted.
Although this contributed to a certain transitory success, it could not disguise the fact that Muscovite culture was facing decay and internal dissolution. By the mid century much had disintegrated, and what was left was a
peasant culture.

The process whereby 17th-century Russians popularised and prolifer-
ated their art forms may be followed clearly in the development of
ecclesiastical architecture. Plans, already complex enough, are now ob-
scured by ornamentation. Cupolas sprouted like swollen buds on slender
stems. *Kokoshniki* multiplied and lost all structural purpose.

The Church of the Georgian Mother of God 'in Nikitinka' was built in
Moscow by Grigorii Nikitinov, a wealthy merchant from Novgorod. The
imposing external staircase and ornamental porch, features adopted from
wooden architecture, provide a buoyant, joyful, and even homely effect.
The Church of the Nativity of Putniki, with its imaginative ornamentation, also evokes clearly the spirit of the 17th century—a joyful and lively
rendering of a national and popular idiom.

During this period of cultural confusion the pro-Greek tendencies of the
higher clergy found a spokesman in the energetic patriarch Nikon who
held office from 1652 to 1666. Nikon believed in the necessity of preserving
the purity of Byzantine achievement as the basis of the national culture and
thought that Byzantine discipline could still counteract the worst excesses
of national cultural aberration. Accordingly, he reasserted the impreg-
nability of canonical painting and opposed the awakening tendency to
turn for inspiration to sentimental Western naturalism. He likewise for-
bade the use of the tent spire over the main structure of church building,
since he claimed that this device distorted the symbolic meaning of Orthodox worship. Nikon then made his intentions for the future of art and
architecture clear by launching an extensive programme of building.
With his patriarchal Church of the Twelve Apostles in the Moscow **106**
Kremlin, Nikon reverted to the traditional Byzantino-Russian cube surmounted by five cupolas. This building is connected to a sumptuous
palace which the patriarch devised to mirror the new notion of the dignity
of his office—a notion which has more in common with Latin than Greek
religious tradition. During his fourteen years of office, Nikon was also a
prodigious builder of monasteries; prominent among them are the
Valdaiskii, Novospasskii, Krestnyi, and the New Jerusalem monasteries.
His lead in planning grandiose architectural complexes was followed by

other Church hierarchs, notably the metropolitans of Suzdal' and Rostov.

109   The Rostov Kremlin was built between 1652–92 by Metropolitan Jonah Sysoevich, who, like Nikon, was the son of a simple parish priest. Churches, flanked by defensive towers, are grouped at intervals along the ramparts. Within the compound five more churches encircle the metropolitan's white palace. A raised, covered corridor, painted with frescoes, connects one part of the compound with the other. The Rostov Kremlin is the last, the most complete, and most monumental expression of Nikon's ideals of defensive religious architecture. (A kremlin is a citadel within a town).

While Nikon's assertions about art forms and his fierce polemics against Western aesthetics were powerless to infuse new life into Russian art, his famous controversial remark 'I am a Russian, but my faith is Greek' provoked a further crack in the Byzantino-Russian culture he sought to defend. It called in question the whole theory of Moscow as the third Rome, since it implied that the Russians were less the chosen people of Orthodoxy than they had supposed. Nikon now suggested that the Greeks, even under Turkish domination, had been more successful than the Russians in safeguarding the Byzantine Christian heritage. Consequently, he proceeded to 'correct' Slavonic 'errors' by bringing Russian rites into line with Greek practice. Nikon's view, both tactless and historically incorrect, provoked the Church schism of 1654 which gave rise to the division between Old Believers and Nikon's followers. It proved to be a further stage in the breakdown of old Russian culture.

In the same year Little Russia (present-day Ukraine) adhered to Russia, and in 1667 Kiev followed suit. These ancient Russian lands, which had for so long been within the cultural orbit of Poland, were a source from which the attitudes and ideas most feared by Nikon were to infect Muscovy. Meanwhile, Alexis, 'the gentle tsar' (1645–76) was caught between his love of traditional spiritual values and a penchant for the technical skill of the West. He was by no means opposed to the spreading of this pseudo-Byzantine culture. When Nikon caused Frankish icons to be smashed on the floor of the Dormition Cathedral and consigned to flames, Alexis wept and meekly asked that they should be reverently buried in the ground. After Nikon's fall Ukrainian literature, painting and church music and Ukrainian Baroque architecture were increasingly accepted by the tsar and the family of his second wife, the Naryshkins. When the tsar appointed Khitrovo, a man of decidedly pro-Western sympathies, to take over the supervision of the Armoury Palace workshops, he ensured the victory of the new aesthetics.

The ablest painter to adopt the new tendencies was Simon Ushakov. Appointed court painter when only twenty-two, Ushakov's interests ranged over a wide field. He tried his hand at fortifications, map-making, portrait painting and casting cannon. Subscribing to an ideal of earthly, as

139 opposed to transcendental, beauty, Ushakov felt a particular fascination for the human face. His meticulously rendered portraits of Christ, with their cold pale colours, are both of historical and artistic interest. They represent the first stage in the evolution of a Russian secular art. In the conflict between the West and Byzantium Ushakov resorted to compromise. Where composition was concerned, he adhered to strictly Byzantine precedents, but adopted naturalism in the painting of faces. Although he mastered much of the technical skill of Western painting, he never renounced tempera for oil paint.

137, 141   The understanding of Western realism by Russian artists was slight. Even the circulation of such books as Piscator's Bible, with its eight-

ST CYRIL OF BELOOZERSK
16th and 17th centuries
tempera on wood, with metal
and precious stones
13·5 × 6·5 in (34·3 × 16·7 cm)
Armoury Palace, the Kremlin, Moscow

A disciple of St Sergii of Radonezh and the founder of a monastery at Beloozersk north-west of Moscow, St Cyril played a leading part in the monastic revival of the 14th century. This icon was first painted in the 16th century, but it was repainted a century later and also embellished with jewels and oval plaques engraved with the patron saints of the Glagolevskii family, to which it belonged.

109

THE CHURCH OF ST JOHN
THE EVANGELIST
1683
Rostov

The Church of St John the Evangelist is one of a series of churches towering over the ramparts and covered passages of the Rostov Kremlin. Constructed by Jonah Sysoevich, metropolitan of Rostov, and friend of Patriarch Nikon, the kremlin complex is an impressive example of a form of architecture which combines features of monastic, civil and military building. The fortified gateways flanked by towers are made more secure by the sacred precincts of a church, in accordance with the Byzantine concept that the spiritual and material worlds are not distinct, but harmonised.

110 *right*

THE GREAT REGALIA OF MIKHAIL ROMANOV

1627–28, Armoury Palace, the Kremlin, Moscow

The Great Regalia were worn for state occasions, at religious
ceremonies and for the reception of foreign ambassadors.
Although Russia was only just emerging from a period of chaos,
no effort was spared in the production of the regalia, since they
epitomised the prestige of the newly elected tsar and of the
country. The biblical scenes in relief on the orb are in the manner
of the Italian Renaissance, but Eastern jewellers were also
responsible for its workmanship.

111 *below*

GOSPEL COVER

late 17th century
gold and enamel, 18·5 × 11·5 in (47 × 29 cm)
Armoury Palace, the Kremlin, Moscow

The technique of applying enamel with a brush reached Russia
during the late 17th century. A good example of the technique is
seen in this superb gospel cover. Between the gold-relief corner
plaques of the evangelists and the centre motif of the Deisis
long-stemmed intertwining flowers, painted in enamel, weave a
pattern of unusual beauty. The rendering of the figures in high
relief by repoussé work is also typical of the same period.

115 *left*
SADDLE

1637–38
velvet, gold, enamel and precious stones
Armoury Palace, the Kremlin, Moscow

In early 17th-century Russia saddles were
of Persian design. This saddle, made in the
imperial workshops of the Silver Palace for
Mikhail Romanov by the craftsmen
responsible for the Great Regalia, has a
frame studded with precious stones and is
worked in finest quality enamel. The seat,
of crimson Italian velvet, is embroidered
with gold and silver thread.

112 *above*
PECTORAL ICON

12th and 16th centuries
onyx, pearls, rubies, gold and enamel
Armoury Palace, the Kremlin, Moscow

Evidence of the high esteem in which Byzantine art was held is
provided by this superb Greek 12th-century onyx cameo, which
was richly mounted four hundred years later as a pectoral icon.
Iov, the first metropolitan of Moscow to be elevated to the rank of
patriarch, received it from Tsar Fedor to mark his consecration
in 1589. The brilliant interplay of polychrome enamel and jewels is
typical of the taste of the late 16th century.

113 *left*
EMBROIDERY OF THE HOLY TRINITY

late 16th century
embroidered textile
Armoury Palace, the Kremlin, Moscow

In Muscovite Russia fine textiles were as highly prized as painted
panels or silver. The exacting needlework and subtle colour
harmonies raise them to the level of a great art form. Although
the design and supervision of the work was entrusted to icon
painters, the execution provided one of the few creative pastimes
open to women. Here, the use of gold and silver threads, and the
seed pearls employed for the lettering and to emphasise the
outline, convey an impression of opulence and festive solemnity,
which is especially characteristic of embroideries from the
Godunov workshops. This embroidery was presented to the
Ipatiev Monastery by O. I. Godunov in 1593.

114
THRONE

late 16th century
gold, rubies, turquoises
35 × 23·5 in (89 × 61 cm)
Armoury Palace, the Kremlin, Moscow

Tsar Boris Godunov was presented with this magnificent throne
by the Persian Shah Abbas in 1604. The wooden frame, which is
overlaid with sheets of gold, is studded with rubies and turquoises.
Under the present damask seat covering, which dates from 1742,
the original Persian velvet has been preserved. A characteristic
example of Persian palace furniture, it appealed to the taste
prevailing in Muscovy during the early 17th century.

116
CENSER

1674
silver-gilt
State Historical Museum, Moscow

Until the transfer of the capital to St Petersburg, the trading towns
along the Volga were distinguished not only for the construction
of splendid churches, but also for their fine silver. The silver
produced in the workshops of Kostroma is stylistically closely
related to that of Novgorod and Pskov. Repoussé and chiselled
work, as on this censer, was much admired during the 17th century.

117 NOVODEVICHII MONASTERY

16th and 17th centuries, Moscow

Founded by Vasilii III in thanksgiving for the recovery of
Smolensk from the Poles, Novodevichii Monastery was a vital
link in the chain of fortress-monasteries which encircled Moscow
at strategic points. As many of its members belonged to the high
nobility, and even occasionally the royal house, it received
unsurpassed endowments both of land and of precious objects.

118 TWO KREMLIN CHURCHES

*Chapel of the Deposition of the Garments and cupolas of the
Chapel of Christ behind the Golden Grille
1484–86 and 1679–81 respectively, Moscow*

The golden cupolas, which crown a network of small chapels
built to serve the Kremlin Palace, contrast sharply with the
austerity of the neighbouring late 15th-century church.

hundred wood-cuts of Western painting, could not fully initiate icon painters into the complexities of Renaissance art to which their ideals, and their training, had so long been diametrically opposed. Russian patrons and artists alike concentrated on depicting elaborately patterned damasks, trompe l'oeil scenes and miniature work. Inferior Western artists employed in the Kremlin received salaries greatly in excess of those earned by Russian icon painters. When an icon painter is recorded as having received a high salary, it is because 'he executes minute heads for the adornment of holy icons'. In his treatise on aesthetics Ushakov compares the ideal work of art to the reflection of nature in a mirror—a view inimical to any Italian artist of that period. Despite the increasing infiltration of secular themes during the 17th century, art continued to maintain its primary religious character. With the exception of the royal residences in the Kremlin, and a few substantial stone dwelling-houses in Moscow, there was little secular art to attract our attention, and most of what there is has been much restored. Even during the second half of the century, when traditional values were being challenged, the most important architectural monuments were still ecclesiastical.

119, 120   A number of churches, built between 1620–90 along the Volga trade route, notably at Iaroslavl', Rostov, Kostroma and Romanov-Borisoglebsk, surpass anything in Moscow at the time. They were erected as *ex vota* offerings by both guilds and individual merchant families, such as the Skripin brothers, jewellers of Iaroslavl'. A keen spirit of rivalry is apparent; every structure vies with its neighbour both in height and spaciousness.

The churches of the Volga towns represent a conservative tendency, but imperial favour gave preference to the Moscow Baroque and other styles imported from the West. And, as time passed, the entire elite was quite content to live with a borrowed culture. Native art, deprived of aristocratic patronage, continued, nonetheless, to display life and vigour, although reduced to the level of a popular culture. The wooden Church of the Transfiguration built at Kizhi, on the shores of lake Onega in 1714, bears witness to the tenacious survival of the popular ideal. With its twenty-two cupolas and its silhouette recalling the outline of a giant fir tree, it may be said to represent wooden tent architecture in its most developed form.

Nestor, the peasant craftsman who supervised its construction, grasped its significance in the history of Russian art. Surveying his creation, he declared that Russia would never again witness such a building, and so saying, hurled his axe into the lake. The church at Kizhi did not entirely represent the end of an era. In 1764, the Church of Pokrov rose majestically alongside it, and the superb belfry was added in 1874. Both these structures, although they do not surpass Nestor's creation, at least demonstrate the undiminished vigour of the tradition which he represented.

In retrospect, Nestor's action in casting his tools into the lake had not been without symbolic meaning and prophetic import. While Kizhi was under construction, Peter the Great was laying out a new city which was to replace Moscow as the capital of his empire. Peter had entrusted the plans to Dutch architects, and it was quite clear to Nestor, as it must have been to his contemporaries, that the skills of native craftsmen were neither appreciated nor required by the Russian tsar. This fact did not prevent people from continuing to build churches and paint icons for their own use, but more than a hundred years were to elapse before the Russian sovereign and the elite were to show interest once again in the Byzantino-Russian tradition.

John Stuart

119

CHURCH OF
ST JOHN CHRYSOSTOM
1644–54
Iaroslavl'

The architects of the towns along the Volga used contrasting materials and vivid colours rather than elaborate gables to beautify the outside of their churches. Warm, red brick sometimes laid in patterns, ceramic tiles, external frescoes and golden cupolas produced stunning effects.

120

CHURCH OF THE RESURRECTION
1652–70
Romanov-Borisoglebsk

Romanov and Borisoglebsk are two small villages separated by the Volga. The rivalry of two merchant families led to the building of two splendid churches, the Erection of the Cross on the left bank and the Resurrection facing it. The latter, consecrated in 1652, was enlarged by Metropolitan Jonah of Rostov in 1670. In its present form it is an outstanding example of the architecture of the Volga towns during the late 17th century.

121
CENSER IN THE FORM OF A CHURCH
1598, gold, Armoury Palace, the Kremlin, Moscow

Irina, sister of Boris Godunov, commissioned this censer for the Cathedral of the Archangel Michael in the Moscow Kremlin, where her husband was buried. The style recalls the contemporary Stroganov school of painting, and the delicacy and precision of the niello work has seldom been surpassed. During the early 17th century, this censer was so highly esteemed that a patriarchal decree limited its use to nine times a year.

122 *below right*
BISHOP'S MITRE

early 17th century, gold and precious stones
Museum of History and Art, Zagorsk

Mitres were unknown in Eastern Europe before the conquest of Constantinople. Thereafter the patriarch of Constantinople assumed a head-dress resembling the crown of the late Byzantine emperors, and by the mid 16th century similar 'mitres' had been adopted by all the higher clergy, Russian as well as Greek. During the second quarter of the 17th century the crown had become higher and was usually resplendent with jewels, enamel and miniature icons. Such mitres were designed to sparkle during the service, thus enhancing the solemn grandeur of the liturgy.

123 *below*
GOSPEL COVER

1571, gold, enamel and precious stones, 10·25 × 17 in (27 × 43 cm)
Armoury Palace, the Kremlin, Moscow

This gospel cover was presented by Ivan the Terrible to the Annunciation Cathedral in 1571. With its enamel executed in white and delicate tones of blue and green, and the rhythmic flow of its design, which encircles massive emeralds, sapphires and rubies, the cover reflects the late 16th-century taste for the sumptuous and the resplendent.

124 *left*

GOLD PLATE

1561
diameter 16 in (40·5 cm)
Armoury Palace, the Kremlin, Moscow

This plate was given by Ivan the Terrible
to his second wife on their wedding day in
1561. It is an excellent example of the
desire of 16th-century Russian silversmiths
for simplicity of form which they
combined with meticulously executed
decorative designs enhancing the basic
shape of the vessel. A vigorous pattern of
flowing curves offsets the circular outline
of the dish. The flowers and inscriptions
around the rim testify to the skill with
which mid century craftsmen handled
niello.

125

VIRGIN OF TENDERNESS

17th century
tempera on wood, framed in gold, with
precious stones
Armoury Palace, the Kremlin, Moscow

This gold triptych has side panels engraved
with the archangels Michael and Gabriel.
The icon itself is practically concealed by
the profusion of enamels, pearls and
precious stones. The triptych originally
belonged to Ivan Griazev, a government
official in the second quarter of the 17th
century

ОА ПЕТР · ΜΗΤΡΟΠΟΛΙΤ

126 *left*

THE METROPOLITAN PETER

early 16th century
Dionisii
tempera on wood
77·5 × 59·75 in (197 × 152 cm)
Tret'iakov Gallery, Moscow

When in 1472 the old Dormition Cathedral was levelled to its foundations prior to its reconstruction under Ivan III, the masons caused a stir by uncovering the remains of the sainted metropolitans Peter and Alexis, who had died in the previous century. About thirty years later Dionisii painted the two imposing icons which established the prototype for their likeness. By these images, he lauded them as men of God and architects of Muscovite unity.

127

THE ENTOMBMENT

late 15th century
tempera on wood
Tret'iakov Gallery, Moscow

This icon conveys some of the intensity of Russian religious emotion. Its message, expressed through a subtle interplay of colour, is moving in its sincerity. Mary Magdalene's upraised hands have the poignancy of a lament whose echo lingers in the stylised rocks forming the background.

128

THE DEPOSITION FROM THE CROSS

late 15th century
tempera on wood
35·75 × 24·5 in (91 × 62 cm)
Tret'iakov Gallery, Moscow

This icon is by the same unknown artist responsible for *The Entombment* (**127**). No superfluous detail is permitted to destroy the epic quality of the work, and this is part of the impact of the icon. The beautiful, sweeping curve described by Christ's body, juxtaposed to the horizontal beam of the cross, succeeds in heightening the sense of sharp dramatic tension.

129 *far left*

WOODEN ROOFS

1714
Church of the Transfiguration, Kizhi

Ridged gables such as these originally evolved from the vaults of Byzantine architecture. The *kokoshnik* gable (named after the head-dress worn by unmarried girls) was primarily devised to meet the climatic conditions in the north, since the steep slope easily sheds snow. However, architects were quick to perceive its potential as a decorative device.

130 *above left*

THE CHURCHES OF KIZHI

18th and 19th centuries
wood

In spite of the indifference of the elite after Peter the Great's Westernisation, Russo-Byzantine religious artistic traditions continued to survive on the level of popular culture and in remote areas such as the north, the Urals and Siberia. The magnificent complex of wooden churches at Kizhi was built over a period of 150 years. On the left is the Church of the Pokrov (1764), on the right the Church of the Transfiguration (1714), and between them the bell tower completed in 1874.

131

CHURCH OF THE ASCENSION

1532
Kolomenskoe

The church built for Vasilii III on his country estate at Kolomenskoe near Moscow reproduced in masonry the tent-shaped silhouette of wooden architecture for the first time. By a brilliant feat of engineering, the difficult transition from cube to octagon is implemented by the use of a receding bank of gables and corner buttresses. On entering the building the worshipper is immediately struck by a new and unfamiliar impression. Far from feeling himself transported under the vault of heaven, as in the Byzantine tradition, he stands encompassed and trapped in a confined space which soars over his head like the neck of a giant bottle. It was for this reason that Patriarch Nikon banned the building of tent-shaped churches in the mid 17th century.

132 *top far left*

WATER POT

1615–16
silver-gilt
Armoury Palace, the Kremlin, Moscow

133 *bottom far left*

LIVERY POT

1604–05
silver-gilt
Armoury Palace, the Kremlin, Moscow

134 *left*

LEOPARD FLAGON

1600–01
silver-gilt
Armoury Palace, the Kremlin, Moscow

135 *right*

FLAGON

1619–20
silver-gilt
Armoury Palace, the Kremlin, Moscow

Relations between England and Russia
were particularly close during the second
half of the 15th century and into the 16th.
English and Russian monarchs exchanged
presents through ambassadors and through
the agents of the Muscovy Company in
Russia to negotiate trading rights. As a
result, the Armoury Palace has a superb
collection of Tudor and Stuart silver.
Many of the pieces are the finest of their
type, and some are unique. The livery pot
and the flagon were brought to Moscow
by the English ambassador Sir John
Merrick in 1615 and 1620 respectively; the
former was probably presented to the tsar
Mikhail. The leopard flagon and the water
pot were purchased by the Russian
treasury through Fabian Smith, an English
agent for the Muscovy company in
Moscow.

136 *left*

ST BASIL'S CATHEDRAL, *1555–60*

Postnik and Barma
Moscow

Ivan IV and Makarii planned this church
as a memorial to eight saints on whose
name days victories over the Tartars had
been won. Its tent shape expresses this
national and Orthodox triumph. The need
to construct eight independent, yet inter-
communicating, units resulted in a compact
group of tent towers, each treated
differently, yet balanced. The result was a
new look in Russian architecture and the
prototype of many subsequent churches.

137

THE MOTHER OF GOD
IN THE GARDEN OF PARADISE

c. 1670
Nikita Pavlovich
tempera on wood
13 × 11·5 in (33 × 29 cm)
Tret'iakov Gallery, Moscow

The strange mingling of East and West
present in this icon throws light on the
cultural orientation of 17th-century
Moscow. The walled garden recalls a
Persian miniature, but the landscape
behind owes its origins to Western art.
The treatment of the faces represents a
compromise between Byzantine tradition
and sentimental Western naturalism.

138

ST NIKITA *detail*

1593
Prokopii Chirin, active in Moscow 1620–42
tempera on wood
Tret'iakov Gallery, Moscow

Chirin was among the foremost of the
tsar's icon painters who were extensively
patronised by the wealthy Stroganov
family. The taste of the Stroganovs
reflected and in some measure influenced
the artistic tendencies of the Kremlin
painters. The emphasis is on exquisite
miniature work, a profusion of gold and
silver ornamentation and the delicate
colour of contemporary enamel. These
icons are not so much traditional objects
for prayer as works of art for the elite.

THE VLADIMIR MOTHER OF GOD

1668
Simon Ushakov 1626–86
Tret'iakov Gallery

The base of the icon is fringed by the crenellated pink walls of the Kremlin, with the five domes of the Dormition Cathedral visible in the background. Metropolitan Peter, together with the grand prince Kalita, are seen planting a giant oak tree from whose spreading branches are suspended portraits of hierarchs and pious tsars – the builders of the Russian State. The largest centre medallion is an icon of the Vladimir Mother of God – the holiest relic of the Dormition Cathedral and the protective palladium of the tsardom (**44**). Tsar Alexis and his wife are shown to the left and right of the composition. Ushakov's icon unfolds the Muscovite conception of history and reflects the cultural and ideological harmony of Russia before the mid 17th century.

140 *below*
THE CHURCH MILITANT
mid 16th century
tempera on wood
Moscow school
Tret'iakov Gallery, Moscow

Like the Cathedral of St Basil, this icon
commemorates the capture of Kazan'. It
was probably executed for Ivan the
Terrible in the workshops of the
metropolitan Makarii in the Kremlin.
Cavalcades of Muscovite horsemen are
seen advancing towards a garden of
paradise, where the Mother of God is
seated. The garden may also be
interpreted as Moscow – the third Rome –
whilst the town of Sodom, behind the
horsemen, represents Kazan'. Angels,
bearing laurels of victory, fly out to meet
the horsemen, among whom the sainted
princes and warriors of Russia's past can be
distinguished.

141 *bottom left*
THE ANNUNCIATION
1652
Spiridon Timofeev
tempera on wood
15·5 × 13·5 in (39 × 34 cm)
Tret'iakov Gallery, Moscow

The detailed embellishment and the
delicate, brittle figures on this icon testify
to the continuing popularity of the
Stroganov tradition in mid 17th-century
Moscow. The architecture filling the
background includes vistas with colonnades
and other features of Renaissance
architecture familiar to the artist through
Western engravings. The architecture is
none the less still treated as decorative
fantasy, with but scant attention paid to
naturalistic perspective.

142 *bottom right*
ST ANTHONY THE ROMAN
late 16th century
12·25 × 10·25 in (31 × 26·3 cm)
Tret'iakov Gallery, Moscow

St Anthony came from the West and for
this reason became known in the country
of his adoption as 'the Roman'. Popular
tradition relates that he floated on a stone
down the river to Novgorod where he
founded the monastery which still bears
his name. The walled monastery is shown
in the background; such topographical
icons were popular during the late 16th
century.

Until recently Russian art has been divided into two distinct epochs by the accession in 1682 of Peter the Great, who was credited with breaking open a window onto Europe. In actual fact, however, he was merely hastening a process which had been inaugurated earlier. During the 15th and 16th centuries Russia had actively come into contact with Western Europe. Such an association demanded a subtle rethinking of Russia's role as a modern state. Not only were trade and diplomatic relations required, but also military measures and sensible economic, social and religious reforms. Yet more important still was the need for the importation of skilled engineers, specialists in the art of war, surgeons and a whole variety of knowledgeable teachers and experienced artisans from abroad.

These early essays in Westernisation were first felt in the sphere of iconography and architecture at the end of the 17th century during the reigns of Fedor (1676–82) and Sophia (1682–89). The regent Sophia's favourite, Vasilii Golitsyn, not only quite brazenly conducted his way of life on a Western European pattern within his own mansion, but startled foreigners with the luxurious style of his household, as well as with his skill in both Polish and German and by being a fluent reader of foreign books. Western European building methods were adopted; portraits of leading boyars were commissioned, private theatricals were instituted, Western fashions in dress became popular, and some of the aristocracy even shaved off their beards. In the eyes of Europe Russia appeared to be growing more civilised, not daily but hourly.

Important Russians realised that it was now essential to maintain a constant connection with Western Europe. The new tsar, Peter the Great, had already determined that 'he would do everything after the example of foreign lands abroad.' Peter raised the tempo, converting the voluntary into the obligatory, the fortuitous into the rule of law. Nevertheless it was not his intention to turn Russians into slavish imitators of foreigners. He invited strangers in on condition that they would instruct the Russian workmen in the expertise that they had acquired in Europe, so that, once this had been absorbed, then there should no longer be any need for foreigners to command positions of trust.

The foundation of St Petersburg

Peter, however, realised that the new experiment must have a new capital. Moscow represented the old Russia. The break away from the conservative tradition still lingering there was achieved by the founding of St Petersburg (now called Leningrad). The city and her fortresses, the bold exit to the sea on ground wrested from the Swedes, a frank face to face with the Western world created a logical link in the sequence of events which led towards the military, naval and cultural might of Russia. The building of St Petersburg marked a decisive step forward in the entire life and culture of the Russian empire, and perhaps most particularly, in her art.

Peter's first concern was the defence of the site for his new city. The foundation of the first fortress on Peter's Day, 1703, marks the official beginning of the city. Inside the fortress Peter desired to build a new cathedral with a campanile which would dominate his city. Domenico Trezzini was called in to plan it, with the help of Grigorii Ustinov. The first church was of wood, but from 1712 a stone cathedral began to rise. The composition shattered previous Russian concepts of ecclesiastical architecture as the church was built on a threefold nave basilican plan with a dome above the sanctuary. Foreign influence had made itself felt, yet Russian traditional forms may be discerned in the general scale.

The monumental nature of the cathedral was enhanced by the addition

144

Peter the Great and the New Capital

1700–1762

143

THE GRAND PALACE OF PETERHOF

1714–52
Johann Braunstein and Bartolomeo Francesco Rastrelli 1700–71
Petrodvorets

Peter the Great started to plan his country residence after his decisive victory over the Swedish army at the Battle of Poltava in 1709. The original palace, on a ridge overlooking the canal and Grand Cascade, had two storeys and a high hipped roof. It corresponded in width to the Grand Cascade, and had a modest exterior designed by J-B. A. Leblond. Between 1747–52 the palace was enlarged by Rastrelli, who added a third storey to the central section and built wings facing the Upper Park. He also added galleries terminating in a tall domed pavilion on either side. The accented rectilinearity of the alleys and the symmetrical distribution of the park structures with the façade of the Grand Palace provide a vivid architectural composition embellished with innumerable delightful fountains.

of the tall, slender bell tower with its gilded ninety-foot spire surmounted by an angel. It is a landmark in the history of a nation dominated architecturally by the onion-shaped Byzantine dome. It represents a final statement of Peter's intention of discarding traditional Russian architecture and a worn-out way of life. In the shallot-shaped cupola, a heritage from Byzantium, Peter detected a hostile force, and he determined that the elongated Protestant Nordic needle should be a monument to his endeavour.

Many Russian craftsmen were called upon to work on the building, gilders from Moscow (already experienced in the application of gold leaf and beaten gold), carvers and decorators. On the icon screen Ivan Zarudnyi of Moscow displayed his skill in carving. The icons were painted by Ivan Merkulev among others. An ivory candelabrum was carved by the tsar himself. It was not surprising that Peter ordered that he should be buried in his new cathedral, rather than in the Dormition Cathedral in the Moscow Kremlin, and his successors followed his example.

Meanwhile, on the shore opposite the fortress, the Summer Garden (Letnii Sad), another memorial of the early years of St Petersburg was being developed. The Summer Garden with its shady walks and innumerable marble statues—many of which had been collected from Italy on the personal order of the tsar—was to become the favourite haunt of all St Petersburg, the original site for open-air assemblies, music, fireworks and all kinds of gala occasions. The gardens were of a formal, geometrical design to begin with, and this scheme was laid out with fountains and conduits. The idea for the fountains was promoted by Peter himself who selected suitable sculptural groups modelled on themes taken from Aesop's Fables. The first garden contained over 250 statues, and there were many busts, basins, aviaries, canals, grottoes and bridges. 'If I should live for three years,' Peter declared, 'I shall have a garden finer than the French king has at Versailles.' Despite changes, the Summer Garden remains today essentially as it was in those early days. The statuary survives, and the whole area along the river front is now adorned with the famous gate and railings cast in severe Classical style by the architect Iurii Veldten in 1784.

The early palaces of Peter the Great

153 The very first palace occupied by Peter the Great was the Summer Palace (Letnii Dvorets). It was built on a modest and intimate scale by Trezzini in 1710–12 in a part of the Summer Garden. The interior of the palace differed greatly from the arrangement customary in Russian mansions of preceding centuries. Rooms were regulated by an *enfilade* plan, and separate chambers were set aside for special purposes—there was a dining-room,
154 a study, a nursery, a main bedroom, a drawing-room, a saloon, a ballroom and a kitchen. Silk coverings for the walls, *boiseries*, glazed tiles were included into the scheme of decoration. Plain wooden floors were replaced with marble or with ornamental inlaid wood. In the ballroom there is a large looking-glass set in a carved mahogany and rosewood frame of the early 18th century. The inscription states that Peter himself had a hand in the design, which was executed—possibly partly by him too—during 1710–11. An assortment of tapestries hang upon the walls. As early as 1717, near St Petersburg, at Ekaterinhof, a tapestry manufactory had been established with French tapestry makers, but already by the end of the first quarter of the 18th century Russian weavers had taken over from the French, and Russian tapestries soon acquired a notable reputation throughout Europe.

Another mansion connected with the personal life of Peter I is the Little House of Peter I (Dvorets-Domik). Like in so many of the St Petersburg

144

CATHEDRAL OF ST PETER
AND ST PAUL

1712–33
Domenico Trezzini 1670–1734
Leningrad

Trezzini had endeavoured to break away from the traditional concept of Russian ecclesiastical architecture by creating a more Nordic style of building. The design and rectangular basilica-style plan of the building was novel to Russia at the time. He attached a tiered campanile crowned by a slender spire covered with gilded metal plates to the western façade of the church. The needle-like spire thus served to remind Russia of her rupture with the past and provided a symbol for the new city of St Petersburg.

145
THE EMPRESS ANNA
WITH HER NEGRO PAGE

begun 1733
bronze
Carlo Bartolomeo Rastrelli 1670–1744
State Russian Museum, Leningrad

The empress is portrayed pointing at an orb proffered to her by a charming little page with a curved sword and a turban on his head. Anna is majesty personified, yet her stout figure, flamboyance and blowsy vulgarity shows up accurately without giving offence. The statue is admired for its technical virtuosity – the elaborately decorated dress with full skirt and extended pointed bodice, the ermine cloak, the small crown on her flowing hair and the sceptre in her right hand. However, the group is not entirely successful as a composition. No bond between the two persons has been devised except for the page's attitude of presentation. Such separate postures, although acceptable in a formal portrait on canvas, seem less happy in sculpture.

early dwellings, it shows strong Dutch influence as a result of the tsar's impressions of architecture gathered from his visits abroad. Although brick and stone were not yet available for building construction, Peter ordered the wooden walls to be painted red outside to resemble brick and the fenestration to imitate the procedure followed in Holland. Only the metalwork on the doors recalled the portals of Moscow palaces of the 17th century. Peter used this dwelling as a summer resort from which he could keep a watchful eye on the progress of the city's building programme.

In the early style of Dutch architecture, which influenced the architecture in St Petersburg, Trezzini designed the notable range of the Twelve Colleges on Vasil'evskii Island, while Georg Johann Mattarnovi and Mikhail Zemtsov worked on the building of the Kunstkamera, the first library and museum in Russia. Its collection was an odd mixture of curiosities ranging from Chinese manuscripts to stuffed birds, but to us the most important item is the Scythian jewellery. Peter's interest had been aroused by a gift of Scythian gold, and he immediately banned the robbing of ancient tombs and ordered all objects found in the ground to be sent to him. The governor of Siberia financed a special expedition of discovery and sent Peter a hoard of a hundred beautiful items. Not far from the Kunstkamera is situated the first really grand mansion to have been constructed in the city. This was the Menshikov Palace, built for Prince Menshikov, Peter's favourite, by the architects Giovanni Mario Fontana and Gottfried Schädel. It is a handsome building, more Italianate in style than any other earlier palace, and, although its lines have been simplified in later years and the exuberant ornament restrained, much remains as it was conceived.

Carlo Bartolomeo and Bartolomeo Francesco Rastrelli

Perhaps no other name in Russian architecture has had such an effect upon the appearance of St Petersburg as that of Rastrelli. Carlo Bartolomeo Rastrelli, of Florentine origin, whom Lefort had met in 1715 in Paris, had been invited to accompany Jean-Baptiste Alexandre Leblond, Peter's Architect General, to St Petersburg where from that year onwards he was expected to carry on duties as architect, medallist and sculptor. He was required to execute sculptures in bronze and portrait busts of living notables in both wax and plaster. This was a fortunate commission, for he emerged as an admirable exponent of the artistic trends then reigning in France and Italy, which was exactly what Peter had wanted, there being no Russian tradition.

Carlo Bartolomeo Rastrelli was responsible for a plaster life mask of Peter the Great which served as a model for various busts, as well as for the powerful equestrian statue, which is a major monument to the tsar-reformer and is now situated at the end of the Summer Garden.

More celebrated by far, however, than Rastrelli the Elder was his genius son, Bartolomeo Francesco Rastrelli. The younger Rastrelli's activities cover the very last years of the reign of Peter the Great (he was assigned the planning of the decor for the Shafirov Palace in 1723 and seems to have directed the erection of a palace for Prince Antiokh Kantemir, the satirist), the reigns of Anna, Elizabeth and the first decade of the reign of Catherine the Great. His early training and background remains something of a mystery, but he may have travelled both before and after coming to Russia with his sculptor father. He was influenced by the German Baroque, and he looked to his foreign contemporaries rather than to earlier masters. Neumann and Pöpplemann were his models in preference to Bernini and Borromini, and Fischer von Erlach's Viennese palaces also seem to have captivated him. His first commission for work on an imperial

146
BUST OF PETER THE GREAT
1723
iron
Carlo Bartolomeo Rastrelli 1670–1744
State Russian Museum, Leningrad

The sculptor has rendered a masterly portrait of Peter I as the impetuous tsar, conveying all the energy, ruthlessness and determination of his character. The folds of the mantle and streaming ribbons strengthen the feeling of a mobile and restless monarch. The bust is regal and fierce, with exquisitely detailed chased armour and lace and a splendid swaggering composition.

147.
PORTRAIT OF CATHERINE I
1717
Jean Marc Nattier 1685–1766
oil on canvas
43 × 56 in (142·5 × 110 cm)
State Hermitage Museum, Leningrad

Peter the Great decided that the most successful way to encourage Russian painting was to persuade good European painters to live in St Petersburg. In 1715 he asked his agent in Paris to discover whether any of Louis XIV's artists would be willing to work in Russia. Two years later, when he visited Paris, he met the French painter Nattier, whom he was keen to employ at his court. Nattier painted portraits of Peter and his wife, Catherine I, but declined his invitation.

residence was the enlarging of the great palace at Peterhof (now called Petrodvorets).

The palace of Peterhof

The construction of Peterhof was conceived by Peter the Great after the victory over the Swedes at Poltava in 1709. Extensive work was begun in 1714 following the Russian victory over the Swedish fleet in the battle of Hangö. The tsar spared no pains to make his palace the equal of Versailles. He had personally drawn the preliminary sketches. Thousands of peasants drawn from all over Russia were set to work on the landscape, so that within a few years the shore of the Gulf of Finland was converted from a dreary waste into a pleasance of flowering gardens, pavilions and palaces.

Numerous foreign experts supervised the building programme; a Russian, Ulian Siniavin, was appointed clerk-of-the-works, while J. F. Braunstein became chief architect. The original palace on the ridge had two storeys and a high double roof. It corresponded in width to the Grand Cascade. Its exterior was modest. Leblond, who replaced Braunstein in 1716, later added side galleries with pavilions and enriched the exterior decoration. The Grand Palace ties the Upper and Lower Parks with an 'architectural knot'. It is visible from the town, from the piers of the main entrance to the Upper Park, from the sea along the Sea Canal and the picturesque Fountain Alley, and from other points of the Lower Park. With a graceful, clear-cut silhouette the impressive palace beautifully surmounts the ridge. Its middle part under a hipped roof of complex pattern is connected through glazed galleries to the two domed pavilions.

Progress on the interior continued until 1724. Peter's study contained notable carved panels by the sculptor Nikolai Pineaud, and the other apartments were equally richly adorned. After seven years from the laying of the first stone, in the year of the Peace of Nystadt (8th August 1721) with Sweden, the premiere for the display of the fountains was celebrated. Towards the end of Peter's reign in 1725, the main work of construction was complete—all the palaces, the Upper and Lower Parks together with the many fountains seen today.

Two little palaces placed in the western area of the Lower Park are worth noting for their elegance and interesting interiors. One of them, the Hermitage, is a two-storeyed rectangular building on a massive, high foundation surrounded by a moat designed by Braunstein. It was intended as a palace of seclusion and contained an oval dining table which could be raised and lowered from the kitchen situated below so that guests need not be inconvenienced by the presence of servants. The other use to which this building was put was to house a collection of pictures. The paintings consist of works by Dutch, Flemish, French and German artists of the turn of the 18th century. There are over one hundred canvases by masters such as David Teniers, and also *The Battle of Poltava* by Ivan Nikitin, an artist of the time of Peter the Great, whose ability the tsar much admired. Marly is the name of the other little palace which is reflected in the water of a formal lake. It is a small two-storey building with a hipped roof; the façade is modestly adorned with rusticated joints, a balcony grille of distinctive design and carved brackets. It, too, was built by Braunstein.

Finally, after passing down the radial alleys running east from the Large Flower Beds to the sea-shore, upon an artificial mound framed by a white balustrade, stands Mon Plaisir, the original and favourite summer residence of Peter. Mon Plaisir has survived quite unaltered, both externally and internally, and is complete in its period decoration and furniture. During the seven years from 1714 to 1721 the cream of Russian designers and

143

157

SNUFF BOX WITH A PORTRAIT OF PETER THE GREAT

early 18th century
Andrei Ovsov
gilt and enamel
0·75 × 1·25 × 2 in (2·3 × 2·9 × 5·3 cm)
Armoury Palace, the Kremlin, Moscow

Many members of Peter's entourage were presented with miniature portraits of their tsar painted by Andrei Ovsov, who was one of the finest Russian miniaturists of the period.

149 *left*

SNUFF BOX WITH A PORTRAIT OF EMPRESS ELIZABETH

18th century
Jeremiah Posier
gilt and brilliants
Armoury Palace, the Kremlin, Moscow

Elizabeth is shown here with her palace at Tsarskoe Selo just visible in the background. Below her is the Russian eagle holding an orb and a sceptre.

150

CUP

17th century
gold, enamel and precious stones
diameter 6 in (15·4 cm)
Armoury Palace, the Kremlin, Moscow

Since the 16th century, when an English ambassador had been amazed by the quantity of gold he saw at a banquet in the Kremlin, the tsars had built up a vast collection of precious objects and had commissioned many valuable gifts with which to reward their subjects. This cup was given by Peter the Great to his son Alexis in 1694.

craftsmen worked on this squat single-storeyed palace. During his trips abroad Peter collected paintings for Mon Plaisir. In addition to the central hall the paintings adorned the side galleries, the secretary's room and the naval office. Porcelain from China and Asia were exhibited on the shelves in the Chinese Lacquer Room.

When Elizabeth became empress in 1741, however, she decided that the small size of the palace no longer corresponded to its aims of representing the might of a powerful empire. She had very definite ideas about how she wanted the palace altered, and Rastrelli had to change his plans several times before they were acceptable to her. Building, which did not start until 1747, continued until 1752. The resulting palace is one of many examples of the successful combination of Elizabeth's taste and Rastrelli's imagination.

The task confronting Rastrelli was complicated by the necessity of preserving the old palace. He enlarged the central part of the building and **143** made it three storeyed, built wings facing the Upper Park, constructed large galleries and completed the two tall domed pavilions. Only Peter's **159** study and the great oak staircase were preserved inside, otherwise five reception halls and a suite of guest rooms were built anew. Gilt wood carving, mirrors, painted ceilings and parquetry flooring were used in the decoration throughout. Some of the greatest specialists of the time worked on the execution of Rastrelli's plans. Carvers made decorative wooden statues, vases and garlands. The ceilings were painted by Russian and foreign artists; Russian designers worked in the old rooms in the central part of the palace; magnificent parquet patterned floors were laid.

The patronage of Elizabeth

While Elizabeth, ebullient daughter of Peter the Great, was on the throne (1741–62), Rastrelli held free sway over Russian art. Elizabeth was supreme arbiter of a style of living which demanded the scenic backdrops he was so well able to devise. Rivals to the master could emerge only from **page 6** amongst the pupils and imitators of his art. Yet he is important in the history of world architecture, for he initiated something entirely novel: a style with roots in the ancient Orthodoxy of Byzantium rather than in the traditions of Western Mannerist or Baroque art. He succeeded in fusing the spirit of Baroque and Rococo decoration predominant in the West with the individual character of Russian architecture. This unusual, but effective, mixture may be entitled the Rastrelli style or Elizabethan Rococo, and its mood exactly fits and nicely permeates the exuberant, almost magic atmosphere of Russia during the middle part of the 18th century. This is the period of the powerful Lomonosov and the laudatory ode, of the **165** victorious force of Russian arms, of the growth of national drama, opera and the ballet, of the spread of learning and the cultural consolidation of an empire.

Rastrelli's industry extended to well outside St Petersburg and Moscow. His energies were so expansive that neither taste nor time has succeeded in effacing his achievements. Far away in historic Kiev the empress required him to design a new cathedral. This he did, and the church, dedicated to St Andrew, stands to this day. In the capital and environs he was continually occupied with new building schemes. Among them was the brightening up of Zemtsov's Anichkov Palace, which stands at the point where the Nevskii Prospekt crosses the Fontanka Canal. Not much of Rastrelli's work, however, has been allowed to remain except in the arrangement of the staircase. More representative of Rastrelli's style are the Vorontsov Palace of 1745 and the Stroganov Palace, begun in 1750. Outwardly both buildings are little altered and achieve a luxuriousness of decoration with- **151** out being in the least bit cumbersome. Rastrelli regarded colour as an integral part of every building scheme and would always lay down detailed instructions about the desired effect. St Petersburg architects normally lacked the more conventional materials of marble, stone and granite and were obliged to make use of wood and plaster-covered brick. Nevertheless, the polychromatic rendering of the turquoise-blue, emerald, sage-green, rose, tangerine and yellow stucco, which formed a background to pure white relief ornament, together with shimmering bronze, gold and silver imparted a heightened effect, touched with a fairy-tale splendour, to all their compositions.

156 To Rastrelli, too, does the Smol'nyi Institute, with its fanciful Rococo chapel crowned with gilded onion cupolas, owe its design. The building was later supplemented by the Couvent des Demoiselles Nobles, a superior academy for aristocratic young ladies. Here the architect has modelled his ideas on the normal lay-out of Russian monastic institutions, yet infused something of Trezzini's Baroque projection of the Aleksandr Nevskii Monastery. The result is an exuberant and dynamic recreation of traditional Russian religious houses.

Rastrelli's preoccupation with designing flowing tracery and scrollwork, contorted amoretti, and curvilinear broken pediments was perhaps but a dress rehearsal for his creations yet to come. The final breath-taking glittering mise-en-scène was ultimately revealed in Rastrelli's greatest show of all—Tsarskoe Selo (now called Pushkin)—and the unforgettable finale—The Winter Palace.

The original Tsarskoe Selo passed to Elizabeth on the death of Peter's wife Catherine in 1727. She immediately began feverish building work. Serfs and army recruits were enrolled as labourers, and craftsmen were sent for from all over Russia to help to create a more magnificent palace. In 1744, three years after the palace revolution which placed her on the throne, major operations were put under way. In 1749 Rastrelli had appeared on the scene as chief architect, and the empress came to the conclusion that all these conversion jobs could not provide her with the necessary background to her masquerades, fêtes and banquets. Accordingly in 1752 she ordered Rastrelli to begin a total reconstruction.

For four years Rastrelli toiled, and he finished his commission in 1756. Braunstein's preliminary low semi-circle of single-storey staff and domestic buildings was retained in the plan so as to face on to a colossal courtyard stretching in front of the main corpus of the palace. Three elaborate wrought-iron gates give access through the horse-shoe plan of the outbuildings on to the court. The stunning length of the three-storeyed palace frontage, 326 feet in all, has no parallel in Europe. Rastrelli achieved his effect by endowing the façade with a generous display of columns,

160 pilasters, balustrades and interrupted pediments which allowed light and shadow to provide mobility and interest. The impression is of an unbroken mass, not even disturbed by the unemphatic central position of the building, of cumulative magnificence and of rhythmic regularity.

The interior of the palace at Tsarskoe Selo was fitted out according to the same principles as the exterior—that is of endless vista and extent. From the Great Hall and continuing onward the salons and carved door frames follow in *enfilade*, providing an uninterrupted view through from one to the other; in each portal a similar motif of carving is repeated and appears to grow smaller as the doors recede into the distance, as though reflected in innumerable mirrors.

Successive sovereigns have changed much of Rastrelli's interior decorations, but the original scheme for Elizabeth's, and later Catherine the Great's and Alexander I's bedroom still remains: the charming alcove for

151
THE STROGANOV PALACE
1752—54
Bartolomeo Francesco Rastrelli 1700—71
Leningrad

Unlike the enclosed mansions with extensive gardens erected at the time, the Stroganov Palace was incorporated into the urban panorama and forms part of the ensemble of the Nevskii Prospekt. It is a perfect example of Rastrelli's style before he completed the definitive residences for Elizabeth. It has been little altered outwardly, and achieves richness of decoration without appearing at all ponderous. It was built for S. G. Stroganov, President of the Academy of Sciences.

the bed, with garlanded pilasters, cherubim, goddesses and caryatids still bearing the monograph of Elizabeth.

The decline of Rastrelli and the end of an age

The curtain is rung down on Rastrelli's manifold building activities with the final immensely expensive reconstruction of the Winter Palace. The money was found from a levy placed on wine and salt. The Winter Palace of Anna's reign proved to be too antiquated for the grandiloquent style of Elizabeth. Accordingly, it was demolished in 1754. In spite of the hoards of employees engaged on the building work, the new Winter Palace was not completed in Elizabeth's lifetime. Even after Catherine the Great had achieved her coup d'état and come to the throne, the palace continued to be under construction. Rastrelli, however, took no more part in the progress of its building. Catherine had different tastes and an aversion to Baroque. At the end of the 18th century the interior of the palace was reorganised by Giacomo Quarenghi and was restored completely after the disastrous fire which raged for a week inside the palace in 1837. Only the chapel and Jordan staircase remain out of Rastrelli's initial decor.

152

THE WINTER PALACE

begun 1754
Bartolomeo Francesco Rastrelli 1700–71
Leningrad

In 1754 Elizabeth ordered the demolition of all the buildings of the old Winter Palace and required Rastrelli to erect a vast new palace. In order to enable it to blend with the rest of the city, which it faces on all four sides, the height was to be only 70 feet, despite a length of 450 feet. The result was a magnificent theatrical achievement and the culmination of Rastrelli's Baroque style. The immense cost was met by a state tax on wine and salt.

The Winter Palace is a proud, majestic pile, and no other palace in 18th-century Europe was quite able to compare with it in grandeur and magnificence. It represents the last of the Baroque in Russia. Already there were indications of an approaching change of taste. The flamboyant, elaborate mood of Rastrelli's Baroque was giving way to a more sober preference for quiet Classicism. **152**

Elizabeth's favourite, the all powerful statesman and connoisseur, Ivan Shuvalov, had become displeased with Rastrelli's proposals for the rebuilding of the Gostinyi Dvor, a row of shops by the angle of the Moika and Nevskii Prospekt burnt down in 1736. In his capacity as initiator of a new scheme for the establishment of an Academy of Arts in St Petersburg, Shuvalov awarded the commission for the formulation of the building's design to a young architect just lately arrived from Paris, Jean-Baptiste Michel Vallin de la Mothe. De la Mothe was ably assisted by a Russian architect, Aleksandr Kokorinov. Both men were later appointed professors of architecture, and Kokorinov actually became the director.

Rastrelli retired to Italy in 1763. On his return to Russia a year later he found that the new empress, Catherine, only too clearly showed her displeasure with his work. The old, once successful court architect of Elizabeth, now in his sixties, was dismissed from service with a state pension. The building of the Academy of Fine Arts thus significantly played Rastrelli out with a forlorn farewell, but the orchestrated harmony of the academy's Neo-Classical architecture was the overture for the reign of great Catherine.

Malcolm Burgess

153 *right*

THE SUMMER PALACE

begun 1710
Domenico Trezzini 1670–1734 and
Andreas Schlüter 1665–1714
Leningrad

This, the first palace built by Peter the Great, is a simple two-storeyed rectangular building with rusticated corners. Ceramic bas-reliefs which adorn the façades symbolise Russia's victory over the Swedes during the Seven Years War. In the interior, panelling, silk hangings and tapestries were used for the first time in Russia, and parquet floors, glazed tiles for stoves, and marble, also appeared.

154 *below right*

THE GREEN DRAWING ROOM

The Summer Palace
1713–14
Leningrad

Several rooms of the Summer Palace, including the Green Drawing Room, have retained their 18th-century appearance. The Green Drawing Room has decorative painted panels between columns with carved and gilded capitals. Three bookcases, still filled with the original glass, are let into the walls; they now contain curiosities from Peter's collection formerly in the Kunstkamera.

155 *above far right*

THE MENSHIKOV PALACE

1710–16
Giovanni Mario Fontana and
Gottfried Schädel, c. 1680–1752
Leningrad

Prince Menshikov was the favourite and close friend of Peter the Great and was very much the co-founder of St Petersburg. His taste, which was far more sophisticated than Peter's, determined the early appearance of the city. Menshikov's palace (now slightly altered) was one of the first brick buildings in St Petersburg and was borrowed by the tsar when important visitors necessitated entertainment on a grander scale than was possible in Peter's more modest palace.

156 *below far right*

SMOL'NYI CATHEDRAL

1748–62
Bartolomeo Francesco Rastrelli 1700–71
Leningrad

The Smol'nyi Monastery was very much the creation of the empress Elizabeth. The plans were projected in 1744; work continued throughout the 1750s, but was suspended in 1757 when the empress was taken ill and it was feared that she was about to die. As she recovered, building continued, but Rastrelli's complete scheme was never executed. In 1764 Catherine the Great founded her academy for young ladies nearby.

157 *left* **158** *below left*

THE GRAND CASCADE

early 18th century
gilded bronze
Petrodvorets (Peterhof)

The central figure of the grand cascade is a powerful figure of
Samson in single combat with a lion. As a symbol of Samson's
victory a single jet of water, sixty-five feet high, shoots out of the
mouth of the lion. The group symbolises the decisive victory of
the Russians over the Swedes which occurred on Samson's Day,
27th June 1709; the lion appeared on the Swedish state emblem.

159 *far left*

THE PAVILION UNDER THE COAT OF ARMS

1747–52
Bartolomeo Francesco Rastrelli 1700–71
Petrodvorets (Peterhof)

Rastrelli's extension of the palace added a tall domed pavilion at
either side of the central building linked by glazed galleries. The
Pavilion under the Coat of Arms matches a similar pavilion, a
chapel, on the east side.

160

TSARSKOE SELO

1750–1755
Bartolomeo Francesco Rastrelli 1700–1771
Pushkin

It was Peter the Great's wife, Catherine I, who had persuaded her
husband to develop this site as a residence. On her death it passed
to her daughter Elizabeth, who set about enlarging the property.
Various architects were called in, but from 1749 Rastrelli
supervised the work, and in 1752 the empress commanded him to
reconstruct the palace anew. The great length of the three-
storeyed palace frontage, 326 feet in all, has no other parallel in
Europe.

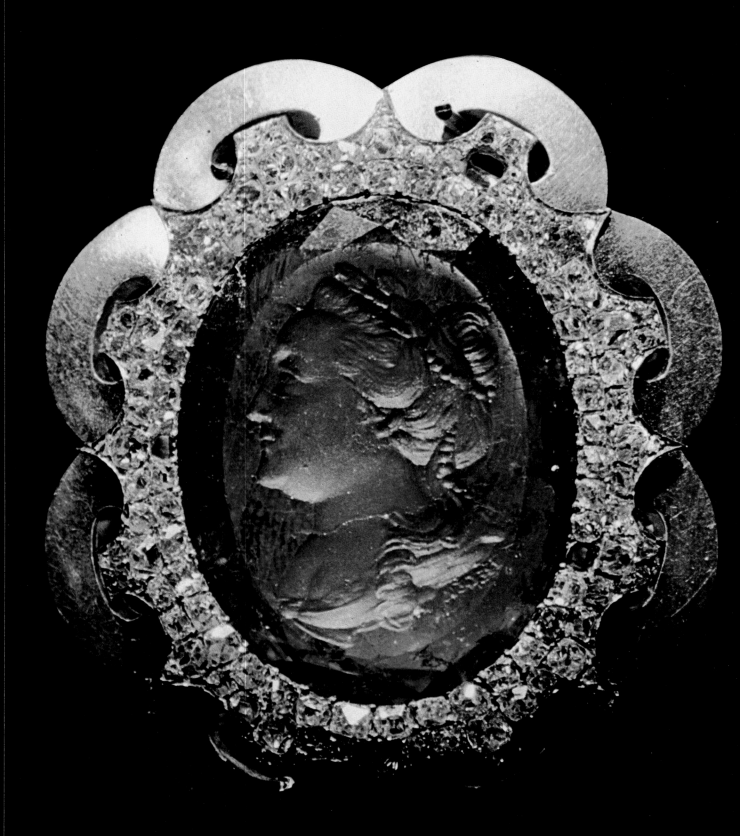

Since the time of Peter the Great succeeding sovereigns have continued to embellish St Petersburg, but none more than Catherine the Great (1762–96), who might be called its second founder. Paradoxically this great empress, who did so much for St Petersburg, who brought Russia further into the radius of Western Europe, and whose understanding of Russian history and tradition was probably deeper than that of any other ruler, was not Russian herself. She was a German princess who went to Russia at the age of fifteen to marry the feeble grand duke Peter; and, though she was in constant touch with Western thought and taste throughout her life, she identified herself totally with her adopted country.

Catherine's favourites and love affairs may have shocked Europe, but we now have great cause to be thankful for them, for she offered witness and recognition of her affections in her buildings. One of the first recipients of her bounty was Grigorii Orlov, who, with his brothers, had been the principal agent of the coup d'état which in 1762 overthrew Catherine's **188** husband Peter III and caused Catherine to assume the authority of empress. **162** For him Catherine constructed at her own expense the magnificent Marble Palace (Mramornyi Dvorets) and the grimly Classical Gatchina Palace. Another beneficiary was Grigorii Potemkin, a later favourite, who received the fine Tauride Palace (Tavricheskii Dvorets) near the outskirts of St Petersburg.

The accession of Catherine gave the necessary impetus to a rising swing towards a revival of Neo-Classical taste. It is strange that it should have been only in England and Russia that a return was made to a style based on the over-civilised revelations of Pompeii and Herculaneum. Nowhere else in Europe of the late 18th century did this style mature with such antiquarian fervour, with such inventiveness, such attention to fine detail, or with such delicate taste as at Osterley Park House near London or Tsarskoe Selo near St Petersburg.

Catherine's architects

Now that Rastrelli had been retired from favour, Catherine sought for architects more suited to the Classical serenity which she desired, and she **162** summoned Antonio Rinaldi to design the Marble Palace. The style of architecture is magnificent yet severe; the front is composed of polished grey granite from a recently opened quarry in Siberia and embellished with many-coloured marble. It is finished with such nicety, and in a style so different from the neighbouring buildings that it seemed to travellers such as Archdeacon Coxe that it had been 'transported to the present spot like a palace in the Arabian tales, raised by the enchantment of Aladdin's lamp'.

169 For Catherine Rinaldi also devised the delicate Toboggan Hill Pavilion (Katal'naia Gorka) of which the main pavilion survives at Lomonosov (formerly Oranienbaum). A taste for Chinoiserie, which came from the West not from the East, had infected Rinaldi while he was working at **168** Lomonosov, and the little Chinese Palace (Kitaiskii Dvorets) expresses his recherché taste most completely. Catherine also had a perfect Chinese village erected at Tsarskoe Selo, including a Chinese bridge and a theatre hung with silk and decorated with lacquer panels and Chinese porcelain.

Giacomo Quarenghi, a most prolific architect who adopted the Palladian manner, was responsible for many of Catherine's Classical edifices; he built the English Palace at Peterhof and the Alexander Palace for Catherine's grandson. He may be said to have been the last of the great architects of Italy, but he managed to Russianise his Palladian buildings and made use of the Russian tradition of a multi-coloured façade. Catherine showered Quarenghi with honours; he was designated coun-

161

PROFILE OF CATHERINE THE GREAT

emerald, late 18th century; frame, later carved emerald, gold and diamonds
1.75×1.5 *in* $(4.5 \times 3.6$ *cm)*
USSR Diamond Fund, Moscow

Among the most striking relics of the magnificence of the world of Catherine the Great are the jewels and precious objects which have survived. The art of the jeweller reached its zenith in Russia of the 18th century, and in its products Catherine found an outlet for her love of display and beauty.

cillor of state, architect to her imperial majesty, and even occupied an apartment in the Hermitage.

The person, however, most responsible for the resurgence of the Pompeian style was a Scotsman – Charles Cameron. He was the designer of what are perhaps the most elegant creations ever built in Russia. The empress appointed him in 1780 as architect-in-chief for the interior decoration of Tsarskoe Selo. He also worked on the Chinese Village there, and erected nineteen small houses with a pagoda in the middle. Cameron's most celebrated works are the Agate Pavilion and the Cameron Gallery (both in the grounds of Tsarskoe Selo), which are superb examples of his style. The decoration of the Agate Pavilion was carried out in polychrome marble and jasper; relief medallions and a gentle Ionic portico adorn the front. The Cameron Gallery, with its grand stairway and balconies, along which the empress loved to walk, houses a series of bronze busts of famous figures from antiquity.

For the grand duke Paul and his wife Maria, Cameron constructed the Palace of Pavlovsk, which was started in 1782. By then English landscape gardens were fully in vogue, and in the grounds were built the circular Temple of Friendship, the Colonnade of Apollo, the Pavilion of the Three Graces, the Pavilion of Elizabeth, a dairy, a cattleshed, an aviary, a hospital, a music room and various villas. The main part of the palace is a cube crowned with a dome (copied from the Pantheon at Rome) resting on a circular row of columns. Lateral wings and pavilions were added at the end of the 18th century. The distinguished patron demanded Classical purism, and Pavlovsk became a scholarly essay in antique revival taste. It is famous for its Grecian Hall, which bears affinities with Kedleston Hall in Derbyshire. There is also an Italian Hall closely modelled on the Pantheon. Pavlovsk was a signpost of the future trend of formal Classicism and the oncoming Alexandrine Empire style. The palace has been meticulously restored after devastating damage to the fabric during the Second World War.

Cameron is particularly remembered for his exquisite interior decors in Tsarskoe Selo: the Lyons Room, with its richly inlaid parquetry floor, a chimneypiece and table of lapis lazuli, the walls and furniture covered in pale yellow Lyons silk woven with a pattern of branches and little birds; the Room of the Arabesques with its Pompeian inspired wall paintings; the Chinese Room with furniture designed by him. All Cameron's domestic salons are intimate and fragile; the hues are iridescent, opaline milky-white, lilac, green and turquoise. Catherine's own bedroom at Tsarskoe Selo has walls inlaid with Wedgwood jasper plaques and medallions decorated with columns of violet glass ending in bases and capitals of bronze. Her 'snuff-box', which is what she called her private boudoir, is panelled with opaline white glass and gilt appliqué ornament. The doors are framed in columns of ultramarine-coloured glass. The effect is brittle, as if the salons had been intended to exist beneath the waters of some enchanted sea.

Catherine's picture collection

Equal to Catherine's desire to live in beautiful surroundings was her passion for collecting paintings. Her wish to own Western painting was part of her attempt, following Peter's example, to promote closer links between Russia and Europe and to take part in Western intellectual life. Her first acquisition was arranged by a Berlin merchant who persuaded Frederick II of Prussia to part with 225 works in lieu of war debts to Russia. Following this, Catherine's ambassadors in Europe were instructed to inform her of collections that were to be sold and to act as her agent at

173, 174

194, 195

172

171

173, 174

189-193

162
THE MARBLE PALACE
1768–85
marble facing, granite base
Antonio Rinaldi, c. 1710–94
Leningrad

Soon after she became empress Catherine rewarded her favourite Grigorii Orlov, who had helped her to the throne, by building the Marble Palace for him. The use of marble on the façade was an innovation of great luxury, since other buildings in St Petersburg were of brick and stucco. The exterior displays an aristocratic, coherent form, emphasised by a single line of Corinthian pilasters set upon a restrained surface. The colours of the marble and the granite cause a delightful, soft interplay of tones.

auctions. Prince Dimitrii Golitsyn, ambassador in Paris and later at the Hague, was particularly active in this respect; he was instrumental in securing for Catherine forty-five works from Count Koblenz, a minister in the Austrian court, and works from the most valuable collection in Paris, that of the Duke of Choiseul. During the 1770s and 1780s purchases were made in Rome, Dresden, London, Holland and, in particular, Paris. Collection after collection left Paris for St Petersburg, culminating in 119 pictures acquired from the Comte de Baudouin. During the 1770s Catherine turned her attention from her first love, Dutch and Flemish works, to Italian paintings. One of her greatest coups was the purchase, through the Russian minister plenipotentiary in London, of 198 Italian masters, as well as paintings by Rubens, Van Dyck, Rembrandt and Poussin, from the heirs of the English prime minister Robert Walpole.

191

199, 200

Catherine's collection was first housed in the Winter Palace or in other galleries in Mon Plaisir or Tsarskoe Selo. In 1768, however, a proper museum, the Little Hermitage, was completed, and later the Winter Palace was extended to contain another gallery, now called the Old Hermitage. Although by no means public museums, the pictures could, with permission, be viewed.

179

Not only had Catherine during her reign built up a superb imperial collection, but she had also encouraged others to collect. The fabulously wealthy Russian nobles such as Ivan Shuvalov, A. M. Belosel'skii, Aleksandr Stroganov and Nikolai Iusupov travelled in Europe, visiting auctions and dealers and competing with each other in their purchases. At the Revolution their collections came to the State to form, with Catherine's, the Hermitage Museum, one of the finest in existence.

The palaces of the aristocracy

During the last half of the 18th century the increased wealth of the Russian aristocracy favoured the development of private estates in the country. Many fine mansions were erected, mostly in the Neo-Classical style, and elegant landscaped parks were laid out around them. The court and nobility were accustomed to retire to these delightful seats for the summer season or for a change of air. Belonging to this period is the palace-park ensemble at Kuskovo, in the Ukhtomskii region, which had belonged to Boris Sheremetev and had then passed to his son Petr Sheremetev. The mansion is interesting in that it was designed and fitted out by serfs from the Sheremetev estates.

175

On the outskirts of Moscow, in the Shcherbakovskii region, lies the famous palace of Ostankino, on a site which passed to the Sheremetevs in 1743. Petr Sheremetev had a chapel, a manor house, a garden, an orangery and a 'House of Amusement' there. His son Nikolai Sheremetev decided to build a theatre and a new mansion beside the chapel. Construction was begun in the spring of 1792, and by the autumn the theatre was ready; but as the stage proved rather small, the Moscow architect, Francesco Camporesi, was called in to redesign the whole interior. The theatre survives intact to this day; it is one of the few complete 18th-century theatres containing all the original fittings anywhere in the world. Other buildings making up this entertainment ensemble are Egyptian and Italian pavilions, both exquisitely furnished and decorated. The Pale Blue Saloon, in the Egyptian style, is a striking example of Russian interior design.

177

Among the estates in the countryside surrounding Moscow distinguished for their architecture is Arkhangel'skoe. Situated in the Krasnogorskii region upon a high bank of the Moscow river twenty-three kilometres from the city, it belonged after 1810 to Nikolai Iusupov. Work on the present house was begun in the 1780s, but was not finally com-

176

pleted, together with the park, until the 1830s. A little known French architect, De Guerne, conceived the original plan. The mansion is painted pale orange, while the columns, cornices and other details and reliefs are left white. A small manor house called Caprice in the western part of the estate survives, as well as a number of unusual grottoes, and many pavilions and sculptural groups in the park. Also in the grounds is a theatre, built in 1817, which still contains four complete drops and settings designed by the Venetian designer Pietro Gonzaga.

The interiors of the mansion are particularly outstanding. The Oval Room is the most elegant saloon. The Imperial Hall has walls lined with portraits of Russian emperors including an excellent painting of Paul I by Stepan Shchukin. A charming bedroom, belonging to Iusupov's sister, is a replica of a typical 18th-century royal bedroom. The grey-green rug of the Music Room, woven to order at Iusupov's mills, matches the grey-green hue of the walls. Among the paintings in the Arkhangel'skoe picture gallery are Tiepolo's *Cleopatra's Feast*, Van Dyck's *Portrait of an Unknown Woman*, a seascape by Claude Vernet and Boucher's *Frightened Nymph*. Iusupov's collection of original Greek and Roman sculpture is to be found in the Antique Hall. The palace also contains a notable collection of works by Hubert Robert; the walls of two rooms are hung with his landscapes and genre scenes.

The nobility, no longer required to reside in St Petersburg, were active in building handsome mansions in the major cities of Russia during the latter part of the 18th century. The Palladian-style Pashkov Mansion, built **178** in Moscow between 1784–86 by the talented architect Vasilii Bazhenov, is a masterpiece of 18th-century design and one of the city's most stately mansions. Similarly in St Petersburg a most attractive house, the Elagin Palace (Elaginskii Dvorets), was built between 1818–22 by the architect Carlo Rossi as one of his first commissions. Soon after his success with this mansion, which had been devised as a summer residence for the empress dowager Maria, Rossi attracted the attention of Alexander I. From 1820–32 imperial favour permitted him to accomplish four great decors of stone, brick and stucco which have no equivalent in any other capital of **163** Europe: the hemicycle of the Winter Palace, the square in front of the **197** Mikhailovskii Palace, the ensemble of the Aleksandrinskii Theatre and then finally the two joint palaces of the Synod and Senate.

The public buildings of Alexander I

The Alexandrine Empire style is the title given to the second phase of Classicism which followed directly upon the swing towards the antique, hastened by Catherine the Great upon her accession to the throne. This ideal of archaic simplicity can be found all over Europe in about 1800. The French origins of the Russian Empire style are well established, just as the influence of France is felt in the development of the English Empire or Regency style; yet it is curious that this type of architecture, paralysed by the troubles of the French Revolution and the Napoleonic wars, was to prove far more fertile in Russia than it was in France. The architects of Alexander I (1801–25) and Nicholas I (1825–55), however, were able, thanks to more favourable conditions, to realise the type of large-scale scheme which in France, more often than not, remained on paper.

Alexander I, a sovereign imbued with taste and discernment, continued his grandmother's work of embellishing St Petersburg with buildings in a consistent and harmonious style. He wanted to make St Petersburg finer than any of the European capitals he had visited. Accordingly a special architectural commission was set up under the chairmanship of General Béthencourt to examine all designs, to accept, reject or alter them and also

163 *above*
THE ARCH OF THE CHIEF STAFF
1819–29
Carlo Rossi 1775–1849
Leningrad

Plans for the area opposite the Winter Palace had been discussed for some forty years, but it was not until the arrival of Rossi that building actually started. Rossi solved the problem of a difficult site with an immense double arch which leads the visitor into the square. The chaste lines of the Empire-style arch contrast dramatically with the green and white Baroque Winter Palace and the red granite column. The arch is a masterpiece of the Alexandrine Empire style.

to attend to the plan of streets and squares, projects for bridges, canals and other construction works, 'in a word to bring about the city's uniform exterior beauty'.

The emperor was more concerned with public buildings than palaces, and his reign is marked by the monumental edifices erected in St Petersburg. Grecian, rather than Roman in conception, yet Russian in spirit with regard to their scale, colour and varied use of texture, these buildings remain unparalleled in any other European capital. The first large building enterprise of the new reign was the erection of Kazan' Cathedral by **164** Andrei Voronikhin. It recalls St Peter's in Rome and the Pantheon or St Geneviève in Paris and is remarkable for the great circular colonnade opening on to the Nevskii Prospekt.

Between 1805–06 the architect Thomas de Thomon embellished the ensemble of the Strelka and Vasil'evskii Island by building the Bourse. It is a handsome rectangular edifice surrounded with a Doric colonnade raised on a granite podium. The main admiralty in St Petersburg is, after the **198** Bourse, perhaps the most perfect example of the Alexandrine Empire style. The architect, Adreian Zakharov, had the delicate task of following the original horizontal lines and elongated stretches of an earlier admiralty by Korobov. Zakharov retained the idea of a needle-like spire and managed to season his new Empire building with a Petrine flavour. The result was the provision of St Petersburg with a most satisfying and homogeneous composition.

For the grand duke Mikhail, the brother of Alexander I and Nicholas I, Rossi constructed the Mikhailovskii Palace as part of a general city planning scheme. A grandiose Corinthian colonnade rests upon a monumental base; side wings, a little lower and in a simplified Doric style, frame the central motif. The square in front of the palace has lower buildings surrounding it, which seem to enhance the effect. Among the buildings and incorporated into the scheme is the former Mikhailovskii Theatre—now the State Academic Malyi Theatre—a beautifully designed structure of grace and elegance decorated inside in a scheme of silver and peach tones.

The conversion of the Mikhailovskii Palace into the Russian Museum by Nicholas II in 1898, according to the wishes of his father Alexander III, necessitated the replanning of many of the internal apartments. The white and gold Grand Staircase, however, survives as Rossi planned it, as does the celebrated White Columned Saloon, together with the furniture which was designed en suite by the architect. An authoritative grille with four granite piers surmounted by bronze military emblems in the Empire manner encloses the forecourt.

It is in Palace Square that the present-day visitor to Leningrad can observe the harmonious amalgamation of the several styles of architecture which have gone to make up the city's appearance. Rossi's grand Arch of **163** the Chief Staff, with the triumphal chariot by Vasilii Demut-Malinovskii and Stepan Pimenov surmounting it, the ministries of Finance and Foreign Affairs close one side of the square, and Rastrelli's magnificent Winter Palace forms the other. Together they create what must be con- **152** sidered as one of the most unified, as well as one of the most spectacular, examples of city planning in the world. The erection of the column of Alexander by Montferrand in 1834, which dominates the centre of the square, and the vista of the gilded dome of the Cathedral of St Isaac to **196** the left, with the Admiralty needle on the right, completes this most **198** extravagant ensemble.

Painting and sculpture and the academy

A great influence over the arts in the 18th century was the academy. The

165

MIKHAIL LOMONOSOV
1792
Fedot Shubin 1740–1805
gypsum
State Russian Museum, Leningrad

Shubin was one of the artists encouraged by Elizabeth's favourite Ivan Shuvalov; it was at the latter's instigation that Shubin entered the academy in 1761. Five years at the academy and several years travelling in Western Europe made him, by the late 1770s, a highly skilled portrait sculptor. This bust of Mikhail Lomonosov, the celebrated savant, scientist, poet and first great modern Russian intellectual, is a splendid example of Shubin's talent. It is a portrait of a vivid, energetic personality with a penetrating intellect.

project to turn Peter the Great's school of drawing into a permanent academy of arts was revived by Ivan Shuvalov, the favourite of Empress Elizabeth, who, as the first president, lost no time in seeking out and admitting talented pupils. Catherine replaced him with a man of her choice when she put the academy on a regular basis in 1764.

From the academy there graduated the architects Ivan Starov who built the Tauride Palace for Prince Potemkin, Vasilii Bazhenov and E. P. Chemesov. These architects supplemented the pleiad of distinguished names such as Savva Chevakinskii, Aleksei Evlashev and Aleksei Kvasov who worked in the Rastrelli mood. Bazhenov and Starov, moreover, together with Matvei Kazakov, had been among the first students at the school of architecture set up in Moscow by Dimitrii Ukhtomskii, who had completed the great campanile of the Monastery of the Trinity and St Sergii at Zagorsk.

Sculpture was also encouraged, and Fedor Shubin and Fedor Gordeev **165** emerged as eminent craftsmen from the academy. Most notable is Shubin's truthful, though unflattering, representation of Paul I. Gordeev later turned his attention to monumental sculpture for tombs and bas-reliefs; examples of his bas-reliefs may be seen at Ostankino in Moscow.

A celebrated Russian sculptor, Ivan Martos, was also soon to have a profound effect upon the plastic arts. His most famous work is the bronze group of Minin and Pozharskii in front of St Basil's Cathedral on the Red Square in Moscow. In 1819–20 Martos, in association with his partner Ivan Prokof'ev and his pupils Stepan Pimenov and Vasilii Demut-Malinovskii, were employed in decorating the vault of the staircase at the Academy **166** of Fine Arts, constructed anew by the young architect Mikhailov the Second. The four sculptors, who became very popular in the 19th century, executed four bas-reliefs in the Neo-Classical idiom. The tradition was continued by another celebrated sculptor Ivan Vitali who, besides carving many busts and statues, was very widely employed upon the sculptural groups in the pediment and elsewhere within the fabric of the vast Cathedral of St Isaac. **190**

The growth and influence of the Academy of Fine Arts soon gave rise to a Russian school of painting. After the early attempts at portraiture at

the end of the 17th century, there followed several painters, among them Ivan Nikitin, Andrei Matveev, Ivan Argunov and Aleksei Antropov, who worked in a Western style. The most striking artist nurtured by the academy was Anton Losenko who became director of the academy in 1772. Losenko represents the advent of the Neo-Classical movement in painting in Russia. One of the great masters of 18th-century Russian portraiture was Fedor Rokotov. His portraits of Peter III are reminiscent of Pietro Rotari, while his wonderfully painted and very bold portraits of Catherine in a white satin crinoline are exceptional examples of state portraiture.

Perhaps, however, the painter who has most appeal to foreign eyes is Dimitrii Levitskii. Levitskii was not among the early pupils at the academy and thus managed to avoid the excesses of a rigid Neo-Classicism which was being inculcated within its walls. He exhibited there, however, in 1770 and taught there from 1771–87. He was also elected official portrait painter to the Russian court. His most notable paintings of these years are **180** seven portraits of young ladies resident at the Smol'nyi Institute, which **181, 183** Catherine had founded on the lines of the seminary of St Cyr set up by Madame de Maintenon. The empress always took a great delight in visiting her new foundation, she presided over all extra-curricular activities and commissioned Levitskii, as court painter, to perpetuate the occasion of an entertainment in these canvases.

A succession of accomplished painters followed after Levitskii. Their names include Vladimir Borovikovskii, Grigorii Ugriumov, Orest Kiprenskii, the last a meticulous artist of the Romantic school; A. O. Orlovskii and the realistic painter Aleksei Venetsianov, who was influenced by sentimentalism; Semeon and Sil'vester Shchedrin, both of whom painted landscapes; and the sensitive topographical artist Fedor Alekseev, who has left many dream-like and enchanted views of Moscow **184** and St Petersburg. The list is made finally complete by the name of Karl Briullov, a graduate from the academy. Briullov was unquestionably the most formidable exponent of the Classical revival of the first half of the 19th century. His composition is masterly, and his style technically assured. Briullov exerted a profound influence on Russian painting during his own lifetime.

The minor arts

Unlike Russian painting, Russian ceramic art was destined to achieve by 1800 an international reputation. The foundation of a porcelain factory in St Petersburg had been one of Peter the Great's ambitions, but it was never realised. It was Elizabeth who succeeded where her father had failed. Orders were sent to the chief of the Russian commercial delegation in China to extort from the Chinese the secret of making porcelain—a secret which intrigued the whole of Europe.

A priest's son from Moscow, Dimitrii Vinogradov, brought success to the porcelain factory which was built outside St Petersburg. By 1752 Vinogradov had become so expert and energetic that not only pots but porcelain figurines were being designed. Although he died in 1758, connoisseurs abroad agreed that St Petersburg was gradually coming to rival even Meissen, and sometimes it was hard to distinguish any difference in quality between German and Russian products.

Elizabethan porcelain offers much variety of design and colour. Tea and coffee services, pierced plates and baskets, animals, statuettes, flower pots and many forms of enamelled snuff boxes with, after 1753, decoratively painted lids, abound in a style which is fresh and cheerful and, perhaps, a little naïve as well. Russian porcelain reflected the changing demands of

166

RELIEF DEDICATED
TO SCULPTURE

1819–20
Ivan Martos 1752–1835 and S. S. Pimenov
plaster
Academy of Fine Arts, Leningrad

Ivan Martos had a profound effect upon the art of sculpture in the Neo-Classical style in Russia at the end of the 18th century and the early years of the 19th century. In 1819–20 Martos, in collaboration with his partner and his assistants, was employed in decorating the vault above the wrought-iron staircase in the Academy of Fine Arts. This relief was executed by S. S. Pimenov, in spite of the legend beneath bearing the name of Martos.

style throughout its history; in the first half of the 19th century it showed a preference for rich and severe Neo-Classicism inspired by Greece and in keeping with Alexandrine Empire taste.

The Imperial Porcelain Factory continued producing first quality wares throughout the following century. Soon, however, the example was followed elsewhere in the empire. Franz Gardner, an experienced merchant and business man, established a porcelain manufactory in the village of Verbilki, near Moscow in the Gzhel'sk district. The enterprise prospered and fine porcelain, besides other wares, was made at cheaper rates than ever before.

Not only were Russian manufacturers adept at creating ceramics to adorn the salons of the wealthy, but they were equally skilful at turning and carving wood and ivory objects. A brilliant worker in ivory, N. Vereshchagin, produced several fine vases of turned and chiselled ivory at the end of the 18th century. Vases and urns seem always to have attracted the Russian craftsman. The rich variety of marbles, stone, granite and other rocks to be found inside the empire offered the designer a perfect opportunity to carve Classical-shaped vases. Some of these are of colossal size and when polished and finished on the lapidary's wheel present a handsome appearance in the halls they were made to decorate. Most of them were executed in the first half of the 19th century.

A most unusual manufactory, which existed in Russia, was the Tula Armaments Factory. Apart from producing military weapons and similar goods, from the 17th century the Tula factory had specialised in the creation of steel furniture. During the 18th century slender chairs and tables of oxydised steel, cut and polished, often with the addition of gilded metal appliqué ornamentation, were being produced. In the time of Catherine the Great much cut-steel furniture was ordered from Tula to embellish the imperial palaces.

At the end of the 18th century Russian bronze work and the manufacture of ormolu vied with the products of Parisian firms. The St Petersburg bronze foundries achieved a reputation which nearly succeeded in cutting out the importation of metal objets d'art from France. The great crystal chandeliers and lustres, which were moulded and cut at the St Petersburg glassworks to designs by leading Russian designers for the residences of the aristocracy and for public buildings, were usually mounted in ormolu or bronze fittings. The incursion of Napoleon Bonaparte, however, caused a set-back to the Russian foundries, thereby re-establishing the former prestige in which the French work was held.

Chandeliers and cut-glass lustres, greatly in favour among the Russian nobility, achieved a rare perfection, and many survive today. Russian chandeliers are often made of glass of two colours; the slender central baluster stem might be of ruby, sapphire or emerald glass, and the branches extending out from it would be hung with white crystal cut-glass drops; the sconces would be ormolu, and gilt-bronze fixtures would carry the weight. Torchères, usually in pairs, were similarly much in evidence. They were of carved and gilded wood or cast in bronze and were executed according to the drawings of such notable architects as Vincenzo Brenna (as in the Saloon of War at Pavlovsk), Charles Cameron or Andrei Voronikhin.

The most spectacular success was accomplished in the sphere of gold and silver work. An important atelier of silversmiths attached to the tsar's residence in the Moscow Kremlin had been in existence for a long time, and during the second half of the 17th century many superb examples of the silver- and goldsmiths' art were produced there. The 18th century also

187

186

167

THE TOBOGGAN HILL PAVILION
1762–74
Antonio Rinaldi, c. 1710–94
Lomonosov

The Toboggan Hill Pavilion is the only building to have survived out of a complex of amusement constructions erected by Rinaldi in the Upper Park at Lomonosov. Originally a thirty-three metre high switchback projected from the three-storeyed pavilion. In summer ornamental cars would run down the track; in winter the track was flooded with water to provide a frozen slide.

168 *below right*
THE GLASS BEAD ROOM
The Chinese Palace
1760–beginning of the 1770s
Antonio Rinaldi, c. 1710–94
Lomonosov

The Chinese Palace, the Toboggan Hill Pavilion and the main part of the Upper Park originally comprised the ensemble of the 'Personal Dacha' of Catherine the Great projected by Rinaldi in the 1760s. It was the third, most significant stage in the history of the construction at Lomonosov. In the Glass Bead Room the unique decoration of the wall surfaces has been preserved intact. Embroidered *panneaux* interwoven with glass-beaded twist portraying fantastic birds, exotic plants and other delights are mounted between gilded carved wood frames.

169 *far right*
THE PORCELAIN CABINET
The Toboggan Hill Pavilion
1762–74
Antonio Rinaldi, c. 1710–94
Lomonosov

The third storey of the Toboggan Hill Pavilion contains the Circular Saloon, the Porcelain Cabinet and the Hunting Cabinet; for these rooms a decorative scheme was carried out in white and gold relief ornament. The floors are remarkable for their fine multi-coloured polished inlay. Rinaldi displayed a sure hand when devising the fusion of architectural form and interior design in this suite of rooms. The entire pattern of decoration is a refined blend of colour, plasterwork and painting.

170

CHAIR

c. 1795–1800

This example from a set of chairs in late 18th century Neo-Classical taste owes much of the design to English furniture styles of the same period. It was probably devised as an integral part of the furnishings for the imperial apartments which Cameron was arranging towards the end of the 18th century.

171
PAVILION OF THE THREE GRACES
1800
Charles Cameron 1740–1812
Pavlovsk

Maria, wife of the grand duke Paul, was captivated by the
landscape 'English' gardens which she saw on her visit to France
in 1782. The numerous pavilions and temples at Versailles
particularly impressed her, and, as the laying out of the grounds
at Pavlovsk progressed, she was able to realise many of the ideas
which she had collected abroad. The Pavilion of the Three Graces
is only one of the numerous buildings in the grounds. The portico
of sixteen columns encloses a sculptured group of the Three
Graces; together they form a very pure and sensitive expression
of the Greek style.

172 *far left*
THE PALACE OF PAVLOVSK
1782
Charles Cameron 1740–1812

Cameron constructed the Palace of Pavlovsk for the grand duke
Paul and his wife the grand duchess Maria. The first stone was laid
on the 25th May 1782. The central block of the palace was
completed first, lateral wings and pavilions being added at the end
of the 18th century. Cameron wished to provide a Pompeian or
Adam-style scheme of decoration, but his patrons, after their
visits to Paris and Rome, had been converted to Classical purism,
and Pavlovsk is thus a signpost of the future trend of formal
Classicism to the oncoming Alexandrine Empire style.

173
THE GREEN DINING ROOM
1779–81
Charles Cameron 1740–1812
stucco, plasterwork, relief-moulding
Pushkin (Tsarskoe Selo)

Catherine did not like the Baroque interior of Rastrelli's palace,
so she commissioned Cameron to decorate three suites of rooms
for her. Cameron completed the first suite, which was not as
lavish as the succeeding ones, between 1779 and 1782. The Green
Dining Room was one of his earliest works in Russia. It seems
to have been inspired by the Villa Albani in Rome, which
Cameron would have visited. The elaborate plasterwork contrasts
vividly with the more modest conventions of his fellow
countrymen Adam and Wyatt, working in England.

174
THE BLUE DRAWING ROOM
1779–81
Charles Cameron 1740–1812
Pushkin (Tsarskoe Selo)

The walls of the Blue Drawing Room are hung with heavy
white silk with blue flowers, and the gilt furniture is covered with
the same material. The candelabrum is of lapis lazuli; the parquetry
floor includes mother-of-pearl as well as wood. This room belongs
to the first suite decorated by Cameron.

THE GROTTO
1755–75
Semeon Argunov 1733–68
Kuskovo

The estate of Kuskovo passed to the Sheremetev family at the beginning of the 16th century, but it was not until 1715 when it was acquired by Petr Sheremetev that it was really developed. It was turned into a residence for summer receptions, for garden parties, firework displays, theatre performances and sumptuous banquets. The park is in the French style and contains an Italian villa, a Dutch House and an orangery, as well as this grotto.

witnessed a further development in the style of working in precious metals. New forms of domestic silver became necessary; samovars, coffee-pots, teapots, cups, saucers and trays made their appearance. Besides Moscow and St Petersburg, there were many other centres throughout Russia where competent smiths could be found; among the best known are Velikii Ustiug, Vologda, Tobo'lsk, Kazan', Iaroslavl'. In Iaroslavl' and Nizhnii Novgorod there were craftsmen who experimented with a form of high-quality engraving almost reminiscent of wood carving. Throughout the 18th and 19th centuries the silverworkers of Velikii Ustiug specialised in silver and black inlaid enamelware; landscape designs, buildings and hunting scenes all appeared in this medium on the tops of snuff boxes and scent bottles.

Perhaps, however, in the historical development of Russian creative energy nothing can quite compare with the skill lavished upon jewellery. The USSR Diamond Fund owns one of the world's largest collections of **161, 185** rare gems of historic, artistic and material value. It includes the gems, jewellery and coronation regalia of the sovereigns of Russia. Diamonds had long been held in esteem, for it was believed that they gave people strength and courage. In the 17th century they were widely used by Russian jewellers, and in the 1680s glittering diamond crowns were made for the tsars Ivan and Peter by jewelsmiths at the ateliers in the Moscow Kremlin. In the 18th century great progress was affected in the cutting and faceting of precious stones and it was then that the art of the jeweller reached its zenith in Russia.

Return to a Russian style

The reign of Nicholas I (1825–55) witnesses a change of direction in the taste of Russia. A return to a 'national style' was encouraged, and an attempt made to recreate the glories of a much earlier period of Russian history. Sometimes the result allowed certain awkward eccentricities to intrude into the design; occasionally, it was successful.

In 1838 all the ancient palace buildings of the Moscow Kremlin were demolished, apart from the Granovitaia Palace, the Terem and Zolotoi Tsaritsyn Palaces. On the site a vast new palace was erected called the Grand Kremlin Palace, which was finished in 1849. The architect of this great project was Konstantin Thon. It is a three-storeyed building consisting of rows of windows facing the Moscow river designed in a pseudo-Russian style; a vast iron roof covers the structure, while a square cupola-tent-shaped projection occupies the central position above the main façade. The iron stanchions were devised by a professor of Moscow University, D. M. Perevoshchikov. There are seven hundred separate apartments within the palace, all luxuriously furnished, and the interior can accommodate over twenty thousand people.

In 1849–51 Thon erected the new Armoury Palace (Oruzheinaia Palata). The outside of this Renaissance-style building, adorned with carved white stone pilasters, cornices and reliefs, appears to be far more assured and picturesque than do the huge façades of the Grand Kremlin Palace. The Armoury Palace now contains the greatest collection of Russian treasures in Moscow.

Thus, by 1850, the last years of the reign of Nicholas I, Russia's treasures were being properly cared for and housed in appropriate surroundings. Taste had veered back in time towards a more national, seemingly more 'Russian', style of decoration. There was now a real feeling for the part which Russia had played throughout her extensive history, and the object of the designer was to recapture such a spirit.

Malcolm Burgess

176

THE PALACE OF ARKHANGEL'SKOE

1780–1812
De Guerne

In the 18th century the estate of Arkhangel'skoe had belonged first to the Sheremetev and then to the Golitsyn families; in 1804, however, it was bought by Nikolai Iusupov, one of the richest and most celebrated connoisseurs of the time. Once building on the main house, which had been designed by the little known French architect De Guerne, was completed, Iusupov began amassing a vast collection of valuable pictures, furniture and porcelain. Much of this collection is still displayed in the palace.

177 *below right*
THE PALACE OF OSTANKINO

1729–99
mainly Vasilii Bazhenov 1737–99
Moscow

The mansions built by the aristocracy in Moscow were rather smaller and less pretentious than the palaces they built themselves in St Petersburg. Ostankino belonged after 1743 to the Sheremetev family, which had risen to prominence when Boris Sheremetev was field marshal to Peter the Great. They remained among the wealthiest Russian families and brought together a fine collection of paintings. Many architects worked on the palace, but it took its final shape from the designs of Bazhenov.

178 *above far right*
THE PASHKOV MANSION

1784–86
Vasilii Bazhenov 1737–99
Moscow

Peter the Great had tried to destroy the prestige of Moscow, but Elizabeth and Catherine the Great, who were both interested in their country's history, held Moscow in some affection. Catherine's plans to reconstruct the Kremlin was perhaps a sign of her recognition of the importance of Moscow. Bazhenov spent vast amounts on designs and models, but the immense task was halted at a very early stage. The Pashkov Mansion was built by Bazhenov within sight of the Kremlin for Petr Pashkov, a member of the bodyguard. It now houses the Lenin Library.

179 *far right*
THE LITTLE HERMITAGE

1764–67
Jean-Baptiste Vallin de la Mothe 1729–1800
Leningrad

In 1764 Catherine started building a hermitage or pleasure pavilion attached to the Winter Palace to house her collection of pictures. The collection increased so swiftly that in 1775 another building, now known as the Old Hermitage, was added. The calm Classicism of the Little Hermitage is in direct contrast to Rastrelli's Baroque Winter Palace. The Little Hermitage still houses part of the collection of the State Hermitage Museum.

180

CATHERINE THE GREAT

1783
Dimitrii Levitskii 1735–1822
State Russian Museum, Leningrad

A series of full-length portraits of Catherine followed Levitskii's success with his Smol'nyi portraits. Catherine stands regally surrounded by symbols of imperial greatness. She looks very different from the benign mother-like figure of Borovikovskii's picture *Catherine the Great walking with her Dog* (**frontispiece**).

181 *below*

PRINCESS KHOVANSKAIA AND E. N. KHRUSHCHEVA

1777
Dimitrii Levitskii 1735–1822
oil on canvas
64·5 × 50·75 in (164 × 129 cm)
State Russian Museum, Leningrad

Of the seven paintings of pupils at the Smol'nyi Institute this double portrait probably achieves the greatest spontaneity and effect. It shows two of the pupils acting in a pastoral opéra-comique performed on 16th June 1777 in the presence of King Gustav III of Sweden. Catherine described the costumes in detail in a letter to Voltaire.

182 *right*

THE APPEARANCE OF CHRIST TO THE PEOPLE

1833–55
Aleksandr Ivanov 1806–58
oil on canvas
State Russian Museum, Leningrad

Enormous historical and religious compositions became the fashion in the first half of the 19th century. Ivanov spent twenty-two years working on this painting, making numerous detailed studies of nature and going through grave religious doubts. The figures in the foreground show an entirely new interest in representing character and emotion.

183

N. S. BORSHCHEVA

1776
Dimitrii Levitskii 1735–1822
oil on canvas
64·5 × 50·75 in (164 × 129 cm)
State Russian Museum, Leningrad

The series of seven portraits of pupils at Catherine's school for daughters of the nobility did much to establish Levitskii's reputation. He recorded with great subtlety, grace and charm the character of each of his sitters. This young lady is shown on the terrace of the institute looking pleased at the success of her dancing.

184 *below*

A VIEW OF MOSCOW

1811
Fedor Alekseev 1753–1824
oil on canvas
51·25 × 43·5 in (130 × 110·5 cm)
Tret'iakov Gallery, Moscow

Alekseev is one of the best masters of the Russian school of landscape painting. During the 1790s he painted many excellent views of St Petersburg, but in 1800 he was ordered by Paul I to execute views of Moscow and other cities and to instruct in his style two students of his own choice from the academy. His works reveal Moscow as a romantic, 'Gothic' city, very different from St Petersburg.

THE GRAND IMPERIAL CROWN

1762
Jeremiah Posier
silver, brilliants, pearls and a single
spinel ruby
10·75 in (27·5 cm)
USSR Diamond Fund, Moscow

The Grand Imperial Crown was made for the coronation of Catherine the Great by the talented court jeweller Jeremiah Posier. The crown is in the traditional form of two silver cowl-shaped half sections divided by a garland and secured by a small chaplet, encrusted with brilliants and pearls. It conveys an impression of pomp and majesty. This crown appears in many of the portraits painted of Catherine.

186 *above*

TULA STEEL FURNITURE

late 18th century
Pushkin (Tsarskoe Selo)

The cut-steel furniture made at Tula was a by-product of the small arms industry there and became widely used in the imperial palaces during Catherine's reign. Catherine's favourite Orlov visited a steel-furniture factory in Birmingham during a visit to England and brought back English styles and methods, and possibly even some workmen. The absence of examples after 1796 suggests that the desire for steel furniture died with the empress.

187 *left*

THE VASE OF THE SEASONS

c. 1785
ivory
N. Vereshchagin
State Hermitage Museum, Leningrad

A brilliant craftsman working in the medium of ivory, N. Vereshchagin produced several fine vases of turned and chiselled ivory at the end of the 18th century. This example has allegorical scenes carved upon the body.

188 *right*

MOSAIC PORTRAIT OF PETER III

1763
Mikhail Lomonosov 1711–65
glass mosaic
State Russian Museum, Leningrad

In 1753, after much persistence, Lomonosov received from Elizabeth a site on which to establish a glass factory. There, on machinery designed by himself, he made glass tesserae and beads and produced mosaics, which he considered vied with the patterns produced at Rome. The mosaic portrait of Catherine's husband, tsar for six months in 1762, shows him as a thoroughly feeble young man.

The first pictures which Catherine purchased set the pattern for the reign; they were a collection of 225 works, most of which were by Dutch and Flemish masters. Catherine bought pictures by the hundred, always unseen, often without knowing what she was actually getting. It is impossible to be certain how far Catherine appreciated her pictures as works of art. She did, however, clearly derive great pleasure from haggling with other collectors and from the envy her success aroused. She also saw that buying pictures was a way of displaying her own and Russia's wealth and power to the French, British and Germans, who were unable to prevent, for instance, the 400 works of Pierre Crozat or the 198 works of Robert Walpole going to Russia. At her death the imperial collection of pictures, most of which had been bought by her, was estimated to total 3926 works.

192 *above*
A BOY BENT DOUBLE

early 1530s
Michelangelo Buonarroti 1475–1564
marble
acquired 1785
State Hermitage Museum, Leningrad

193 *left*
SASKIA AS FLORA

1634
Rembrandt van Rijn 1606–69
oil on canvas
47·5 × 39·75 in (125 × 107 cm)
acquired 1770–74
State Hermitage Museum, Leningrad

194, 195

THE CAMERON GALLERY

1779—94
Charles Cameron 1740—1812
Pushkin (Tsarskoe Selo)

Catherine was particularly fond of this gallery and furnished it
with great care. Between the columns she placed bronze busts of
famous figures. At first these included Voltaire and Charles James
Fox. The bust of Voltaire was destroyed at the empress's orders on
the outbreak of the French Revolution. That of Charles James
Fox, which had stood between Demosthenes and Cicero and
gained a place on the strength of his opposition to war with
Russia, was also destroyed when he showed support for the
revolutionaries in France.

196 *below*

CATHEDRAL OF ST ISAAC

1817–57
Ricard de Montferrand 1786–1858
Leningrad

In 1817 Alexander's architectural commission organised a competition for designs for the rebuilding of the Cathedral of St Isaac. The winner was an unknown young man who had submitted designs in the Chinese, Indian, Gothic and Byzantine styles. This was the last great building erected in accordance with the commission's standard of design, for by the 1840s Nicholas I had to give up imperial censorship of architecture in the face of the eclecticism of mid 19th-century Europe.

197 *bottom left*

THE PUSHKIN THEATRE

formerly the Aleksandrinskii Theatre
1828–32
Carlo Rossi 1775–1849
Leningrad

The character of St Petersburg is as much due to Alexander as to Catherine. He established a special architectural committee to control all aspects of building from the smallest private houses up. These plain Classical dwellings provided a suitable background for monumental public structures. The Aleksandrinskii Theatre, like all Rossi's buildings, was designed as a part of an impressive large-scale ensemble.

198 *bottom right*

THE ADMIRALTY

1806–23
Adreian Zakharov 1761–1811
Leningrad

By 1800 the admiralty built by Peter the Great was not sufficiently impressive for the great maritime city which St Petersburg had become. The task of converting the old admiralty was a difficult one, for it entailed preserving the famous steeple, which balanced that of the Cathedral of St Peter and St Paul on the opposite bank (**144**). Zakharov successfully overcame the problems and designed an original and homogenous building.

199 *above*

A FAMILY GROUP

Anthony van Dyck 1599–1641
oil on canvas
45·5 × 36·75 in (115·5 × 93·5 cm)
acquired 1774
State Hermitage Museum, Leningrad

Flemish and Dutch pictures were more
popular with 18th-century connoisseurs
than the Italian works collected during the
previous century. They were more
plentiful and less expensive; most of
Catherine's early purchases were of
Flemish and Dutch masters. The Brühl
collection bought in 1769 added to the
number of French pictures in her possession, and, although the number of French,
Spanish and Italian works increased,
Rubens, Rembrandt and Van Dyck
remained Catherine's favourite artists.

200 *right*

DANAE

c. 1636
Rembrandt van Rijn 1606–69
oil on canvas
76 × 52·5 in (193 × 133 cm)
acquired 1771 from Pierre Crozat
State Hermitage Museum, Leningrad

The purchase of four hundred pictures
from the Crozat collection in 1771 was one
of Catherine's greatest triumphs. Diderot,
the great French encyclopedist who was a
friend and correspondent of Catherine,
reported that 'the collectors, the artists
and the rich are all up in arms. . . . So much
the worse for France if we must sell our
pictures in time of peace, whereas
Catherine can buy them in the middle of
a war.' Among the most important items
in the collection, apart from Raphael's
The Virgin and Child with St Joseph (**191**)
and this Rembrandt, were several other
Rembrandts, a Giorgione, a Tintoretto, a
dozen works by Rubens and several
Watteaus.

The mid 19th century provides as great a turning point in Russian history as the accession of Peter the Great. Ancient patriarchal Russia, with its agrarian and economic system based on serfdom, did not survive the strain of the Crimean War and the government of the new emperor Alexander II (1851–81) was obliged to pursue a policy which forced Russia into the modern age at an accelerated pace. The far-reaching Great Reforms of the 1860s were bolstered after 1870 by the simultaneous impact of an agrarian and an industrial revolution. Although they entailed much hardship, they also brought about brilliant practical results and were accompanied in the intellectual field by a new spirit of enquiry and rich creative achievement.

The changes, both in the structure of the empire and in the life pattern of its citizens, are paralleled by corresponding changes in the field of art and art patronage. During the first half of the century it was the aristocracy, following the lead given by the monarchy, which had dominated the arts. After the abolition of serfdom by Alexander II in 1861 the aristocracy went gradually into decline, and from then on the taste of the period was no longer dependent on aristocratic patronage. The monarchy also ceased to be the guiding light in the domain of art, as it had been under Nicholas I. Not merely did Alexander II lack the interest of his predecessors, but art was no longer considered of primary importance. In the exacting intellectual climate prevailing in Russia between 1860 and 1890, social issues, humanitarian problems and scientific investigation became almost the sole province considered worthy of attention. Art which did not help to alleviate the social problems of the day was treated with disapproval. It was a small intellectual circle, adrift from the rest of society, which usurped the functions of the monarchy and aristocracy in establishing fashionable trends. Its members did not belong to any class or group, but the nucleus of the movement was made up of the descendants of Peter's Westernised elite and, as it expanded, it attracted the sons of bureaucrats, clergymen, doctors and lawyers. Anyone whose profession implied being under the direct influence of the State, such as army officers or clergymen, were not acceptable.

Both this Intelligentsia and society as a whole was split into two groups – Slavophils and Westerners. The former held that the problems besetting Russia were the result of Peter's too drastic Westernisation – an unnatural development, which had arrested the healthy evolution of indigenous culture. The latter held the opposite view, namely, that it was the indigenous tradition that was at fault, and that progress could only be attained by a closer imitation of the West.

The starting point of the Intelligentsia's philosophy was an idealisation of the peasantry, who, degraded to a status little better than that of beasts of burden, were nevertheless thought to have greater moral qualities than other levels of society. The outstanding characteristics of the Intelligentsia itself were a sense of personal guilt, shared humanitarian sentiments, and common opposition to a bureaucracy which, to them, exemplified social injustice. All of these stemmed from the Intelligentsia's painful awareness of the vast gulf which divided them from the masses they idolised.

Guided by the taste of the Intelligentsia, the public of the 1860s required art to be realistic, to have social content, and to be Russian. Art critics held that the artist's first duty was to probe deeply into psychological and spiritual issues, to arrive at a critical appraisal of men and events and to invest his art with social purpose. For this reason, in the Russia of the 1860s, the theme of a picture was of primary importance, both to the public and to the artist, while the execution was secondary.

Social Revolution and the Arts

1855–1917

201
THE RELIGIOUS PROCESSION
1880–83
Il'ia Repin 1884–1930
oil on canvas
Tret'iakov Gallery, Moscow

An accurate observer of the world around him, Repin succeeded here in bringing us face to face with a vivid cross-section of rural life. The effect is dramatic in spite of its realism. There are peasants, a choir, eager cripples and pilgrims, as well as petty officials, soldiers and police. Certain figures, such as the fat woman with her icon, are treated with telling satire. The soldier portrayed with raised whip is an indictment of military violence.

The paintings of Vasilii Perov are the epitome of the taste of the 1860s. They are imbued with a bitter, hard-hitting satire aimed at the bureaucracy and official classes. Anti-clerical feeling is undisguised in such paintings as

201 *The Easter Procession* and *Tea Drinking at Mytishchakh near Moscow* – works which reflect the prevailing attitude of the Intelligentsia at the time.

202 Perov's painting *The Arrival of a New Governess at a Merchant's House* provides an illuminating pictorial commentary on the social life of the 1860s. Under the gaze of the entire household, a sensitive young girl stands meekly facing her new employer. Portrayed here is the type of grasping, uncultured tycoon whose meteoric rise from the ranks of the richer peasants followed the re-organisation of the empire under Alexander II. Only the rapid development of the country can account for the contrast between the merchant class of the 1860s – a self-sufficient community, generally speaking ultra conservative, both puritan and obscurantist – and the same group a decade later who numbered in the ranks some of the greatest art patrons of the empire.

The Wanderers

While Perov was in Paris (where he ignored the artistic ferment produced by the Impressionists), an event took place at the Academy of Fine Arts in St Petersburg which was the starting point of an organised artistic movement. In 1863 fourteen students left the academy in protest against having to paint subjects completely divorced from real life. A few years later they formed a co-operative society for the exhibition of their work. From 1872 onwards, in a series of ambulant exhibitions, their painting was regularly displayed in provincial towns. In this way, they familiarised the public with the social content of their work and identified themselves with the popular movement headed by the Intelligentsia. These artists, who became popularly known as the Wanderers, established aesthetic standards which were to remain unchallenged until the 1890s.

Il'ia Repin was undoubtedly the greatest artist who subscribed to the ideals of the Wanderers. His paintings, which dominated art during the 1870s, are, compared with those of Perov, less rigid in their approach to doctrinaire realism. Repin was not only an excellent draughtsman, but, as

203 is evident in *The Volga Boatmen*, a master of composition. The fact that his sketches often have greater appeal than his finished work may be due to his inability to experiment with new techniques. As in the case of Perov, Paris failed to inspire him, and he was drawn back to his native Russia where, again like Perov, he devoted his energies to social problems. His work never lacked recognition, however, and in 1898 he was made professor of the academy where his influence was considerable. Particular importance is ascribed by Soviet critics to his role in the evolution of a national Russian school of painting, and as the forerunner of Soviet art.

Although the Wanderers had altered the themes they painted, their technique was little different from that of the academic painters of the early 19th century. The first Russian artist to experiment with a technique more in line with the aspirations of the new movement was Vasilii Surikov.

204 His epic painting *Boyarina Morozova*, finished in 1887 after many preliminary studies, is one of the most significant works of the second half of the 19th century. Surikov thrilled his contemporaries by his painstaking reconstruction of 17th-century Moscow. The critics admired the 'beautiful muddiness of his colours', which they held to be reminiscent of the colour range predominant in ancient icons and decorative peasant work, and of the sky and snow effects observed on a wintry Moscow day.

·Historical painting, of which this is an example, played a significant part in the evolution of Russian art, for it provided a salutary escape from

203 *above*

THE VOLGA BOATMEN

1870–73
Il'ia Repin 1844–1930, oil on canvas
State Russian Museum, Leningrad

This painting caused a sensation, and made the artist's reputation when it was shown at an exhibition of the Wanderers in 1873. It moved the public by its essentially honest portrayal of the bargemen's hard life. The painting was acquired by the president of the academy, Grand Duke Vladimir, for his private collection.

202 *left*

THE ARRIVAL OF
A NEW GOVERNESS

1866
Vasilii Perov 1833–82, oil on wood
17·5 × 21 in (44 × 53·5 cm)
Tret'iakov Gallery, Moscow

Responsive to the mood of the time, Perov gave prominence in his paintings to social questions, and here he provides an interesting commentary on life during the 1860s. The heroine of this 'moral tale' is the young governess, a shy, modest and poetic representative of the Intelligentsia. The villains were the boorish merchant, his family and household. The girl's tragedy is perhaps the tragedy of the whole Intelligentsia.

204 *below*

BOYARINA MOROZOVA

1887, Vasilii Surikov 1848–1916
Tret'iakov Gallery, Moscow

This painting depicts a historical incident during the spiritual and cultural crisis of 17th-century Russia. Conveyed to prison for resisting Patriarch Nikon's ritualistic innovations, Morozova raises her right hand to make the sign of the cross according to the ancient rite. She believed that only by total adherence to tradition could the faith be kept pure.

the stultifying demands of subjects with a social message. The same applies to nature painting, which enabled artists like Ivan Aivazovskii, famous for his seascapes, and Isaak Levitan, the renowned landscape painter, to turn away from mundane, human problems and find solace in nature.

By breaking away from the academy, the Wanderers had made a stand for independence. Nevertheless, in order to make a living, they needed patrons to back their movement. Although they held the view that it was unethical to depict scenes from the lives of the wealthy, curiously, men of wealth and prestige showed them sympathy and bought their work. Lacking the confidence of the aristocratic patron, these men never doubted that the best judge of art was the artist himself. These 19th-century merchants were avid travellers, but the artistic achievements of strange lands only increased their nostalgic love of Russia and the desire to promote her cultural standing.

The age of museums

The best paintings exhibited by the Wanderers at their first public exhibition in 1872 were, in fact, bought by two influential collectors – the future emperor Alexander III, and the wealthy merchant brothers Pavel and Sergei Tret'iakov. The Slavophil tsar Alexander III (1881–94) did much to encourage the collecting of old Russian art. In 1883, he incorporated a hall of Russian medieval art into the Historical Museum in Moscow, founded in the preceding reign. He also made plans for the founding of a new museum, which was to be fully representative of Russian art. To this end, he acquired paintings by the Wanderers and had selected canvases put aside from the various imperial residences. On set days during the summer, dealers brought 18th-century paintings to him at Tsarskoe Selo, and Alexander enjoyed bargaining with them. After the emperor's death, the Mikhailovskii Palace in St Petersburg was acquired by the State, and it was opened in 1898 to the public as the Russian Museum of Emperor Alexander III (now the State Russian Museum). In this superb Neo-Classical setting the collection formed by the princes Gagarin and Lobanov-Rostovskii, paintings from the academy and those set aside by Alexander III were brought together.

Princess Tenisheva, founder of a museum at Smolensk, was one of the outstanding patrons of Russian peasant craft. She donated a collection of sketches and other items to the Alexander III Museum which were catalogued for the museum by Alexandre Benois. Funds provided by the emperor Nicholas II and the grand duke George enabled the museum to purchase the first systematic collection of icons, which had been carefully selected by the Petersburg collector N. P. Likhachev.

The 18th-century idea of art as a private pastime of the aristocracy was replaced in the 19th century by the new concept that art should play a part in the education and cultural advancement of the general public. The foundation and endowment of museums became an important factor in 19th-century art patronage and it was now the ambition of both enlightened governments and wealthy individuals.

The Tret'iakov Gallery in Moscow, opened to the public in 1881, was the counterpart of the Alexander III Museum in St Petersburg. Donated to the city of Moscow by Pavel and Sergei Tret'iakov, it was intended to be representative of the history and culture of Moscow. Not only was it especially rich in paintings by the Wanderers, it also contained a growing number of old icons for which Pavel Tret'iakov paid vast amounts, as well as a noteworthy section of Western art (now in the Pushkin Museum).

In 1903, after Pavel Tret'iakov's death, the painter I. S. Ostroukhov, one of the foremost connoisseurs and collectors of the time, was appointed

205

THE DUCHESS OF BEAUFORT

1775–80
Thomas Gainsborough 1727–88
oil on canvas
30 × 25·5 in (76 × 64 cm)
State Hermitage Museum, Leningrad

In 1916 the Aleksei Khitrovo collection was bequeathed to the Hermitage. Rich in the work of English portrait painters such as Gainsborough, Lawrence, Raeburn and Romney, it filled an important gap in the museum's collection. Among his English portraits was this painting of the Duchess of Beaufort.

director of the gallery. Ostroukhov's marriage to Nadezhda Botkina, in whose father's trading company he had been a humble employee, had made him one of the richest men in Russia. Exacting, temperamental, but generous, he was to use his fortune to build up a fine private collection and to further the cause of Russian art, of which he had acquired a highly specialised knowledge. Ostroukhov's collection of icons, now incorporated in the Tret'iakov Gallery, was a landmark in the appreciation of medieval Russian art at the beginning of this century.

The Imperial Hermitage Museum also acquired many outstanding works of art during this period. One of the most notable was Raphael's *Conestabile Madonna*, purchased for Empress Maria by the director **20(** Kheneonov from the collection of Count Conestabile in Perugia. It remained in the empress's private apartments for ten years before passing as a gift to the Hermitage. Meanwhile the Hermitage, which had for so long been regarded as the personal property of the sovereign, was now emerging as an independent institution. *The Benois Madonna* by Leonardo da Vinci **208** is another masterpiece which entered the Hermitage during this period. The Hermitage acquired entire collections as well as individual canvases; on the eve of the First World War, Nicholas II bought the Semenov collection of almost a thousand Dutch paintings.

The merchant collectors

More amazing than the collectors of old masters were the activities of a small group of millionaire merchants, consisting, in the main, of Muscovites and Old Believers, noted for their generous patronage of both French and Russian contemporary art. Compared with that of Western bourgeoisie, the generosity and avant-garde taste of Russian art patrons were astonishing. Concerned with the changing world around them, they turned to the avant-garde cultural arena of contemporary Europe in an endeavour to find new roots. From the ensuing interaction of trends, new and old, native and foreign, now freely intermingling, emerged what has come to be known as Russia's Silver Age (1890-1917). This was the period of Symbolist literature; a creative period in which the author's medium became the language of moods and nuances, and the painter's brush, unbridled, followed suit.

The most remarkable collectors were Savva Morozov and Sergei Shchukin, pioneer purchasers of Post-Impressionist French paintings. Between them they were responsible for building up a phenomenal collection of modern French art – the most startling importation of paintings into Russia since Catherine purchased her Rembrandts. These collections were, at the time when they were being bought, far more ambitious than any being assembled in Paris, and even now, they form what is perhaps still the finest collection of Post-Impressionist paintings in the world.

Shchukin began his collection in 1897 in Paris. He first bought a number of Impressionist paintings including six Renoirs, but then he turned his attention to later artists whose work, still unrecognised in France, was quite unknown in Russia – Cézanne, Gauguin, Van Gogh and, above all, **218** Matisse. In 1909 Matisse executed the decorative panels entitled *Music* and **221** *Dance* for him. Through Matisse Shchukin met Picasso and in Shchukin's collection (now in the Pushkin Museum of Visual Arts, Moscow) are fifty works by Picasso, covering the stylistic evolution of his Blue and Cubist **242** periods.

The rich collections of Shchukin and Morozov served to reveal the latest **217** developments of the French School of painting to the young Russian artists of the first decade of the 20th century. It was in this way that the

206 *below*

THE CONESTABILE MADONNA

c. 1500
Raphael 1483–1520
tempera on wood, transferred to canvas
7 × 7·25 in (17·5 × 18 cm)
State Hermitage Museum, Leningrad

Alexander II bought this Madonna and
Child in 1870 as a present for his wife
Maria. In accordance with her wishes it
was added to the collections in the
Hermitage after her death in 1880. The
Madonnas of Raphael were thought in the
19th century to be the most perfect
expression of beauty.

207 *right*

EASTER EGG

1899
Carl Fabergé 1846–1920
gold, enamel and precious stones
height 10·5 in (26·5 cm)
Armoury Palace, the Kremlin, Moscow

After 1884 Fabergé devoted a vast amount
of skill and imagination to the making of
eggs which were delivered to the palace
each year for Easter. That made in 1899 for
Nicholas II to give to his consort is in the
form of a clock with a vase of lilies of
quartzite and rose diamonds. The enamel
egg is encircled by a revolving belt
studded with diamond numerals which
indicates the time against a golden arrow.

208

THE BENOIS MADONNA

1478
Leonardo da Vinci 1452–1519
oil on wood, transferred to canvas
19·25 × 12·25 in (49·5 × 31·5 cm)
State Hermitage Museum, Leningrad

The Benois Madonna was brought to Russia by a troupe of itinerant Italian actors early in the 19th century. It was subsequently acquired by the Benois family, and, once Alexandre Benois had succeeded in having it authenticated, Nicholas II consented to its purchase by the Hermitage. The agreed sum was to be paid in instalments, but after the first instalment the 1917 Revolution cut short the payments.

work of the Post-Impressionists, the Fauves, Futurists and Cubists became known in Russia, and for this reason that Russians became familiar with all these movements almost simultaneously.

Meanwhile, in Russia itself there was a growing awareness of the aesthetic value of ancient icons. In the 1890s, artists of the World of Art group had already admired the beauty of line of early icons. The painters of the next decade, Goncharova and Kandinsky, had been struck by their colour. It was not until 1900, however, when the systematic restoration and cleaning of icons started in Russia, a process sponsored by such famous collectors as N. P. Likhachev, I. S. Ostroukhov, and S. P. Riabushinskii, that the richness and luminosity of their true colour really came into its own. In 1913 the first exhibition of cleaned icons was organised to celebrate the tercentenary of the Romanov dynasty. This exhibition opened the eyes of the public to the rich heritage of medieval Russian painting for the first time. Curiously, although Russian 15th-century icons and the Paris school were a far cry from each other, they had one thing in common: they both sought to depict a form of reality through abstract media and oblique impressions.

Mamontov, Serov and Vrubel'

Savva Mamontov played an important part in the story of Russian art patronage in the 19th century. Of peasant stock and self-taught, he became a railway magnate and amassed a fortune. Intensely patriotic, he believed he had a duty to use his wealth for the betterment of his countrymen and the promotion of national culture. Hospitals, schools and the contemporary religious revival interested him and his wife, Elizaveta, no less than the promotion of art with which he was deeply involved. Mamontov aimed always at encouraging youthful talent of the most experimental kind. At his country estate of Abramtsevo near Moscow he attracted around him all the great artists of the time, and many of them came with their families to settle there and work together. In due course, they formed the nucleus of a new cultural movement. It was here that Repin, already an established artist, Serov, the Vasnetsov brothers, Vrubel', Golovin, Korovin and the sculptor Antokolskii gathered to hold discussion groups and practise their skills – encouraged by Mamontov's contagious enthusiasm.

Two artists of Mamontov's circle, Valentin Serov and Mikhail Vrubel', are particularly important. The work of these two painters bridges the gap between the decline of the Wanderers and the emergence of the World of Art group.

Valentin Serov was brought up on Mamontov's estate where he studied under Repin. His handling of light and shade and the freshness of his colours reflect his interest in French Impressionism, ignored by Repin. Indeed, Serov is the first Russian painter of this period whose work shows the technical innovations of Western painting, and his gift as a teacher ensured that this Western trend was passed on to the next generation of Russian artists. At the age of twenty-two he attracted attention as a landscape painter, but it is as the most outstanding portrait painter of the period that he is chiefly remembered today. Serov's portraits of Emperor Nicholas II are among his best psychological studies, justifying his unofficial status of court painter.

Mikhail Vrubel' who had studied with Serov at the Imperial Academy was introduced by him to Savva Mamontov. On leaving the academy Vrubel' was recommended by his professors to undertake a series of frescoes for the Church of St Cyril in Kiev. In spite of this commission Vrubel' owed what little recognition he had during his life-time to the interest shown him by a handful of patrons, in particular Mamontov. The

209
MADAME ERMOLOVA
1905, Valentin Serov 1865–1911
oil on canvas
Tret'iakov Gallery, Moscow

This portrait of the celebrated actress, Ermolova, demonstrates Serov's outstanding gift for rendering on canvas the very essence of human character. Commanding and self-assured, she is clearly a member of the Intelligentsia. The picture was painted for the Moscow Art Circle.

210
THE DEMON
c. 1900, terracotta, Mikhail Vrubel' 1856–1910
State Russian Museum, Leningrad

There is a lapidary quality about the work by Vrubel', who approached painting with the eye of a sculptor. The complex design of Oriental rug patterns or the play of light over the surface of mosaic cubes held an equal fascination for him in his search for new forms.

145

latter's recognition of Vrubel's talent shows him to have been a connoisseur of real flair, for posterity has assigned to Vrubel' a unique place among Russian artists. Apart from painting, he experimented with a great variety of materials such as wood, clay, glass and glazes, all of which he handled with the imagination of a poet. While absorbed on the St Cyril frescoes, Vrubel' fell under the spell of Byzantine art, at the time imperfectly understood. In particular, he was excited by the luminous colour and texture of mosaics and the challenge of tackling drapery. From the Byzantines, Vrubel' learned to appreciate texture and light, and how to build up colour in planes, but the creative flow of his work appeared, at times, to be inhibited by a demanding intellect.

The World of Art

Serov and Vrubel' were pioneers in the cultural revolution in which the World of Art played a key role. Artists of the World of Art group (named after a magazine published by Sergei Diaghilev and other exponents of the movement) reacted against the aesthetic values of the Wanderers and rejected their belief in the primarily didactic and social function of art. Instead, they set themselves the task of removing the narrow and pseudo-national understanding of art, and introduced the West to what they held to be the real artistic expression and achievement of Russian art. It was for this reason that the organisation of exhibitions and the publication of journals assumed such a vital part in the movement, which was above all orientated outwards towards the West.

The group activities were presided over by Alexandre Benois and subsequently by Sergei Diaghilev, both of whom provided leadership and guidance. These men were characteristic of the period in which they lived – a period in which artists tried their hand at a variety of media. Alexandre 212 Benois was not only a water-colourist, a writer and critic, but a notable curator of the Hermitage after the Revolution and an illustrator and eminent theatrical designer. Unlike many of the Wanderers, who were mostly of humble birth, he hailed from an artistic elite with a cosmopolitan background.

Diaghilev was an outstanding patron of the arts. His remarkable flair for spotting talent enabled him to single out the finest contemporary Russian painters, such as Leon Bakst, Mikhail Larionov and Natal'ia Goncharova. Later Diaghilev was to assume the unchallenged leadership of the whole World of Art movement, which he introduced to the West with the panache of an accomplished impresario. Nevertheless the major part of the work of the World of Art artists has remained unfamiliar to the West.

A search for atmosphere often full of nostalgia and poetic symbolism and a kind of theatrical mise en scène are typical features of the World of 212 Art group. Alexandre Benois tried to capture in his imaginative paintings the mood of 18th-century St Petersburg or Versailles. The artist Nikolai Roerich, an archaeologist by training, recreated ancient Russia – a land of primeval forest and mountain peaks, bathed in a strange light and 211 peopled by a frontier people of warriors and hermits. Borisov-Musatov, certainly a most important painter, evoked beautifully sad and nostalgic images of the 1840s with crinolined ladies gliding through overgrown parkland, all in a characteristic pale tone of blue-green. Dimitrii Steletskii skilfully wove a pattern of architectural landscape and figure painting taken directly from icon painting as though the intervening period of 18th-century Westernisation had never existed. The stage designs of Leon 226 Bakst resurrect the distant past of ancient Greece and the splendour of Persia and the East. Golovin adopted the colour harmony of ancient icons 216 in his back-cloth for the Imperial Theatre production of 'Boris Godunov'.

211

REQUIEM

1905
Viktor Borisov-Musatov 1870–1905
Tret'iakov Gallery, Moscow

The work of Borisov-Musatov was revered by a whole generation of Russian artists to whom his early death came as a tragedy. His large canvases have something of the quality of frescoes. His crinolined girls are shown at peace in the green parkland of secluded country houses during the early 19th century. These figures, fragrant, lyrical and poetic, owe nothing to historical reconstruction. They are phantoms, the echoes of a departed world, transmitted to canvas as in a dream.

Brightly painted peasant toys, gay shop signs and quaint carved wood surrounds used by the peasants to decorate their log cabins became a **227** fertile source of inspiration to such painters as Boris Kustodiev, Konstantin Iuon and Sergei Sudeikin.

The symbolism, colour and this search for atmosphere of the World of Art were particularly suited to stage design and it is here that the World of Art scored its most resounding success. Under the stimulus of the revitalising originality of stage design, pictorial art broke away from the trends of the 1870s and 1880s, and a new art movement emerged. It was with stage design that Russia, which had for so long followed in the footsteps of the West, now established a model for the West to copy. The West was stunned by the colour, vitality, exotic Orientalism and 'barbarism' of the Russian stage, introduced by Diaghilev and the Imperial Theatre.

212
FANTASY ON
A VERSAILLES THEME
1906
Alexandre Benois 1870–1960
Tret'iakov Gallery, Moscow

The art movement, the World of Art, which gathered round Alexandre Benois, rediscovered a respectable place for the aristocratic culture of the 18th and early 19th centuries. It was France, and in particular an admiration for the parks and statues of Versailles, which preceded a reappraisal and scholarly interest in Russia's own past. Benois and his followers laid stress on investigation beneath the surface of history, and consulted old engravings, original diaries and documents.

In this field, as in so many others, a key role was played by Mamontov. He was the first to commission a talented artist rather than a stage designer to plan a setting and backcloth. Stanislavsky, a cousin of Mamontov, at the Realistic Theatre and Diaghilev with his celebrated Ballets Russes followed suit a decade later.

Architecture

The changes that took place in the field of architecture during the mid-19th century were no less abrupt than those which had taken place in the sphere of painting. Quite suddenly, with the death of Nicholas I, it became apparent that the official Classicism had only been retained because nobody had found an adequate substitute for it. Now, no longer answering the demands of contemporary life, it was superseded by eclectic and experimental interpretations based either on the Italian Renaissance or on 16th-century Moscow architecture. The St Petersburg residence of the grand duke Vladimir was built by Rezanov in 1867, and conforms to the first category. With its heavy faceted walls pierced by long tiers of arched windows, it resembles a Florentine town house of the early Renaissance.

The simultaneous movement which aimed at reforging a national style of architecture, by copying the picturesque effects and ornamental motifs **224** of 16th-century Russian architecture, was to become the dominant style of the late 19th century. An example of this is the Cathedral of the

KAZAN' RAILWAY STATION
1914–40, A. V. Shchusev, Moscow

In his designs for Kazan' railway station, Shchusev sought to combine 16th-century principles of architecture with a modern functional use. The long, broken frontage, made up of many seemingly independent pavilions, recalls 17th-century wooden architecture. When Shchusev devised the station-palace in 1914, it was designed to harmonise with the unique character of the city at that time.

214
THE CATHEDRAL OF THE RESURRECTION
1883–1907, A. A. Parland, Leningrad

The Cathedral of the Resurrection is popularly known as the Church of the Saviour upon the Blood, as it rises over the blood-stained cobblestones where Alexander II was assassinated on 1st March 1881. The cost of building it was met largely from public contributions. It was inspired by St Basil's Cathedral, Moscow, and with its multi-coloured, bulbous domes, polychrome tiles, tent-shaped spires and gables, it is a glaring assertion of Slavophilism which contrasts oddly with the discreet elegance and restraint of Classical St Petersburg.

215 *right*
THE GIRL WITH PEACHES
1887, Valentin Serov 1864–1911
oil on canvas, 37·75 × 33·5 in (91 × 85 cm)
Tret'iakov Gallery, Moscow

Serov was only twenty-two when, after returning from a visit to Italy with his patron Savva Mamontov, he painted the latter's daughter Vera. Serov said that he had aimed in this portrait to capture 'that freshness which, instinct in nature, is so hard to render on canvas'. The beauty and purity of the colours are astonishing. The picture remained in Mamontov's collection at his estate at Abramtsevo until it was acquired by the Tret'iakov Gallery after the Revolution.

Resurrection built in St Petersburg by Parland between 1883 and 1907. A **214** more genuine adaptation of the principles of old Russian architecture, which had in the meantime been closely studied, was initiated by Viktor Vasnetsov and developed by his followers into a valid architectural style around the turn of the century. In 1900, Vasnetsov designed an extension and a main façade for the Tret'iakov Gallery. The upper part of the building is treated as a background to accommodate a massive spreading inscription. By contrast, Shchusev's treatment of the Kazan' railway station **213** in Moscow, commissioned by Von Meck, chairman of the railway company, is both more mature and self-assured. Shchusev disguised the essentially practical function of the building by adapting a broken frontage consisting of a succession of intricately balanced and symmetrically placed pavilions. Every detail of this station-palace is worked out with the same attention as the overall grouping of the whole. The internal decoration of frescoes and mosaics was of the same high order as the window surrounds, which were inspired by the 17th century.

This synthesis of old architectural motifs showed its best results in ecclesiastical architecture, and during the first decade of this century Shchusev designed a number of churches which show both spirit and imagination. The Convent Church of Martha and Mary was built for the grand duchess Elizabeth, sister of the empress Alexandra, and founder of a nursing order. This boldly proportioned church demonstrates Shchusev's creative ability to re-work old architectural motifs, in this case those of Pskov, in an entirely original manner. The interior is painted with frescoes by Nesterov.

To display the icon collection of Madame Khoratonenko, Shchusev built a highly stylised church on her family estate near Khar'kov. With its exaggerated swollen cupolas and clean curves, Shchusev gave an impression of something both new and archaic, as evocative and full of mystery as a drawing by Roerich. Similar qualities are to be found in a memorial church built in 1913 on the battlefield of Kulikovo. In this case, Shchusev drew his inspiration from the wall and towers of the austere northern monastery of Solovki.

Apart from interpretations of the theme of ancient Russian architecture, two distinct styles are characteristic of the early 20th century – Art Nouveau and Neo-Classicism. Art Nouveau was the most significant European movement of the end of the century, and as such attracted a

STAGE SET FOR 'BORIS GODUNOV'
Aleksandr Golovin 1863–1930
oil on canvas, Tret'iakov Gallery, Moscow

One of the chief designers of the imperial theatres after 1902, Golovin was commissioned by Diaghilev to produce the sets for Mussorgsky's opera 'Boris Godunov', shown in Paris in 1908. Golovin's designs reveal his ability to penetrate not only to the centre of the music and poetry of the opera, but also into the historical background. Like Vrubel', he had experience of handling mosaics, and much of his painting is built up with splashes of colour of equal strength and intensity to give a rich overall carpet-like effect.

Moscow of the early 20th century was
perhaps the best place in the whole of
Europe to see avant-garde French painting.
The collections of the wealthy Moscow
merchants Shchukin and Morozov, which
were familiar to the Moscow art world,
contained works by Post-Impressionist
painters such as Van Gogh, Cézanne and
Gauguin, as well as paintings by Picasso and
Matisse, who were practically unknown at
the time.

217 *above*
THE SMOKER

c. 1859–1900
Paul Cézanne 1839–1906
oil on canvas
36 × 28·25 in (91 × 72 cm)
formerly Morozov collection
State Hermitage Museum, Leningrad

218 *right*
THE WALK

1888
Vincent van Gogh 1853–90
oil on canvas
29 × 36·5 in (73·5 × 92·5 cm)
formerly Shchukin collection
State Hermitage Museum, Leningrad

219 *far left*

AFTER THE BATH

mid 1890s
Edgar Degas 1834–1917
pastel, gouache, charcoal on cardboard
32·5 × 28·25 in (82·5 × 72 cm)
formerly Morozov Collection
State Hermitage Museum, Leningrad

220 *left*

TAHITIAN WOMAN
WITH FLOWERS

1899
Paul Gauguin 1848–1903
oil on canvas
37 × 28·25 in (94 × 72 cm)
formerly Shchukin collection
State Hermitage Museum, Leningrad

221

THE DESSERT, HARMONY IN RED

1908, Henri Matisse, 1869–1954
oil on canvas
71 × 86·5 in (180 × 220 cm)
State Hermitage Museum, Leningrad

222

THE DANCE

1910
Henri Matisse 1869–1954
oil on canvas
102·5 × 154 in (260 × 391 cm)
State Hermitage Museum, Leningrad

Sergei Shchukin was one of Matisse's most important early collectors; he owned thirty-seven of the artist's works. He bought *The Dessert* in 1908 at the Paris Salon d'Automne. *The Dance* was painted especially for the staircase of his Moscow house. 'Entering the house, the visitor sees the first flight of stairs,' wrote Matisse, 'the effort of climbing them demands a feeling of release. The panel therefore represents the dance, a ring flung over a hilltop.'

contingent of followers in Russia who were anxious to participate fully in European culture. Many of them came from the versatile Muscovite merchant class. The collector, Mikhail Riabushinskii, engaged Shekhtel, a Russian exponent of Art Nouveau, to design his villa in 1900. The same architect adopted Art Nouveau flowing curves and faded colours, combining them with the high-pitched roofs characteristic of north Russian wooden architecture for his assignment of the Iaroslavl' railway station in Moscow.

If Art Nouveau may be associated with the Moscow merchant class, then the revival of Neo-Classicism owes much to the patronage of the St Petersburg nobility, who never ceased to admire the style which gave the northern capital its character. A revived interest in Neo-Classicism was simultaneously popularised by such gifted artists of the World of Art group as Benois and Somov.

The architect who most thoroughly assimilated the spirit of Neo-Classicism was M. A. Fomin. The elegant house built by Fomin on an island in the Neva, its façade lined with white Ionic columns, is a delightful building in the pure Classical tradition. Fomin understood that this style demanded adherence to rules which could not be disregarded without jeopardising the fastidiously calculated proportions of Classical architecture. He followed his model so carefully that one might easily mistake it for a building of the early 19th century.

Imperial patronage

The aristocracy's predilection for the Neo-Classical is reflected in the work of Carl Fabergé, a Russian jeweller of French extraction. Although he worked for a very wide, and indeed international clientele, and used a variety of styles, Fabergé really set out to please the Russian aristocracy. His greatest patrons, however, were the emperors Alexander III and Nicholas II. In 1884 Alexander III commissioned a bejewelled and enamelled egg as an Easter present for his consort, which was to be the first of a series of fifty-six. After his father's death in 1881, Nicholas II continued the practice, commissioning two surprise eggs every year, one for his wife and the other for the dowager empress. Fabergé was given a free hand in the design and choice of materials, and until it was finished the creation of each egg remained a closely guarded secret. Although more acceptable by 1900, the assignment seemed strangely out of keeping with the socially useful art prevalent at the time when Alexander III commissioned the first of these eggs. This was one of the few instances when Alexander and Nicholas ordered what appealed to them personally. If they so rarely indulged their own taste, it may well have been due to the pressure of public opinion. On the other hand these two tsars were unsophisticated, and the Russian court was never so unassuming, not to say austere, as during their reign.

However, to uphold the prestige of the monarchy, it was necessary for the emperor to support, not the most avant-garde art, but that which had established its worth. The artists whom the public esteemed received imperial commissions; museums were founded and endowed; the Hermitage added to its collection. Nicholas II paid out a yearly subsidy of 12,000 roubles for the cultural art journal 'World of Art' for five years; he also supported Nikodim Kondakov's scheme for assisting contemporary icon painting by subsidising the village centres where it still survived as a living art. In 1901 he appointed a commission which was entrusted with the cleaning and restoring of ancient monuments. It is not surprising that in spite of substantial imperial revenues, the finding of funds presented a considerable problem. Not only the Imperial Academy of Art, but the non-

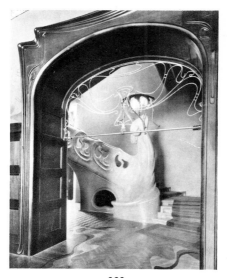

223

THE RIABUSHINSKII HOUSE
1902–06
Fedor Shekhtel, 1859–1926
Moscow

The Art Nouveau movement aroused great interest in Russia, and was fostered by many wealthy merchants. One of the more successful buildings in this style is the house of Mikhail Riabushinskii, icon collector and patron of the artist Vrubel'. The capricious, rhythmic spirals decorating the staircase spread like exotic creepers, forming an integral part of the architecture.

224

THE CHURCH OF ABRAMTSEVO
1880–82

The construction of a church on Mamontov's estate at Abramtsevo was fostered by Elizaveta Mamontov, who was interested in the current religious and liturgical revival. The entire colony of artists enthusiastically took up the project, and made sketches and detailed plans of forgotten buildings. Although all this was part of a medieval revival movement, serious research into the past had barely begun. The artists of Abramtsevo were, therefore, pioneers in their break away from a pseudo-Russian style and began a fresh examination of Russia's medieval heritage.

profit-making imperial theatres, porcelain and glass factories were financially dependent on the crown. The problem might have been solved if they could have become profit-making organisations, engaged in mass production. But they were obliged, instead, to maintain standards of craftsmanship and excellence which were rarely found elsewhere in Europe at that time.

The emergence of avant-garde movements

The accelerated pace of Russian life, which had been working up to a crescendo, reached its creative climax during the first decade of the 20th century. Painting, writing, poetry and even conversation were now fraught with the same measure of feverish excitement – the one stimulating the other but with painting firmly in the lead.

Against this background, two avant-garde movements of painting emerged. They are Rayonism, whose chief exponents were Mikhail Larionov and Natal'ia Goncharova, and Suprematism led by Kazimir Malevich and Liubov' Popova. The same period witnessed the birth of abstract painting with Kazimir Malevich, Vasilii Kandinsky, Larionov, and Goncharova to the fore. The first abstract reliefs of Vladimir Tatlin and the Cubist sculptural work of Aleksandr Archipenko, also belong to this period.

The short-lived Rayonist style of painting was the creation of Mikhail Larionov and of Natal'ia Goncharova, his lifelong companion and outstanding pupil. Larionov's consuming desire to produce something new that might startle an apathetic public led him to adopt shock tactics. He paraded with his followers in strange clothes, his face covered in curious inscriptions, a nosegay of radishes in his buttonhole. His famous series of paintings of prostitutes overwritten with bawdy words were intended as a rebellion against the age-old morality prevalent in Russian art. In 1912 he presented to the public his paintings embodying his fully developed theory of Rayonism at the famous 'Donkey Tail Exhibition' contributed to by Goncharova, Malevich, Tatlin and Chagall.

When the public received the 1913 exhibition of Rayonism with disgust, Larionov announced, 'We do not demand attention from the public, but we ask it not to demand attention from us'. This remark summarised the new relationship between the artist, engaged in revolutionary techniques, and the public, unable to see the significance of such experiments. Larionov bowed to the situation and was deprived of artistic patronage. The Russian public had given support to the Wanderers without imposing conditions; it had also supported the World of Art in spite of accusations of decadence. In the period 1910–17, however, art was too far in advance of public taste to be palatable.

In 1917 the artists of the World of Art group were only just reaching maturity, while for the artists of the next generation, their major achievements lay before them. However, following the exodus of the old patrons and the emergence of the new Soviet society, many artists were obliged to change their subject matter and therefore, indirectly, the style of their painting. Some, like the architect Shchusev, succeeded in adapting themselves, but there were many who lost heart and produced nothing more. The majority of the World of Art group who left Russia for Paris were uprooted from their native land, and found themselves deprived of what had been their greatest source of inspiration – Russia. For those artists who believed that the cataclysm of revolution could unleash a new epoch of creativity, as well as for those who forsook their native land for a life of exile, after 1917 nothing was ever to be quite the same again.

John Stuart

232, 240
237, 239
234
240

225 *above*

THE DEMON SEATED

oil on canvas
Mikhail Vrubel' 1856–1910
Tret'iakov Gallery, Moscow

The Demon Seated was painted as a result of a competition sponsored in 1890 by the banker Konchalovskii to commemorate the writer and poet Lermontov. The contestants were asked to illustrate Lermontov's poem *The Demon*. To Vrubel', who became obsessed by this theme, the Demon was not the spirit of evil, but a racked and anguished spirit – an outcast. At times, Vrubel' turned away from his easel in despair and tried to carve the theme in wood. Enriched with new ideas, he then reverted to his canvas.

226 *right*

COSTUME DESIGN FOR 'SALOME'

1908
Leon Bakst 1866–1925
Tret'iakov Gallery, Moscow

The World of Art movement scored an undoubted triumph in the sphere of stage design, elevating it to the standard of a high art form. In St Petersburg and Moscow alike, theatrical productions came to resemble art exhibitions incorporating movement and sound. Exotic and sensuous, Leon Bakst's vividly colourful designs captivated audiences in the West with their irresistible exuberance.

227 *above*

THE FAIR

1906
oil on canvas
Boris Kustodiev 1878–1927
Tret'iakov Gallery, Moscow

Whereas Benois and Somov turned for inspiration to 18th-century aristocratic culture, so long despised, Kustodiev preferred to paint scenes from the lives of the common people. In this he continued the tradition of the Wanderers. However, far from showing the distressing aspects of peasant life as the Wanderers had, he painted the peasants' own gay, creative world; a world reflected in their brightly patterned textiles, stamped gingerbread and jaunty wood carvings. Kustodiev depicted popular peasant culture on the eve of its destruction.

The Revolution of 1917 itself gave birth to no significant new movement in art, with the partial exception of Constructivism, the basic principles of which had been anticipated, if not proclaimed, on the eve of the First World War. However, it brought the artist into a new relationship with society and allowed him to make public, and at the outset virtually to impose as a norm, the truly revolutionary art of the preceding five years.

The Revolution and the avant garde

Rayonism had been developed and practised by Mikhail Larionov from 1911 to 1914. More significant, in Munich his compatriot Vasilii Kandinsky was evolving his abstract mystical-musical art from 1910; and Kazimir Malevich, influenced possibly by some of Léger's pre-war writings as well as by his Russian contemporaries, was at work on his pioneer Suprematist compositions from 1913 (if his own retrospective dating is to be accepted). Not only Russian, but European and American art of the succeeding half-century was to be profoundly affected by their work. Probably at no other time has Russian art been so integral or so significant a part of the Western European art world than in the period 1910–22.

In addition to Rayonism, Suprematism and Kandinsky's Abstract Expressionism, several other tendencies were well established before 1913: Russian Primitivism, with Larionov as its principal exponent; Russian Futurism, best represented by the pre-war paintings of Natal'ia Goncharova; and Russian Cubism, associated with the name of Liubov' Popova, among others. Further, Vladimir Tatlin, who has been described as 'the first rigorously non-figurative sculptor', was creating his essentially Constructivist reliefs from 1913. Remarkable foundations had thus been laid. While none of these movements had yet begun to affect the Russian architectural scene, their impact could already be discerned (and, by the general public, resented) in the literary and theatrical worlds.

Malevich represented the view held by much of the avant-garde when, in 1919, he wrote, 'Cubism and Futurism were revolutionary movements in art, anticipating the 1917 Revolution in political and economic life'. The belief that political and social renewal must be accompanied – or even provoked – by renewal in the arts motivated the post-Revolutionary dissolution of the old academies of art and the establishment of progressive ('Left') artists in key administrative positions. For their coups d'atelier these artists found support among prominent Bolsheviks – A. V. Lunacharskii foremost among them. 'You are a revolutionary in music,' he is reported to have said to Prokofiev in 1918, 'We are revolutionaries in life. We belong together'. Lenin was markedly less enthusiastic. For the present, however (though Naum Gabo noted that 'we were not favoured by the government, we were tolerated'), progressive artists were in a position to dominate the scene.

The role of art: the artist's view

Among the artists there was no unanimity as to the role their work was to perform in the new society. While some aimed to serve the Revolution by bringing down art from its pedestal into the factories and streets, there to be assimilated to industrial production and to everyday life, others, however dedicated to the Revolution or accepting of it, insisted on the autonomy of art.

Vladimir Tatlin (an 'assimilationist') proceeded from easel painting, via constructions 'in real materials and in real space', to the design of clothing, pottery and furniture. Paradoxically, this pioneer sculptor-constructivist is often remembered for two ambitious projects that were never to be realised: his vast Monument to the IIIrd International, a building of steel and glass, twice the height of the Empire State Building, with a complex

240
237
232
239
234
235

The Artist and the State

1917 to the present day

228

WOMAN WITH RAKE
c. 1930–1935
Kazimir Malevich 1878–1935
oil on canvas
Tret'iakov Gallery, Moscow
(reserve collection).

Towards the end of the 1920s, in semi-retirement, Malevich again reverted to easel painting and, moreover, to some of the subject matter ('the ballast of the objective world') which had occupied him in his pre-Suprematist days. At the same time his manner of presenting it was necessarily conditioned and refined by his Suprematist experience. Little is known of Malevich's later work. This example suggests that it was chaste, dignified and, in its way, compelling.

157

series of independently revolving and (above all) functional units; and a glider, on which he was to work painstakingly during the last two decades of his life.

Associated with him were such Constructivists as Aleksandr Rodchenko and El Lisitskii. It was Rodchenko who, with his wife and colleague Varvara Stepanova, was to issue a 'Programme of the Productivist Group' in 1920: among other things, it declared that 'the group stands for ruthless war against art in general. . . . Down with art! Long live technology! . . . Long live the Constructivist technician!' Art, as understood in pre-revolutionary times, was to be abandoned in the service of the people. Rodchenko turned to design work; he excelled in typography. Lisitskii is also remembered as a typographer: by his pioneer work, and by his travels in the West during the twenties he made a notable contribution to Bauhaus and De Stijl typography in particular, and to European, as well as to Russian, concepts of design in general.

Lisitskii's early works were visually, at least, Suprematist creations, and this is a reminder of his one-time association with Malevich. However, Malevich was one of the principal 'autonomists', who insisted on the visionary, as opposed to the practical role of the artist in society. On this question he was at one with the otherwise dissimilar Kandinsky (who was to leave Russia for the Bauhaus in 1921) and the brothers Anton Pevsner **229** and Naum Gabo – both of whom were to follow him to Europe during the next two years, where they were to propagate Constructivism.

Admittedly Malevich believed that he had completed his work as an easel painter by 1918. 'In my desperate attempt to free art from the ballast of the objective world, I flew to the form of the square', he wrote of his earlier Suprematist work, in which squares, circles, triangles and rectangles in black and primary colours were assembled on a white ground (on 'infinite white', as he described it). However, in 1917–18 he progressed to the painting of white squares on a white ground: he was soon to declare the end of Suprematism, the end of easel painting. Not unlike the Productivists he asserted that 'painting was done for long ago, and the artist himself is a prejudice of the past' (1920). Nevertheless, he was not to become a simple Productivist. He devoted himself principally to teaching and to the design of ideal architectural models; during the final seven years of his life **228** he even reverted to painting (one of his last works was the decoration of his own coffin).

The architectural projects of artist like Malevich, Lisitskii or Tatlin had no more chance of being implemented than those of professional architects in a period of acute shortage in labour and raw materials. The old buildings that survived the Revolution and the civil war were welcome, no matter what their style, as long as they were sound. During the later twenties, however, conditions improved sufficiently for a number of plans to be realised. The Lenin Mausoleum in Red Square, Moscow (re-built in reinforced concrete, brick and granite, 1928–30) approximated in its outlines to Constructivist principles, though its architect, A. V. Shchusev, was hardly a Constructivist at heart. Typical of the period were **230** the Moscow Pravda building by P. A. Golosov and Le Corbusier's build-ing for the Ministry of Light Industry, subsequently allocated to the Central Trades Union Administration. One of the most significant and ambitious undertakings was the Dzerzhinskii Square ensemble in **231** Khar'kov, including the Gosprom buildings and the House of Projects, among the principal architects for which was S. S. Serafimov. The Khar'kov complex has been noted as a parallel to its pioneer contemporary in Germany, Gropius's Bauhaus at Dessau.

229 below
TOWER
c. 1921
Naum Gabo, b. 1890
glass and metal
At this early stage in his career Gabo was already concerned principally with linear and kinetic factors in his sculpture: 'We renounce the mass as a sculptural element', stated a manifesto which he issued in August 1920 together with his brother, Anton Pevsner (1886–1962). Of towers like this one he wrote, 'My works of this time, up to 1924, are all the search for an image which would fuse the sculptural element with the architectural element into one unit'. The purity of Gabo's construc-tions contrasts with the more earthy, less refined character of Tatlin's reliefs. Gabo left Russia in 1922.

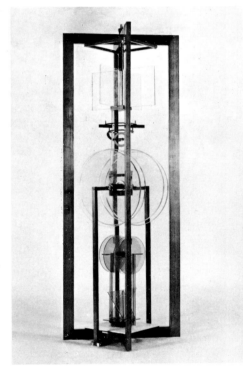

230 *right*
THE PRAVDA BUILDING
1929–1935
P. A. Golosov
Moscow

During the twenties Golosov was one of the outstanding practitioners of the Constructivist school of architecture. His Pravda Building was an exact con-temporary of Le Corbusier's Moscow building for the Ministry of Light Industry, with which it may be compared. This type of building was soon to lose favour. Golosov himself abjured his former principles in the 1930s and, reverting to his training in the Classical school, he designed prosaic works in the accepted style of the Socialist Realist period.

It should not be thought that Russia was served at this time exclusively by avant-garde artists and architects. Artists trained in the older traditions were also at work in the twenties. M. V. Nesterov and B. M. Kustodiev continued to paint, though much of the work by which they will be remembered was already behind them. Such artists as V. A. Favorskii and A. I. Kravchenko were responsible for some distinguished graphic work.

238 K. S. Petrov-Vodkin produced some admirable paintings in the twenties, such as his renowned *1918 in Petrograd* and *Death of a Commissar*. His emotional restraint, his drawing and his use of colour inevitably bring to mind the medieval tradition of icon painting on which Petrov-Vodkin manifestly drew, albeit with discretion.

A different, and more overt dependence on the medieval tradition is to be noted in the case of the miniature paintings of such a centre as Palekh. The exquisite work of masters like I. I. Golikov or I. V. Markichev, both of them, like many of their immediate colleagues, trained as icon painters in the local tradition before the Revolution, maintained a curious and distinguished enclave of non-Socialist-Realist art throughout the period. For this reason it was to be barely tolerated by the authorities in the late thirties and forties. Nonetheless, the products of Palekh found a ready

231 *below left*

THE HOUSE OF CULTURE
FOR RAILWAYMEN

1927–32, A. I. Dmitriev
brick and concrete
Khar'kov

Ambitious plans were made in the late 1920s for the replanning of Khar'kov, which was then the capital of the Ukraine. One of the most significant undertakings was the Dzerzhinskii Square ensemble, in which A. I. Dmitriev participated. His elegant House of Culture for Railwaymen was also constructed at this time. Behind the restrained rhythm of the façade were located numerous recreation rooms and an auditorium with seating for an audience of two thousand.

232 *below*

THE RELAXING SOLDIER

1911
Mikhail Larionov 1881–1964
oil on canvas
46·75 × 48 in (119 × 122 cm)
Tret'iakov Gallery, Moscow

Larionov's Rayonist period followed and coincided with a Primitivist phase, of which this work is an outstanding example. Soldiers and prostitutes were his favoured subject matter at this time, and man's naïve carnality his refrain. In his earlier works Larionov's brushwork was carefully controlled and sensitive in the Impressionist mode. His new subject matter corresponded to, and demanded, a freer and less cultivated manner of painting. Larionov made his contribution to Russian painting before the First World War, and he emigrated to Paris several years before the Revolution, never to return.

market, both at home and abroad, and have a museum devoted to them.

Unfortunately, the majority of traditionalist artists did no more than echo the ethos and techniques of late 19th-century Russian art, despite their introduction of contemporary themes. A painter like M. V. Grekov, who specialised in realistic representations of civil war scenes, is a typical representative of the academic school. It was this school which was soon to gain the unequivocal and exclusive support of the state authorities.

The role of art officially defined

With the beginning of the Five Year Plans, the Party authorities began to impose firm controls in the artistic world. Private groupings of artists were dissolved. Artists whose work was unacceptable to the authorities found themselves unable to exhibit. The 1929 retrospective exhibition of the remarkable and disturbing 'Analytical' painter, Pavel Filonov, for example—its 306 items assembled and catalogued by the Russian Museum—was never to be opened to the public, and he was to continue his work in obscurity. His true stature has yet to be revealed.

Museums were pruned of avant-garde works, which were relegated to their reserve collections ('Our museums possess superlative collections of the "Left art" of the early post-Revolutionary years,' noted Il'ia Erenburg in 1961, 'It is a pity that these collections are not open to the public'). In April 1932 the Party issued a decree 'On the Reconstruction of Literary and Artistic Organisations': each of the arts was to set up a single organisation, through which all artists were to be employed by the State, their principal patron, and through which the Party was to insist with ever-increasing rigour on conformity to the principles of Socialist Realism, first propounded in 1934. The artist, in a phrase attributed to Stalin, was required to be 'an engineer of people's souls', and his task was to produce exclusively 'art that is national in form and socialist in content'. In those arts which could immediately reflect aspects of the Soviet environment (literature, drama, or painting) it was less difficult to insist on Socialist Realism than is the more abstract arts (music or architecture). Here (as is now acknowledged) the criterion for acceptability was too often Stalin's personal taste, and Socialist Realism in architecture, for instance, came to mean grandiose buildings in a ponderous Neo-Classical style (Proletarian Classicism was a term introduced by the architect I. A. Fomin).

Official patronage and non-conformist art

Socialist Realism has retained official support in the period since Stalin's death. However, recent years have witnessed the growing acceptance (as in Leningrad's Moskovskii region) of architectural styles, furniture and decor that would have been condemned only a few years previously as formalistic. Similarly, while a sculptor of Ernest Neizvestnyi's stature remains virtually unacknowledged officially, others—such as the members of Lev Nusberg's Kinetic Group (founded 1962)—are receiving occasional official patronage, although their acknowledged precursors are the Constructivists of the distant twenties. If the state does not support experimental artists, there exist private patrons who will purchase the works of such artists as Vladimir Iakovlev, Rabin or Neizvestnyi. In 1962 the first (and short-lived) public exhibition of avant-garde work since the beginning of the thirties provoked a violent reaction from N. S. Krushchev, but at least the holding of such an exhibition is no longer an inconceivable possibility. Nor, in the seventies, is it entirely vain to hope for some renewal of official art, for the recognition by the establishment of the existence and potential of experimental art, and for the diminution of the barriers that separate the two.

Sergei Hackel

233 *right*
MARCHING SOLDIER
1916
Marc Chagall, b. 1882
oil on canvas
30·25 × 34·25 in (77 × 87 cm)
Tret'iakov Gallery, Moscow

Chagall was able to hold as many as three major exhibitions in 1916, the year in which this little known painting was produced. It is executed in a somewhat freer and more dynamic manner than most of his work of the preceding two years. The wooden house in the background suggests that the setting may be Chagall's native Vitebsk, the town which is so often and so affectionately depicted by him. After the Revolution he was to be head of its art school, until he was displaced by Malevich. Chagall emigrated from Russia in 1922.

234 *far right*
RELIEF
1917
Vladimir Tatlin 1885–1953
wood and zinc on iron
c. 39·25 × 25 in (100 × 64 cm)
Tret'iakov Gallery, Moscow
(reserve collection)

Tatlin has been described as 'the first rigorously non-figurative sculptor'. He began work on his Constructivist reliefs in 1913, delighting in the use of 'real materials in real space'. In these Constructions he demonstrated none of Gabo's concern for pure forms and pure textures. He preferred rather to explore the tense co-existence of contrasting materials and imperfect, unsophisticated textures—as in this relief. Much of Tatlin's work in this sphere has disappeared, or is not displayed, but of its importance there can be no doubt.

235 *right*
THE FISHMONGER
1911
Vladimir Tatlin 1885–1953
gum paints on cardboard
30 × 38·5 in (76 × 98 cm)
Tret'iakov Gallery, Moscow

Tatlin, who worked for some years as a sailor, painted a number of pictures on nautical themes before the First World War. In his work of this period there is an interesting convergence of two major influences, that of icon painting, and that of Cézanne. Two years after the completion of *The Fishmonger* Tatlin was to visit Picasso briefly in Paris; from this visit he returned ready to embark on his work as a Constructivist.

237 right
WHITE OVAL (BLACK BORDER)

1919
Vasilii Kandinsky 1866–1944
oil on canvas
31·5 × 36·75 in (80 × 95 cm)
Tret'iakov Gallery, Moscow
(reserve collection)

Kandinsky returned to Russia from Munich at the outbreak of the 1914 war, and he was to work there until his emigration in 1921. *White Oval (Black Border)* is one of the comparatively few works he completed in Russia after an eighteen-month fallow period from 1917 to 1919. Despite Kandinsky's insistence that 'beauty of colour and form . . . is not a sufficient goal for art', he is too often considered simply as an abstract artist. Yet in such a painting as this, the occult teachings of theosophy and anthroposophy (which influenced Kandinsky) find their visual expression.

238 top far right
1918 IN PETROGRAD

1920
K. S. Petrov-Vodkin 1878–1939
oil on canvas
28·75 × 36 in (73 × 92 cm)
Tret'iakov Gallery, Moscow

Against the background of a restive city, a Mother and Child are enthroned on a balcony. Though she wears a Russian peasant kerchief and a simple dress, her posture, the inclination of her carefully modelled head, and the gentle melancholy with which, as in medieval icons, she gazes at the spectator, all speak unobtrusively of the Virgin Mother's presence. Inevitably, the name *1918 in Petrograd* has been displaced in popular usage by the title *The Petersburg Mother of God*.

236 above
DYNAMIC SUPREMATISM

1916
Kazimir Malevich 1878–1935
oil on canvas
Tret'iakov Gallery, Moscow
(reserve collection)

Suprematism, the creation of Malevich, was one of the most significant of Russian art movements to mature on the eve of the Revolution. 'In my desperate attempt to free art from the ballast of the objective world, I flew to the form of the square', wrote Malevich. Squares, rectangles, triangles and circles, in flat colours and on flat colour – these were his vocabulary. By 1918, before turning aside from painting altogether for a decade, he had reduced it to a single square in white on white. This painting was used by Malevich in 1919 as the basis for a lithograph.

239 right
THE TRAVELLER

1915
Liubov' Popova 1889–1924
oil on canvas
41·75 × 56 in (106 × 142 cm)
Private Collection, Moscow

Before she turned to Suprematism, and eventually to Productivist art, Liubov' Popova was the outstanding proponent of Cubism in Russia. With another Russian Cubist, Nadezhda Udaltsova (1886–1961) she had studied with Le Fauconier and Metzinger in Paris. *The Traveller* is one of her most monumental works. The central figure of the traveller merges with his setting in her analysis and redistribution of planes and colours. The lettering gives some indication of the setting, a railway station.

240 *above*

THE COCKEREL

c. 1912
Mikhail Larionov 1881–1964
oil on canvas
Tret'iakov Gallery, Moscow

Rayonism was a short-lived movement, and even in its heyday (1911–14) it did not absorb all the creative energy of its principal practitioners, Larionov and Goncharova. Yet Rayonist paintings were among the first purely abstract works to be exhibited in Russia, and they have an important place in the history of Russian art. *The Cockerel* is not yet an abstract, but the subject is about to be absorbed in the rich pattern of reflected rays, for which it is the starting point. At the same time, and with equal justice, the painting may be appreciated as almost a Fauve celebration of the cockerel's energy and colour.

Museums and Monuments

An index of museums, churches, palaces, castles, Islamic monuments and archaeological sites, listing some of the major treasures they contain and corresponding to the places marked on the maps at the front and back of the book.

Illustrations on this page

left

241 Badge of the Order of St Catherine, 18th century. USSR Diamond Fund, Moscow.

242 Pablo Picasso *The Acrobat and the Ball* 1905. Pushkin Museum, Moscow.

centre

243 The monastery of Guedhard in Armenia, 13th century.

244 *St George and the Dragon* 15th century, school of Novgorod. Tret'iakov Gallery, Moscow.

245 Etienne Falconnet, statue of Peter the Great, 1782. Leningrad.

right

246 Enamel and niello goblet inscribed with the name of Tsar Alexis, 17th century. Armoury Palace, the Kremlin, Moscow.

247 Wrought-iron gates to the courtyard of the palace of Tsarskoe Selo (Pushkin), 18th century.

248 Paul Cézanne *Self-portrait* 1873–75. State Hermitage Museum, Leningrad.

ABRAMTSEVO, Russian Federation
1 **Church** 19th c, built in old Russian style by members of Savva Mamontov's artists' colony.
ALMA ATA, Kazakhstan
2 **Kazakh T. G. Shevchenko State Art Gallery** Local, Russian and Western artists.
3 **Museum of the Kazakh Republic** Housed in a former cathedral, one of the tallest wooden buildings in the world.
ALUPKA, Ukraine
4 **Crimea State Museum of Fine Art** Housed in fine 19th c Alupka Palace. N façade Tudor style; s façade Mauresque.
ANANURI, Georgia
5 **Medieval fortress** Sacked in 1739. Noteworthy inner ramparts, characteristic of medieval Georgian military architecture. Two churches: one built at the beginning of the 17th c in a mixture of rolled stone and brick; the other shows the excess of decoration of a later period.
ANBERD, Armenia
6 **Fortress** 7th–13th c, the remains of one of the largest fortresses in medieval Armenia. One surviving church, 1026, is a fine example of contemporary architecture.
ARKHANGEL'SK (Archangel) Russian Federation
7 **Novodivina Fortress** 1701–05.
8 **Residences** Several early 18th c Neo-Classical buildings.
ARKHANGEL'SKOE, Russian Federation
9 **Palace** Stucco-covered wood, constructed from the end of the 18th c by several different architects. Splendid interior with rich furnishings and French and Italian works of art; ingenious painted ceilings. Collection of paintings and china. Park in Classical style.
ASHKHABAD, Turkmenistan
10 **Mausoleum of Khan Abul Kazim-Babur** 1435; now in ruins.
11 **Nisa** Remains of a Parthian city including a palace and several temples.
ASHTARAK, Armenia
12 **Church of Karmravor** 7th c, retains the original roofing tiles. A unique example of this type of church with Greek-cross plan, as seen in Greek Byzantine churches.
13 **Church of Mariane** 1281, very pointed conical roof.
AVAN, Armenia
14 **Church** Ruins, built 590–609.
BAGINETI (formerly Armazis-Tsikhe) Georgia
15 **Castle** Once belonged to the emperors of Iberia; ruins dating back to the 4th c BC.
BAKHCHISARAI, Ukraine
16 **Palace** Formerly belonged to khan of the Crimea.
17 **State Museum of History and Archaeology** Contains art collections and exhibits relating to architectural monuments and the cave towns.
BAKU, Azerbaidzhan
18 **Azerbaidzhan A. Mustafaev State Art Museum** Local and Western painting.
19 **Maiden's Tower** 12th c, 28 metres high. Part of the original system of complex fortifications on the Apsheron Peninsula.
20 **Sinik Kala Minaret** 11th c.
21 **Town of the Shirvan Shahs** Divan-khan, polyhedral pavilion surrounded by columns, believed to go back to the main tradition of near Eastern mausoleums, with delicate stone carving. Mausoleum of Seide Yahia Bakuvi 15th c. Mosque of the Shirvan Shahs 1441. Palace of the Shirvan Shahs 14th and 15th c, the best example of medieval Azerbaidzhan architecture. Mausoleum of the Shirvan Shahs 1435–36.
BARDA, Azerbaidzhan
22 One of the most ancient towns of the Caucasus. Fine mausoleum of 1322 and remains of a second.
BEDZHNIN, Armenia
23 **Church of the Virgin** Built in 1031 and still intact. Huge drum topped by a corrugated conic roof.
24 **Fortress walls** 11th c.
BOGOLIUBOVO, Russian Federation

25 **Monastery of Our Lady** Present buildings date from the 17th–19th c, except for the Church of the Nativity of Our Lady, of which part of the N tower and connecting passage are the original 12th c. They represent the only existing example of early domestic architecture in stone. Includes a museum.
26 **Pokrov on the Nerl'** (Church of the Intercession of Our Lady) 1165. The most graceful of all old Russian churches, set on an artificial mound outside Bogoliubovo; very simple lines with restrained decoration on the outside.
BOLNISI, Georgia
27 **Basilica of Sion** Largest basilica in Georgia; an inscription dates it to 493–494.
BORZHOMI, Georgia
28 **Museum** in a former 5th–6th c Georgian monastery and two palaces which belonged to the Georgian nobility.
BREST, Belorussia
29 **Fortifications** Remains of fortifications which surrounded the town in the 18th c.
BUKHARA, Uzbekistan
30 **Abdul Aziz Khan Mosque** 1652, finished with majolica, brick, mosaics, wood carvings and glazed ceramics.
31 **The Ark** Ancient citadel on the central hill. Extensive walls built much later. Former jail, now houses the museum: Bukhara carpets, gold embroideries, pottery, chased copper and silver ware.
32 **Bazaar** Three cupolas dating from the 16th c, in addition to the covered market.
33 **Chor-Bakr** (outside the town) The Balyand and Khodza mosques are particularly beautiful inside.
34 **Faizabad Mosque** (outside the town) 1598–99.
35 **Kalyan Cathedral Mosque** Founded 12th c, rebuilt 1514. One of the biggest and most magnificent in Central Asia. Noted for its formal portal and great turquoise cupola.
36 **Kalyan Minaret** 1121–22; over 145 feet high.
37 **Kukeldash Madrasah** 16th c, the largest in Central Asia. Still operates as a Moslem seminary.
38 **Lyabi-Khaus ensemble** 17th c, madrasah, mosque and reservoir.
39 **Magaki Attar Mosque** 12th c.
40 **Mausoleum of Bayan Kuli Khan** 1359.
41 **Mausoleum of Shah Ismail** 9th–10th c, fired decorated brick.
42 **Mir-i-Arab Madrasah** 1535–36, traditional plan, with several important innovations. Coloured decoration, mosaic and ceramic facings.
43 **Ulugh Beg Madrasah** 1417–18, restored in 1585. Austere lines and elegant proportions, the oldest madrasah preserved in Central Asia.
CHERNIGOV, Russian Federation
44 **Cathedral of the Transfiguration** 11th c, sumptuous building with a severe exterior. Vivid mosaics and frescoes of great beauty.
CHERNOVTSY, Ukraine
45 **University** Architectural ensemble by Iosif Glavka, formerly the residence of the metropolitan of Bukovina.
DATHEV, Armenia
46 **Monastery** (suffered from a severe earthquake 1931) Church of St Peter and St Paul 885, tower added 17th c. Church of St Gregory the Illuminator 848, radically reshaped 1295. Church of the Virgin 10th–11th c. Votive Monument 895, unique of its kind: cross on column with hinged base for protection against earthquakes.
D'IAKOVO, Russian Federation
47 **Church of St John the Baptist** 1529.
DMITROV, Russian Federation
48 **Dmitrov Local Museum** Ancient icons.
DNEPROPETROVSK, Ukraine
49 **Hydro-electric station and dam** Pre-war, of impressive design and proportions.
DUBROVITSY, Russian Federation
50 **Mansion** Late 18th c, containing many works of art. **Cathedral** Baroque style, built 1690–1704 by Italian architects.
DVIN, Armenia
51 **Remains of old capital of Armenia** Citadel

with buildings dating from 9th–13th c, built over 5th–9th c palace. Foundations of large cathedral.
DZHVARI, Georgia
52 **Church** 6th c, one of the first sanctuaries in the shape of a cross. Façade covered with bas-reliefs.
ECHMIADZIN, Armenia
53 **Cathedral** Founded 303, rebuilt 5th c and 7th c on a Greek-cross plan with central cupola on four pillars. Belfry, with Oriental-style decoration, added 1653. Interior paintings reminiscent of Persian art. Sacristy, added 1868, contains the treasury. Round the cathedral are monastic buildings.
54 **Gayana** 630, restored but not disfigured 1652, gallery added 1683.
EGHVARD, Armenia
55 One of the oldest and archaeologically richest sites in Armenia includes ruins of late 6th c basilica and 14th c two-storeyed church-tomb.
EREROUYK, Armenia
56 **Ruins** Vestiges of the most interesting buildings in Armenia: basilica with nave and two aisles, related to the Syrian basilicas. Regarded as 4th or 5th c, the peak of antique Christianised art, perhaps also the transition from Roman to Armenian architecture.
EREVAN, Armenia
57 **Arinberd** Stronghold erected 783 BC. Recent excavations have revealed palaces and temples in Assyrian style, modified later, especially by the Persians.
58 **Historical Museum of Armenia** Exhibits include discoveries from numerous archaeological sites in Armenia, and show the evolution of Armenian art and architecture.
59 **Irepuni** (near the town) Remains of a palace.
60 **Karmir-Blur** (near the town) Ruins of the vast Urartian city of Teishebaini dating from 7th c BC. Systematic excavations since 1939 have revealed many rooms completely intact.
61 **Martanadoran Library** Includes fine miniatures and bindings 10th–17th c; the most splendid are 13th–14th c.
62 **Museum of Fine Arts** Large number of pictures by past and modern Armenian artists. Western painting of 17th and 18th c, including Tintoretto, and good examples of French 18th and 19th c.
FRUNZE, Kirgizia
63 **Kirgiz State Museum of Fine Art** Kirgiz, Russian, Chinese and Western Art.
GARBANI Georgia
64 **Basilica of St George** Early 10th c, built of tufa.
GARNI, Armenia
65 **Fortress** Dates back to 3rd c BC; its remains, together with those of a Roman temple, the ruins of a 7th c church, 12th–17th c dwellings and a 3rd c royal baths, with multi-coloured mosaic pavements, constitute the best examples of the Hellenisation of Armenia.
GATCHINA, Russian Federation
66 **Palace** 1770, by Rinaldi, park laid out with English gardens. Several buildings in the grounds, including a priory and an amphitheatre by L'vov.
GELATI, Georgia
67 **Monastery** Buildings of 12th and 13th c survive, with mosaics and frescoes.
GERGETI, Georgia
68 **Sanctuary** Early 14th c, richly decorated.
GOR'KII (formerly Nizhnii Novgorod) Russian Federation
69 **Gor'kii State Art Museum** 6,500 works. Wide selection of paintings of most Western schools from the Sheremetev and Abemelek-Lazarev collections. Also Soviet artists.
GOSHAVANK, Armenia
70 **Goshavank Monastery** (also called Nor-Guetik). Church of the Virgin 1191, narthex 1200–1203. Church of St Gregory c.1230–1241. Church of St Gregory the Illuminator mid 13th c, basilica style with richly decorated outside walls.
GUEDHARD, Armenia
71 **Guedhard Monastery** (formerly called Airivank) 1215–25 and 1283–88: main church

Classical in style, with a wealth of stone sculpture; two rock churches, and other monastic buildings.

GURZUF, Ukraine

72 **Genoese fortress** Dates from the Middle Ages.

HAGHARTSIN, Armenia

73 **Haghartsin Monastery** Founded 11th C. Church of the Virgin 1071–1281, s entrance decorated with stalactite reliefs, narthex in ruins. Church of St Gregory, plain limestone building, the oldest in the group, narthex added end 12th–beginning 13th C. Church of St Stephen, small cruciform church with cupola, built 1244 in blue basalt. Refectory *c.*1248, immense, a masterpiece of medieval architecture.

HAGHBAT, Armenia

74 **Haghbat Monastery** Enclosed by fortified ramparts. Main church 967–991, enormous domed interior, covered with frescoes and inscriptions, narthex added 1201, original roof. Churches of the Virgin and St Gregory 1005, immense separate narthex 1257. Tower 1245 very attractive. Large refectory probably 2nd half 13th C. Fountain outside the monastery 1258, well preserved.

HOVHANNAVANK, Armenia

75 **Hovhannavank Monastery** Main church 1216–21, cupola and s wall collapsed; narthex completed 1250, façade decorated with characteristic 13th C ornaments. Gives access to 5th C basilica, spoilt by later restorations.

IAKUTSK, Russian Federation

76 **Iakutsk Museum of Fine Arts** Western, Russian and Soviet art of 17th–20th C, also folk art.

IALTA (Yalta) Ukraine

77 **Ethnographic Museum** Mainly devoted to Eastern art.

78 **Castle** Crenellated walls, standing on rock overhanging the sea.

IAROSLAVL', Russian Federation

79 **Church of the Annunciation** 1688–1702, austere. Murals by local artists 1709.

80 **Church of the Archangel Michael** 1657–80, vast ground floor contains frescoes typical of the 18th C.

81 **Church of St Dimitrii of Salonica** Much altered since construction in 1671, noted for murals 1686.

82 **Church of the Epiphany** End 17th C, with significant deviations from the current norm, mural paintings 1692–93 by local artists. Icon screen has remarkable wood sculptures and late 17th C icons.

83 **Church of the Nativity** 1644, rearranged beginning of 19th C; murals painted 1683 by local artists; icons 17th–18th C. Pyramidal tower 1650–60, probably once a separate church. A group unique in Russian architecture.

84 **Church of Nicholas Nadein** 1620, typical church with onion domes and pyramidal towers.

85 **Church of Nicholas Rublenyi** (on the Ramparts) 1695.

86 **Church of Our Lady of Vladimir** 1670s.

87 **Church of the Prophet Elijah** 1650, onion domes and pyramidal towers. Interesting interior: early 18th C icon screen; fine mural paintings 1680–81; interesting decoration of the galleries.

88 **Church of the Saviour** 1672; partly destroyed 1851, rebuilt in Classical style. Remarkable murals 1693.

89 **Church of St John the Baptist** 1671–87, Baroque style, considered the perfect example of Iaroslavl' religious architecture. Lively frescoes *c.*1700.

90 **Church of St John Chrysostom** 1648–54 influenced all Iaroslavl' architects; murals 1732–33, beautiful icon screen with icons of late 17th C.

91 **Church of St Nicholas Mokryi** 18th C, with 16th C murals.

92 **Church of St Vladimir** 1669, and a pyramidal tower 121 feet high, late 17th C.

93 **Consistory Courts** 1825, façade typical of the period.

94 **Deiulin Mansion** Typical early 19th C private residence.

95 **House of the Meshchanstvo Representatives** Typical early 19th C mansion.

96 **Ivanov Mansion** Example of a rich dwelling in the early 18th C.

97 **Juridical School** 1805, designed by Mel'nikov.

98 **Kudasov Mansion** 1780–90, re-arranged to be typical of first half of 19th C.

99 **Lopatin Mansion** Wealthy residence in Classical style, late 18th and early 19th C.

100 **Monastery of the Saviour and the Transfiguration** Founded 12th C, damaged 1918, restored after 1920. Part of 17th C wall remains, with two towers and belfry, 16th–19th C; also one entrance of composite style, beginning 1516, wall paintings 1564. Cathedral of the Saviour 1516, only the east front retains original appearance, large-scale wall paintings 16th C refectory and apartments. Church of the Miracle Workers of Iaroslavl', 1831–33.

101 **Old Kremlin** Palace of the Metropolitan, late 17th C, contains the Iaroslavl'-Rostov Museum of History and Art, with ancient icons. Tikhon Church early 19th C Classical style. Volga Tower, 1658–68, reconstructed end 18th C.

102 **Vakhrameev Mansion** 1780, Baroque, completely rebuilt a century later.

IRKUTSK, Russian Federation

103 **Church of the Cross** 1758, richly decorated inside.

104 **Church of the Saviour** 1706.

105 **Institute of Foreign Languages** Unusual building *c.*1930, body framed by two symmetrical peristyles with four external columns.

106 **Museum of Fine Arts** Russian and some Western art.

107 **White House** 18th C, Classical style with Corinthian columns. Now contains the university library.

ISTRA, Russian Federation

108 **Monastery of the Resurrection** (known as the New Jerusalem) Principally mid 17th C, suffered severely in last war.

IUR'EV-POL'SKOI, Russian Federation

109 **Cathedral of St George** 1230, last important church in Vladimir-Suzdal' style. Lavishly adorned with carvings on the outside. Repaired in 1471 by Vasilii Ermolin, who re-arranged the carved stones haphazardly.

KALININ, Russian Federation

110 **Assembly of the Nobility** 1841, fine room with columns.

111 **Church of the Ascension** Built 1813 to plans by L'vov, now the Kalinin Ethnography Museum.

112 **Church of the White Trinity** 1564.

113 **House of the Nobility** 1766–70, and Magistrate's House 1770–80.

114 **Monastery of the Nativity** 14th C.

115 **Palace of Catherine the Great** 1763, architect Kazakov, rebuilt by Rossi, 1809.

116 **River Station on the Volga** Typical example of Stalinist architecture.

117 **Young People's Theatre** 1786, a former school.

KARABAGLAR, Azerbaidzhan

118 14th C mausoleum, a pair of minarets and a 12th C connecting portal.

KAUNASS, Lithuania

119 **Kaunass M. K. Churlionis State Art Museum** Large number of items of Lithuanian art, also Russian, French and Italian artists. Notable collection of Belgian painters of first half of 20th C.

KEM, Russian Federation

120 **Church** 1714, wooden tent-shaped church, with original log walls.

KHAR'KOV, Ukraine

121 **Archbishop's Palace** By Iaroslavskii, now the History Museum.

122 **Cathedral of the Assumption** 1783, icon screen designed by Rastrelli, belfry added beginning 19th C.

123 **Church of the Dormition** End 19th C, Neo-Byzantine.

124 **Dzerzhinskii Square** Massive, modern architectural complex, which includes the House of Projects and the Gosprom buildings.

125 **House of Scholars** Early 20th C by Bekekov.

126 **Khoratonenko Church** (outside the town) 19th C by Shchusev.

127 **Monastery of the Intercession** Dates from 1689, as does the church of the same name.

128 **Palace of Catherine the Great** Sometimes attributed to Rastrelli. Now incorporated in the university.

129 **South Station** Example of recent Soviet architecture.

KHERSON, Ukraine

130 **Old Fort** Late 18th C, only the earth ramparts and main gate remain, together with the old arsenal. Basilica of St Catherine 1780.

KHIVA, Uzbekistan

131 **Ishan-Kala** (inner town) The centre of the old town, preserved as a historic site with its walls, gates and old houses.

132 **Religious buildings** Mosques and madrasahs of mid 19th C.

KHOREZM OASIS, Uzbekistan

133 **Fortified town** Dates from 1st C BC–AD 6th C, remains of a temple for fire-worship and a bazaar. Ruins of the palace very important, walls preserved to 82 feet, state rooms decorated with frescoes and sculptures.

KIDEKSHA, Russian Federation

134 **Church of St Boris and St Gleb** 1152.

KIEV, Ukraine

135 **Cathedral of St Andrew** 1747–48, after plans by Rastrelli, who also designed the icon screen.

136 **Cathedral of St Sophia** Original exterior completely concealed by 18th C Baroque restoration; 12 rebuilt cupolas. Interior: gilt wood Rococo icon screen, 1754, with similar entrance doors. Otherwise the interior dates back to 1037, and is decorated with magnificent frescoes and mosaics, both religious and secular, of Byzantine complexity and magnificence, 1046–47 and 11th and early 12th C. Iaroslav's sarcophagus, 11th C marble work. Small museum in the galleries, including frescoes, mosaics and capitals from Kievan churches. Tower, replacing the belfry, rebuilt 1744–48 and decorated with delicate Baroque stucco work. Refectory 1722–30. Metropolitan's Palace early 18th C Baroque now belongs to the Academy of Architecture. Zaborovskii Door 18th C, only surviving part of the cathedral outbuildings.

137 **Cathedral of St Vladimir** 1882, Neo-Byzantine. Interior decorated by Vasnetsov and Nesterov.

138 **Church of St Cyril** 1146, damaged by Mongols, restored 17th C, cupolas and an attractive pediment added mid 18th C. Interior includes frescoes from beginning of 17th C, and others by Vrubel'.

139 **Church of the Saviour in Berestovo** End 11th–beginning 12th C. First brick church in Russia, shows movement away from Byzantine style. Partly destroyed 1640–43; apse, altar and façade restored; frescoes repainted. Only the narthex dates from 12th C.

140 **Council of Ministers of the Ukrainian Republic** 1938, by Fomin, semi-circular façade.

141 **Golden Gate** 11th C, once the principle entrance to the city.

142 **Imperial Palace** Built at the same time as Cathedral of St Andrew, by the same people. First floor wood, burned and replaced in stone 1870 in Rastrelli's style.

143 **Kreshchatik** Large architectural complex built immediately after the war. Some ceramic decoration in imitation of local decorative art.

144 **Kiev Academy** 18th C, Baroque façade onto the courtyard. Now houses a library.

145 **Kiev State Museum of Russian Art** Ancient and more recent icons; 18th C portraits, including Argunov, Levitskii, Borovikovskii; Romantic portraits, including Kiprenskii, Briullov; Ivanov sketches, 1830. 19th C painters, including Serov, Kustodiev, Vrubel'.

146 **Kiev State Museum of Ukrainian Art** Includes interesting examples of old Russian art and some drawings by Shevchenko.

147 **Kiev State Museum of Western and**

Oriental Art Particularly interesting early Italian Renaissance works and a few outstanding examples of 17th c painting, mainly Flemish and Spanish. Artists include Tiepolo, Rubens, Jordaens; etchings by Rembrandt and Reynolds. The Eastern section has a wide selection of Indian, Chinese and Persian art.

148 **Klovskii Palace** 1753–55, by Michurin and serf Stefan Kovnir. Attractive park and lavishly decorated interior. Now houses the administration of Ukrainian geological research.

149 **Monastery of the Caves** Founded 1051. Church of the Trinity built over the entrance gate of the monastery, exterior stucco work and roof in Baroque style, old church of 1103 well preserved inside, icon screen and frescoes by 18th c Ukrainian craftsmen. Ruins of the collegiate Church of the Dormition, masterpiece of the late 12th c. Reconstruction planned, as of the Baptistery of St John the Baptist. The Church of All Saints, 17th c, pentagonal ground-plan traditional in Ukrainian wood architecture. Belfry, 315 feet high and in perfect proportion, by Schädel 18th c. Former printing room and Kovnir building, by serf Stefan Kovnir, both 18th c. Refectory, massive Russo-Byzantine building of 1900, spoils the ensemble. The buildings of the Lavra house the Ukrainian Museum of Folk and Decorative Art, 46,000 exhibits from 16th c onward.

150 **Monastery of Vydubitskii** Collegiate Church of St Michael has survived with rebuilt apse. Also Church of St George, monastic refectory and single-storeyed belfry dating from end 17th–beginning 18th c.

151 **Statues** The Arsenal Workers 1923. Bogdan Khmel'nitskii planned 1869 erected 1889. General Vatutin 1948. The Magdeburg Rights 1802. Nicholas Shchors 1954.

152 **Paton Bridge** 1953, the first completely welded bridge in the world.

153 **Supreme Soviet of the Ukraine** 1938, Classical portico and glass cupola.

154 **Town Wall** Built under Iaroslav; remains consist of mud ramparts supported by a wooden framework.

155 **University** Heavy red façade and colonnade of main building by Beretti. Rebuilt 1948.

156 **War Memorial** Obelisk of impressive sincerity.

KIRILLO-BELOOZERSK, Russian Federation

157 **Monastery of St Cyril** 1635, outer walls of superb proportions, elaborate decorative brickwork.

KIRILLOV, Russian Federation

158 **Monastery of St Ferapont** Church of the Nativity of the Virgin 1500–2. Paintings by Dionisii and his two sons.

KIROVABAD, Azerbaidzhan

159 **Jomard-Kassab Mausoleum** 9th c.

KISHINEV, Moldavia

160 **Great Cathedral** 1840, by A. I. Mel'nikov, noteworthy belfry, Classical style which can be seen in other buildings of the town.

KISLOVODSK, Russian Federation

161 Several 20th c sanatoria.

KIZHI, Russian Federation

162 **Outdoor Museum** Secular and religious buildings in wood from all over N Russia, including the Church of the Transfiguration 1714, a magnificent creation with elaborate roof of many cupolas. Also Church of the Intercession.

KOLOMENSKOE, Russian Federation

163 **Church of the Ascension** Consecrated 1533, restored 1880; finest church with steep conical roof in Russia. Inside is a small museum with works of art of the 16th c.

164 **Church of Our Lady of Kazan'** 17th c.

165 **Fortified tower** 18th c brought from N Russia with high conical wooden roof.

166 **Museum** Models of wooden buildings, and many objects, mainly in wood, typical of old Russia. Wooden house 18th c; brought from Arkhangel'sk. Carefully reconstructed interior.

KOSTROMA, Russian Federation

167 **Trinity Cathedral** 1652, part of the Ipatevski Monastery.

KRONSTADT, Russian Federation

168 **Cathedral of St Andrew** Built under Catherine the Great by Zakharov.

169 **Iun'skaia ulitsa** (June Street) Row of houses built under Peter the Great, ending with the Italian Palace, built at the beginning of the 18th c for Prince Menshikov.

KURSK, Russian Federation

170 **Cathedral of St Sergii and Our Lady of Kazan'** Example of Russian 18th c provincial Baroque in the Rastrelli style. Curious architecture of several storeys, restored with very bright colours inside and out.

KUSKOVO, Russian Federation

171 **Palace** 1769–75, by serf architects Argunov and Mironov, after plans by De Wailly, in wood but looks like stone. Rooms well furnished and decorated, with Western and Russian works of art. Includes the Porcelain Museum: French, German, English, Chinese and Russian china. Park with numerous pavilions.

KUTAISI, Georgia

172 **Cathedral** Built 1003, destroyed 1691.

173 **Historico-Ethnographical Museum** Medieval Georgian minor arts.

KUZ'MINKI, Russian Federation

174 **Palace** Only the Egyptian wing remains of the palace of 1820, by Gilardi. Park and outbuildings in Empire style.

LENINGRAD (formerly St Petersburg) Russian Federation

175 **Academy of Arts** Imposing main building by De la Mothe and Kokorinov 1764–88. Splendid vestibule and conference hall. Museum with section on the history of Russian painting. On the quay, two rare sphinxes from Thebes about 1500 BC.

176 **Academy of Sciences** 1784–87, Quarenghi. Inside mosaics by Lomonosov.

177 **Admiralty** Started 1704, present appearance dates from 1823, by Zakharov. Architectural centre of the city, where the main avenues converge. Gilded spire 230 feet high.

Aleksandrinskii Theatre see **Pushkin Theatre**

178 **Anichkov Palace** Begun by Zemtsov, completed by Rastrelli 1741–50, later remodelled several times. Portico by Quarenghi 1803–09.

179 **Armenian Church** 1770–72, by Veldten, transitional style between Baroque and Classical.

180 **Bourse** (Stock Exchange) Now the Navy Museum. By Quarenghi and Thomon.

181 **Cathedral of Our Lady of Kazan'** 1801–11, Neo-Classical, Voronikhin's masterpiece. Colonnade copied from St Peter's, Rome. Decorated with many sculptures. Inside, icons by 19th c masters and museum of religion and atheism.

182 **Cathedral of St Isaac** 1817–57, by Montferrand in Imperial Russian style. Great splendour and size, impressive dome. Its interior is outstanding for the richness and variety of marble and other semi-precious stone.

183 **Church of the Ascension** 1760–77, by Rinaldi, Baroque.

184 **Church of Our Lady of Vladimir** 1761–83 by pupils of Rastrelli and Rinaldi. Contains interesting icon screen and icons of the Rublev school. 18th c bell tower.

185 **Church of the Resurrection** Completed 1907, by Parland.

186 **Elagin Palace** 1818–22, by Rossi, noteworthy Neo-Classical building in an English-style park. Very fine frieze on the austere façade.

187 **Engineer's Castle** 1796–1800, by Brenna in Renaissance style. Now a military academy.

188 **Fontanka Palace** 1752 by Chevakinskii and Argunov, remodelled later several times. The only monument of aristocratic culture preserved in its entirety.

189 **Gostinnyi Dvor** (Bazaar) 1785, by De la Mothe; remodelled 1886.

190 **Horse Guards Riding School** 1804, by Quarenghi in Classical style. Beside it, two statues by Rauch, 1844–45.

191 **Iusupov Palace** Main part built end 18th c by Quarenghi, later remodelled several times. Left wing and interior decoration c. 1830.

192 **Kunstkamera** (Cabinet of Curios of Peter the Great) 1718–25, by Mattarnovi, rounded Baroque façade. Exhibits based on Peter I's collection of Chinese, Indian and other art.

193 **Law School** Chapel built 1833 by Stassov, contains a crystal icon screen and a painting attributed to Rubens.

194 **Marble Palace** 1768–85, by Rinaldi. Notable for use of marble rather than stucco. One wing by Briullov mid 19th c contains remarkable staircase.

195 **Menshikov Palace** Begun 1710–15 by Trezzini, finished later by Schädel; Baroque, luxurious interior.

196 **Mikhailovskii Palace** see **State Russian Museum**.

197 **Monastery of Aleksandr Nevskii** 1710–16, from plans by D. and P. Trezzini. All eleven churches suffered considerably during the war. Cemetery of Lazarus early 19th c Neo-Classical graves; monumental and commemorative sculpture. Church of the Annunciation 1717. Basilica of the Holy Trinity 1776–90, Neo-Classical, by Starov, contains pictures by Russian and Western artists, including Ivanov, Rubens, Van Dyck. Remarkable altar ensemble and silver.

198 **Monument to Peter the Great** 1800, designed by Rastrelli the elder.

199 **National Bank** 1793–88 by Quarenghi. Beautiful friezes. Now the State Bank for the North-West.

200 **Nevskii Prospect** Mixture of 18th, 19th and 20th c buildings, most of them in Neo-Classical style.

201 **New Holland Arch** De la Mothe, 18th c.

202 **Palace of Count Bobrinskii** End 18th c, by Rusca. Prototype of the contemporary mansion.

203 **Palace of Labour** 1835–61, by Stakenschneider.

204 **Palace of Senator Polovtsev Fomin** 1911–13, Classical style. Interesting façade and portico.

205 **Palace Square** Contains the former Chief Staff Headquarters, Rossi's masterpiece of 1819–47, including a Roman-style triumphal arch. To the E the barracks of the Household Guard 1840 by Briullov; in the centre column of Alexander by Montferrand, 1834. Sculptures on the plinth by Orlovskii.

206 **Peter and Paul Fortress** Begun 1703, completed 1710 by Trezzini. Later became a prison. St Peter's Gate 1718–18, by Trezzini, bas-relief by Osner. **Peter and Paul Cathedral** 1713–21, by Trezzini in Dutch style with a dome. Rebuilt after a fire by Rastrelli and Chevakinskii 1750. Tower with spire 400 feet, surmounted by metal angel by Rinaldi. Noteworthy Holy Door by Sarukhyi in Russian Baroque style. Tombs of tsars since Peter the Great. Small house nearby by Vist 1761. House of the Commandants of the Fortress, mid 18th c. Mint early 19th c by Voronikhin.

207 **Polovtsev House** 1911–13, by Fomin.

208 **Pushkin Theatre** (formerly Aleksandrinskii Theatre) By Rossi in Empire style, 1828–32.

209 **Saltykov Shchedrin State Library** 1796–1801. Rectilinear façade 1828–32 in Empire style, by Rossi.

210 **Sampsonievskii Basilica** 1740, contains very fine 18th c Baroque icon screen.

211 **Senate and Synod** Joined by an arcade. Rossi, 1829–34.

212 **Smol'nyi Monastery** Baroque style by Rastrelli 1744–57; very fine Cathedral, the interior remodelled by Stasov. Smol'nyi Institute is attached.

State Hermitage Museum see **Winter Palace**.

213 **State Museum of the History of Leningrad** Exhibits featuring the architecture of Leningrad, branches also at the Peter and Paul Fortress and St Isaac's Cathedral.

214 **State Russian Museum** (formerly the Mikhailovskii Palace) Neo-Classical style by Rossi 1819–25, with ornamental railing and decoration disc by Rossi. Wall paintings and ceiling decorations by the Medici brothers. This is the central museum of Russian art and life and contains: Russian and Soviet paintings and drawings; decorative and applied arts from the

18th C; folk art and craft; 12th–17th C icons, including some by Rublev.

215 **Statues** General Suvorov-Kozlovskii 1808. Nicholas I 1859, to designs by Klodt, helped by Montferrand and Efimov. Peter the Great by Falconet 1775. Puskin by Anikushkin 1957.

216 **Stroganov Palace** Baroque style by Rastrelli 1752–54.

217 **Summer Palace** Dutch style by Trezzini 1710–12, sculptures by Schlüter. Interior later, restored. Summer Garden laid out by Peter the Great 1706–12, in the French and Dutch style. Railings made *c.*1780 by Veldten and Egorov.

218 **Tauride Palace** 1783–89 by Starov. Murals by Scotti.

219 **Underground Stations** Decorated with marble and mosaics; note Vladimirskaia, Ploshchad' Vosstaniia and Pushkinshaia stations.

220 **Vorontsov Palace** By Rastrelli. In the courtyard the Chapel of the Order of Malta, Neo-Classical style by Quarenghi 1799.

221 **Winter Palace** Successful example of Baroque architecture, with two façades by Rastrelli 1754–64. Interior restored 1839 after a fire by Stasov and Briullov. Adjoined by the Little Hermitage by De la Mothe 1764–67; next is the Old Hermitage by Veldten 1775–84, and, across the canal, the Hermitage Theatre by Quarenghi 1783–87. **State Hermitage Museum** Collections housed in the Winter Palace and the Little, the Old and the New Hermitage buildings. The chief sections of this include: art of the primitive civilisations of the USSR, art of the peoples of the USSR and of the peoples of the East, and the ancient world. History of Western European art and history of Russian art. Collection of Scythian art. Outstanding examples by Raphael, Leonardo da Vinci, Titian, Rubens, Van Dyck, Rembrandt, Renoir, Monet, Picasso.

LIVADIIA, Ukraine

222 **Two royal palaces** Both rebuilt about 1865 by Monighetti.

LOMONOSOV (formerly Oranienbaum) Russian Federation

223 **Palace** Russian Baroque 1710–25, by Fontana and Schädel.

224 **Toboggan Hill Pavilion** by Rinaldi 1762–74. Chinese Palace in Rococo style by Rinaldi 1768; ceilings by Venetian painters, including Tiepolo.

225 **Palace of Peter III** 1757–62, by Rinaldi, completely restored 1953, now contains exhibition of Chinese objets d'art.

L'VOV, Ukraine

226 **Armenian Cathedral** Begun 1363, completed 15th C.

227 **Boimi Chapel** 1609–17. Richly decorated with sculptures, some features derived from N schools.

228 **Campiani Chapel** End 16th–beginning 17th C, influence of Italian Renaissance.

229 **Catholic Church of the Benedictines** First half of 17th C; influenced by Italian Renaissance.

230 **Church of the Benedictines** End 16th C; blend of Italian and Byzantine features.

231 **Church of the Dominicans** 1744–65, by Urbanik and Witte; exuberant sculptures, characteristic example of Rococo.

232 **Church of the Jesuits** 1610–38, copied from the Gesù in Rome.

233 **Church of St George** 1743–58, by Meretyn.

234 **L'vov State Picture Gallery** Western painting, including the collections of Ianovich, Liubomirskii and Pininskii families. Renaissance art, particularly German. Baroque art, Austrian and German the most interesting. A few good 19th C paintings.

235 **Valacca Greek-Catholic Church** 1591–98, blend of Italian and Byzantine features.

MARMASHEN, Armenia

236 Typical 10th–11th C complex of three churches, the main one being Vahram 986–1029, beautifully preserved and one of the most elegant Armenian buildings.

MASTARA, Armenia

237 **Church of St John** 6th–7th C, one of the first central-plan churches in Armenia, probably used as a prototype.

MERV, Turkmenistan

238 **Complex of ruins** Preserved as a state museum. Includes remains of towns of 1st millennium BC, classical Parthian period 9th C AD and Timurid period.

239 **Mausolea** Those of Sultan Sanjar and of Muhammad ibn-Zaid particularly impressive.

MINSK, Belorussia

240 **Belorussian State Art Museum** Russian and Belorussian painters. Socialist Realist paintings.

MOSCOW, Russian Federation

241 **Academy of Medical Sciences** (formerly Hospice for Waifs and Strays) Built 1823–25 by Gilardi and Grigor'ev, ornamental sculptures by Vitali.

242 **Andronikov Monastery** Rebuilt in stone 1410–27. Church of the Saviour 1425–27 still stands. The monastery now houses the Rublev Museum containing originals and copies of many early icons.

243 **Bol'shoi Theatre** Rebuilt in its present form in 1856 by Cavos. Magnificent hall with gilt and red plush.

244 **Cathedral of St Basil** (officially, Pokrov Cathedral or Cathedral of the Intercession) Exuberant shape and brilliant colour characterise the exterior, built 1554–60 by Barma and Postnik; twice restored. Undistinguished interior set out as a small museum of Old Russian architecture.

245 **Church of All Saints of Kulishkii** Rebuilt during 16th and 17th C.

246 **Church of the Archangel Gabriel** (better known as the Menshikov Tower) 1704–07. Spire destroyed by lightning. Highly decorated façade; fine example of Baroque religious architecture.

247 **Church of the Dormition of the Potters** Mid 18th C; mosaics and decorative brickwork in perfect condition.

248 **Church of the Intercession of the Virgin, Fili** Built 1693; the prototype of Moscow Baroque.

249 **Church of John the Warrior** 1709–13, by Zarudnyi, typical of the Moscow Baroque style.

250 **Church of Jehosophat** 1678, one of the oldest Moscow Baroque buildings.

251 **Church of the Metropolitan Philip** 1771–73, semi-circular Classical building by Kazakov; richly decorated interior.

252 **Church of the Nativity of Putniki** 1652, completely restored. Good example of 17th C monumental style, pavilion roof.

253 **Churches of the Old Believers at Rogozhskoe Kladbishche** Contain a priceless collection of icons up to the 18th C.

254 **Church of Georgian Mother of God 'in Nikitinka'** 1635–53, very richly decorated. Interior decorated by frescoes by Ushakov.

255 **Church of the Prophet Elijah** 1702; a fine octagonal Classical tower.

256 **Church of St Anne** 1490–93; the original style preserved intact.

257 **Church of St Gregory Neokessariiskii** 1667–69, by Kuznechik and Guba; with a beautiful sanctuary.

258 **Church of St Nicholas of the Weavers** 1679–92; graceful and quite detailed in the colourful exterior, completely restored.

259 **Church of St Nikita the Martyr** 1751, by Ukhtomskii. Restored 1962, revealing the original outline.

260 **Church of St Trifon** 15th C; later additions removed during restoration.

261 **Comecon Building** (Council for Mutual Economic Aid) Tall steel and glass office block of fairly imaginative design, completed 1968.

262 **Crimea Bridge** 1958, technically remarkable suspension bridge of grace and strength.

263 **Danilovskii Monastery** Four churches of the 17th and 18th C, and vast surrounding wall in the style of the Kremlin.

264 **Don Monastery** Fine surrounding walls, 1686–1711; seven churches, including a very well preserved small church of 1593, with one cupola, and the New (or Great) Cathedral,

1684–93, in Moscow Baroque, with a beautiful icon screen and 18th C murals. This now houses the Museum of Architecture, with plans and models of the 16th to 19th C.

265 **Frunze Military Academy** Austere building decorated with low relief, 1936, by Rudnev.

266 **Golitsyn Hospital** 1796–1801, by Kazakov; well proportioned Classical building.

267 **Golovin Palace** 18th C, Rinaldi, Bazhenov and Quarenghi helped to design this superb building, with its fine peristyle to the E.

268 **House of the Boyar Saltykov** 18th C.

269 **House of Friendship** Early 20th C, formerly belonged to Morozov; exuberant pseudo-Portuguese Moorish, with decoration over the entire façade.

270 **House of Unions** 1785, Kazakov; famous Empire style column room.

271 **Ivanovskii Monastery** Founded 16th C, rebuilt 1861, still retains the original walls and tented towers.

272 **Kalinin Prospekt** 1968, imaginative avenue built of glass, brick and concrete, tall blocks are widely spaced along two unbroken two-storey buildings.

273 **Kazan' railway station** 1914–40, by Shchusev.

274 **Kremlin** Surrounded by a high, thick wall with numerous towers which were rebuilt and added to at various times; modelled on the walls of the Sforza Palace in Milan by Ruffo and Solario, 1485–1508. Arsenal 1702–36, by C. Konrad. Columned portal by Prince D. V. Ukhtomskii. Belfry of Ivan the Great completed 1600. **Cathedral of the Annunciation** 1482–90, by architects from Pskov. Contains paintings attributed to Feofan Grek and Rublev, and a collection of early icons. Enlarged 1564. **Cathedral of the Archangel Michael** 1505–09, by Novi. A turning point in religious architecture with its rich decoration, two-storeyed construction and shells replacing arcades. Inside, frescoes of 1557; sculptured icon screen and most of the icons date from the 1680 restoration. Portrait of tsar Dimitrii, carved in gold. **Cathedral of the Dormition** 1475–79, by Fiorovanti. Freely copied from the Cathedral of the Dormition in Vladimir. Italian innovations, such as the terrace with twin arcades. Frescoes completely restored. Icon screen contains some original icons, including 12th C St George, from Constantinople. **Chapel of the Deposition of the Garments** 1484–86, by architects from Pskov, restored to its former beauty, contains ancient wooden sculptures. **Church of the Resurrection** Contains a fine 18th C icon screen. **Facets Palace** 1491, by Ruffo and Solario in Florentine style. Original frescoes restored by Ushakov, sumptuous royal apartments. **Church of the the Twelve Apostles and Patriarch's Palace** Both built by Nikon 1660s. **Great Kremlin Palace** Houses the Supreme Soviet, 1839–49 by Thon. Richly decorated royal apartments of the 16th, 17th and 18th C, and a vast meeting hall redone by Ivanov-Schitz in 1934. **Armoury Palace** Now the Museum of Decorative Arts 1849–51, in pseudo-Russian style by Thon, contains items from the court treasury and ancient museum, as well as ecclesiastical treasures, tapestries, metalwork, jewels. **Palace of Congresses** 1961, by M. V. Possokhin, well proportioned, functional building using much glass, with marble columns. **Senate Building** (now the official headquarters of the Soviet government) 1777–88, by Kazakov. **Terem Palace** Three storeys added 1635–36, so that it appears to be typical of 17th C architecture.

275 **Krutitskii Monastery** Rebuilt 17th C. Church of the Dormition 1685, with a long gallery in brick, 1693. Krutitskii Teremok, 1694, by Startsev and Kovalev; unusual tile decoration on the façade.

276 **Lefortovskii Palace** 1697–1708, built to the austere design of Aksanikov and Fontana; altered at the beginning of the 19th C.

277 **Lenin Library** (formerly the Pashkov Mansion) 1784–86, by Bazhenov. Elegant building of oak faced with stucco, with a large flight of steps. Adjoined by the main building, built by Shchuko and Guelfreich in 1939.

278 **Lenin Mausoleum** 1929–30 by Shchusev; Constructivist style, red granite.

279 **Leningrad Hotel** Completed 1954, by Poliakov and Domnikovskii. With its external ornamentation and wasteful ostentation, typical of the Stalin era.

Menshikov Tower see **Church of the Archangel Gabriel.**

280 **Metropol' Hotel** 1899–1903, in the modern style of the period.

281 **Monument to Karl Marx** 1961, by Kerbel. A head emerging from a block of granite.

282 **Monument to Iurii Dolgorukii** 1947–53, by Orlov and assistants.

283 **Moscow State University** 1949–53; largest of the Stalinist sky-scrapers. Central block and symmetrical wings, total height 787 feet. External impression of colossal grandeur not repeated inside.

284 **Moskva Hotel** 1932–35, by Shchusev. Massive, red granite with white marble.

285 **Municipal Hospital** (formerly a palace, then the English Club) 1786–90, by Kazakov in the form of an imposing Greek temple. Damaged by fire, rebuilt with frieze by Bovet.

286 **Museum of Folk Art** Items from 18th to 20th C, including experimental decorative art.

287 **Museum of Oriental Culture** Chinese, Japanese, Indian, Korean, Mongolian, Persian etc. paintings, sculptures, engravings, mosaics and applied art. Eastern republics of the USSR represented mainly by contemporary work.

288 **Novodevichii Monastery** Founded 1524. Gardens, high brick walls and domes are in the same style as the Kremlin. The Great Belfry end of the 18th C Italian Baroque. Cathedral of Smolensk 1524–25. Church of the Transfiguration 1687–88. Church of the Assumption 1685–87. Interesting cemetery outside the walls with the 19th and 20th C graves of famous people. A branch of the History Museum at the monastery contains ecclesiastical and other treasures.

289 **Novospasskii Monastery** Rebuilt 1466. Surrounded by a fine brick wall. Church of the Transfiguration 1645, contains outstanding frescoes. Belfry 1785, 236 feet high.

290 **Ostankino Palace** Built 1790 by serfs to the design of Quarenghi, adapted to the Classical Russian style of the 18th C. Moulded stucco on wood looks like stone. Luxurious interior, with beautiful proportions and decorations. Rich collection of works of art of all kinds. Ingenious theatre, 1791–98. One wing now houses the Museum of Serf Art. Next to the palace is Trinity Church, built 1678–93. A fine example of Russian Baroque, with interesting decoration.

291 **Palace of Prince Razumovskii** 1790–93, a beautiful Classical residence by Kazakov.

Pashkov Mansion see **Lenin Library.**

292 **Patriarchal Cathedral of the Epiphany** Rebuilt 1793; striking exterior, but interior in 19th C style. Interesting icons.

293 **Petrovskii Monastery** Rebuilt 17th C, façade characteristic of the period. The Church of the Metropolitan Peter, 1690, has been restored; belfry in Russian Baroque.

294 **Petrovskii Palace** 1776, by Kazakov in a curious Lombardo-Gothic style; stone and red brick.

295 **Pushkin State Museum of Fine Arts** 1812, by Klein, marble building in Neo-Greek style. Collection based on that of the Rumiantsev Museum; pictures from the Hermitage and other Moscow and Leningrad museums; private collections of Shchukin, Sheremetev, Brokar, Kharitonenko, Iusupov, Shuvalov, and the Impressionist collection of Morozov. Fine collection of Egyptian sculptures, and archaeological finds from the N Black Sea coast. Dutch 17th and 18th C, Flemish and Italian 17th and 18th C, Venetian school, some Italian icons of 13th and 14th C. The richest collection is of French painting and sculpture, particularly of the Impressionist school, including major works by Picasso (pre-1914), Matisse, Degas, Van Gogh, Cézanne, Gauguin and others.

296 **Riabuskinskii House** c.1905 in Art Nouveau style by Shekhtel.

297 **Riding School** Built in 1817 by Bovet. Regarded at the time as a technical marvel.

Rublev Museum see **Andronikov Monastery.**

298 **Shcherbatov House** 1911–13, by Tamanian.

299 **Shchusev Museum of Russian Architecture** Models and photographs of past, present and projected Russian architecture.

300 **Sheremetev Hospital** (now the Sklifovskii Institute) Started by Nazarov in 1794, completed by Quarenghi in 1807. Magnificent building with two curving wings.

301 **Sovetskaia Hotel** 1951, in ostentatious Baroque.

302 **State Historical Museum** Contains icons and Russian applied arts.

303 **Statue of Pushkin** 1880, by Opedukin.

304 **Statue of the Worker and the Collective Farm Worker** 1937, a mammoth creation in steel by Vera Mukhina.

305 **Tret'iakov Gallery** Mid 19th C building by Vasnetsov in curious old Russian style. Collection of Russian painting is based on that of the Tret'iakov brothers. It contains the finest collection of Russian icons, including *The Vladimir Mother of God*. 18th C portraits; 19th C historical paintings, including Ivanov and Vereshchagin; landscapes, including Levitan; Vrubel', Serov etc. Socialist Realist painting. A collection of late 19th–early 20th C Russian painters, including Chagall and Kandinsky, is not on public display.

305 **Ukraina Hotel** 1956, by Mordvinov in Stalinist sky-scraper style, with a spire and Pseudo-Classical ornamentation.

307 **Underground** Started in 1933, stations are palatial and extremely varied. Sculptures, mosaics, chandeliers and other decoration abound in the earlier stations; more recent ones are much plainer. Much of the marble has been taken from old churches.

MTSKHETA, Georgia

308 **Samtavro Monastery** Church dates from 11th C, has richly decorated façades.

309 **Sveti-Tskhoveli Cathedral** Early 11th C, incorporating elements of earlier royal basilica. Fine frescoes, delicate decoration on S wall, geometric on N.

MUG, Uzbekistan

310 **Sogdian Castle** Several rooms have been excavated.

NAKHICHEVAN, Azerbaidzhan

311 12th C tomb-towers of Yusuf ibn-Kuseyir and of Mumineh Khatun by Ajem.

NEREDITSA, Russian Federation

312 **Church of the Saviour** 1198, contained very important wall paintings.

NISA see under **ASHKHABAD.**

NIZHNII NOVGOROD see **GOR'KII**

NORAVANK, Armenia

313 Group of typical 13th and 14th C ornamented two-storey churches. Karapet Church (St John the Baptist) 1221–27, narthex added 1261. Church of St Gregory 1275. Memorial Church of great beauty, 1339; W façade covered with elaborate decorative sculpture.

NOVGOROD, Russian Federation

314 **Cathedral of St Sophia** see **Kremlin.**

315 **Court of Iaroslav** The economic centre of old Novgorod. Church of the Dormition 12th C plan, refashioned 15th C. Church of the Annunciation 1362, transformed several times, but general appearance preserved. Church of St John recently completely rebuilt to the 12th C plan. Church of St Nicholas 1113, on the plan of Kievan churches, severe façade cluttered by 19th C additions, contains the remains of 12th C frescoes. Church of St Praskovia in Smolensk style of 12th and 13th C.

316 **Church of the Annunciation** 1179, cupolas rebuilt 16th C; 12th C murals damaged in the war.

317 **Church of the Nativity** 14th C, remarkable frescoes, recently cleaned, showing the diversity of artistic influences in Novgorod.

318 **Church of St Dimitrii of Salonica** Typical early 15th C Novgorod style.

319 **Iur'ev Monastery** Church of St George 1119, an important departure from Byzantine style. Monumental proportions revealed by restoration. Fragments of wall paintings in the Byzantine tradition.

320 **Church of St John the Divine** 14th C, restored 19th C.

321 **Church of St Nicholas the Miracle-Worker** 1292, a new departure from normal Byzantine influence with its use of materials, single dome on a slender drum, plain external walls and other features.

322 **Church of St Nicholas Stratilates** Fine example of 14th C architecture; traces of mural paintings, attributed to Feofan Grek or his pupils.

323 **Church of St Nikita the Martyr** 16th C.

324 **Church of St Peter and St Paul** 1406, in the style of the two preceding centuries.

325 **Church of St Philip** 14th C, restored 1526 to its original plan.

326 **Church of St Simeon** 1468; 15th C frescoes in very bad condition.

327 **Church of St Theodore Stratilates** 1360–61, characteristic of the classical N style.

328 **Church of St Thomas** Rebuilt 1463 in the style of the 12th C.

329 **Church of the Saviour and of his Transfiguration** 1378, a perfect example of 14th C Novgorod architecture; striking murals by Feofan Grek.

330 **Church of the Trinity** 1365; the upper part was replaced in the 18th and 19th C.

331 **Kremlin** Stone walls of the 11th C, modified 14th and 15th C and rebuilt after the war. Belfry of St Sophia 1439, restored 18th C. **Cathedral of St Sophia** 1045–50, modelled on the cathedral in Kiev; local stone and brick in an austere, dignified building restored after the war; bronze gates from Magdeburg, an interior of imposing proportions; interesting fragments of 11th C painting. 16th C icon screen.

332 **Facet Palace** 1433, rebuilt after the war, contains the Museum of History and Art with icons of the Novgorod and Pskov schools, wood carvings and 19th C Russian landscapes.

333 **White Tower** End of the 15th C.

334 **Znamenskii Cathedral** 17th C, with five cupolas; frescoes of 1702 only partly uncovered.

ODESSA, Ukraine

335 **Monument to the Duke of Richelieu** 1826, by Martos.

336 **Odessa Museum of Western and Eastern Art** Considerable range of Western painting, with many 17th and 18th C works; the collection includes Caravaggio, Rubens, Bruegel and Franz Hals. Interesting Eastern and antique sections.

337 **Odessa State Picture Gallery** Russian and Ukrainian artists, including Repin, Serov, Levitan and Aivazovskii.

338 **Odessa Workers' Soviet** (formerly the archaeological museum) Classical building by Boffo.

339 **Potemkin Steps** (formerly the Richelieu Steps) Built between the boulevard and the port 1837–41 by Boffo.

340 **Theatre of Opera and Ballet** 1884–87, by Felner and Gelmer from Vienna, and the Russian engineer Gonsiorovskii. Composite style, with many statues. Recently completely renovated.

ODZUN (or Uzunlar) Armenia

341 **Basilica** With a gallery, 6th–7th C; to the N an unusual tomb with fine columns and engraving.

ORDZHONIKIDZE, Georgia

342 **Alan Necropolis** Catacombs of the 6th–9th C.

OSTROVO, Russian Federation

343 **Church of the Transfiguration** Fine mid 16th C tower church.

PALEKH see **SELO PALEKH**

PANILOVO, Russian Federation

344 **Church of St Nicholas** 1600, a decorative wooden church.

PAVLOVSK, Russian Federation

345 **Palace** Transitional style between Baroque and Classicism by Cameron, 1782–86. Side wings added later by Brenna. Badly damaged in the war, exterior and part of the interior now restored. English Park designed by Cameron, ornamented by Gonzaga in c.1800. Numerous houses, pavilions and monuments in the styles of various countries and epochs.

PECHORA, Russian Federation
346 **Monastery** Founded 1472, remarkable 16th c ramparts, 16th c bell tower, catacombs, several churches of 16th–19th c.

PERESLAVL'-ZALESKII, Russian Federation
347 **Church of the Transfiguration of the Saviour** 1152, severe, plain walls and a single dome; one of the earliest examples of Vladimir-Suzdal' architecture.
348 **Monastery** Now contains the Regional Museum, with a notable collection of icons and wooden articles.

PERM', Russian Federation
349 **Perm' State Art Gallery** (the former cathedral) Contains Western painting, including Dutch, Flemish and Italian. Another section contains a unique collection of Perm' wooden sculptures of 17th–19th c.

PETERHOF see **PETRODVORETS**.

PETGHNI (or Petghnavank) Armenia
350 **Church** 6th c; first surviving rectangular building with a cupola. Decorative friezes on the outside.

PETRODVORETS (formerly Peterhof) Russian Federation
351 **Grand Palace** Built after Leblond's plans 1715, enlarged by Rastrelli 1750. Destroyed during the war together with the ensemble of fountains. Exterior completely reconstructed, work on the interior in progress. The park contains numerous smaller palaces in a variety of styles including: Mon Plaisir, the Hermitage, Marly.
352 **Strelna Palace** (nearby) Transformed by Voronikhin 1804.

PIATIGORSK, Georgia
353 **Lermontov Baths** (formerly the Nicholas Baths) 1826–31, in Classical style by Bernardazzi.
354 **Monument to Lermontov** End 19th c, by Opekushin.
355 **Mud Baths** 1913–14, by Peretiatkovich.

PITSUNDA, Georgia
356 **Greek Church** Remarkably preserved, considerable size.

POCHAEV, Ukraine
357 **Pochaev Monastery** Founded early Middle Ages, but most of the buildings (among them the seven churches) are of 18th and 19th c. Notable are the Dormition Cathedral 1780 and the unfinished Trinity Church in the old Russian style, begun 1911 by Shchusev.

PODPOROZHIE, Russian Federation
358 **Church of the Trinity** 1725–27, wooden, now boarded over, with a very interesting roof.

POLOTSK, Russian Federation
359 **Cathedral** 18th c icon screen with lavish ornamentation.

PSKOV, Russian Federation
360 **Cathedral of the Trinity** Late 12th c.
361 **Church of the Assumption** 1521, simple and pleasing lines.
362 **Church of St Basil the Great** Typical 15th c Pskov church.
363 **Church of St Basil the Great on the Mound** 1413.
364 **Ivanovskii Monastery** Cathedral first half of the 13th c, with three imposing domes. Related to early 12th c Novgorod churches, but individual in style. Fragments of outstanding frescoes.
365 **Mirozhskii Monastery** Cathedral of the Transfiguration 1156; frescoes.
366 **New Cathedral of the Trinity** 1365–67, to a beautiful design by Kirill. Elaborately reconstructed in 1682–99.
367 **Pogankiny Palace** Best of several 17th c merchants' houses of severe style, well preserved.
368 **Ramparts** Established in the 11th c, dating mainly from a 15th c reconstruction.
369 **Snetogorskii Monastery** Church of the Nativity early 14th c; highly original frescoes painted about 1313, in several different styles.

PUSHKIN (formerly Tsarskoe Selo) Russian Federation
370 **Great Palace of Catherine the Great** Rebuilt by Rastrelli 1752–57. Splendid interior, several rooms designed by Cameron. The Agate Pavilion, the Hanging Gallery, the Cameron Gallery and the Pantheon all designed by Cameron for the grounds. Several other buildings including the Chinese village.
371 **Alexander Palace** 1792–96, by Quarenghi in Classical style.

RHIPSIM, Armenia
372 **Church of Rhipsi the Martyr** 618, one of the purest examples of Armenian art. Slightly elongated cross with central cupola, porch and belfry added 1653, but the basic simplicity is unaffected.

RIAZAN', Russian Federation
373 **Regional Art Museum** Old Russian and Soviet art.

RIGA, Latvia
374 **Church of St James** 12th–13th c, some parts are well preserved.
375 **Church of St John** Mid 13th c, vaulted ceiling and pediment 15th–early 16th c; Baroque altar, 18th c.
376 **Church of St Peter** 13th c, rebuilt several times; wooden spire.
377 **Dom Monastery Church** 13th–19th c. Now houses the Riga State Museum.
378 **Guildhalls** 13th–16th c, the old rooms in the Great Guildhall date back to the beginning of the 14th c.
379 **Lenin Monument** 1950, by Ingau and Bogoliubov, architect Stahlberg.
380 **Powder Tower** (or Sand Tower) 13th–14th c.
381 **Riga Castle** Started 1330 and rebuilt several times, now houses museums.
382 **State Museum of Decorative Art** Porcelain collection, antique objects, French drawings, German and Dutch paintings.
383 **State Museum of Foreign Arts** Western painting, some old masters, but particularly minor Dutch artists of the 17th c and 19th c, German paintings; also contemporary Belgian collection.
384 **State Museum of Latvian and Russian Art.**
385 **State Museum of Folk Crafts** 17th–19th c; vast open-air display of folk architecture.

ROMANOV-BORISOGLEBSK (or Tutaev) Russian Federation
386 **Church** Fine 17th c building.

ROSTOV-ON-DON, Russian Federation
387 **Bank** 1910, by Peretiatkovich.
388 **House of the Municipal Council** 1896–99, by Pomerantsev.
389 **Museum of Fine Arts** Paintings by Vereshchagin, Aivazovskii, Levitan and Repin.
390 **Pioneer's Palace** (formerly the Bank of the Volga and the Kama) By Beketov.

ROSTOV VELIKII, Russian Federation
391 **Kremlin** Thick walls of whitewashed brick, end of the 17th c. Cathedral of the Assumption rebuilt 1408, but style is that of the 17th c modifications. Church of the Resurrection 1670. Church of St John the Evangelist, 1683, above a gate in the wall. Church of the Hodigitria (Virgin of Smolensk) 17th c. These and two other churches are decorated throughout with frescoes by Moscow painters.

SAMARKAND, Uzbekistan
392 **Bibi Khanum Mosque** 1399–1404, partially ruined but still magnificent, of gigantic proportions. Well preserved dadoes of beautiful colour and design.
393 **Gur-i-Mir Mausoleum** Started 1404; elegant lines and magnificent cupola, now restored in the original brilliant colours. Contains the tombs of the Timurid dynasty.
394 **Mausoleum of Ishrat Khan** 1464; note the monument to Shaibani Khan in the madrasah.
395 **Namazgah Mosque** 17th c, and the Khoja-Akhrar Madrasah, which contains the Ottoman Koran.
396 **Observatory of Ulugh Beg** In ruins, but the subterranean astrolabe is preserved.
397 **Registan** (Sandy Square) One of the finest

examples of 15th c architecture in Central Asia. **Shir Dar Madrasah** first half of the 17th c; strikingly intense colours in the ceramic facing. The design conforms generally to that of the **Madrasah of Ulugh Beg** opposite, built in 1420 by Ulugh Beg. Magnificent entrance arch flanked by two minarets. Richly decorated pediment, and the parts of the building that still stand are covered in coloured ceramic and marble. **Tila Kari Madrasah** 17th c, has an imposing entrance and a mosque on one side of the courtyard.
398 **Shah-i-Zind** A magnificent collection of 14th and 15th c buildings arranged haphazardly along a central passage; the most notable is the Shah-i-Zind Mosque, built in the 14th c. The walls, arches, colonnades and pediments are covered in tiles, the predominant colours of which are blue and green. There is also a gateway, and thirteen mausolea, including the Rukhabad Mausoleum of the first half of the 14th c.

SANAHIN, Armenia
399 **Bridge** 1234.
400 **Fountain** End of the 12th c.
401 **Monastery** Built between the 10th and 13th c to symmetrical design. Church of the Saviour 967–972; narthexes added 1158 and 1211, forming a vaulted room. Church of the Virgin early 10th c. Belfry, 13th c. Library 1063, has an unusual vaulted roof. Three other churches, and several family tombs.

SARATOV, Russian Federation
402 **A. N. Radishchev State Art Museum** Western painting, large quantity, but with almost no major artists represented. Many French works of the 17th–19th c, together with Dutch, Flemish, and some Italian and German.

SELO PALEKH, Russian Federation
403 **State Museum of Palekh Art.**

SERPUKHOV, Russian Federation
404 **Fortress** Built for Ivan the Terrible in 1556; now badly damaged.

SHAKHRISYABZ, Uzbekistan
405 **Ak Saray** Tamerlane's palace with beautiful decorated portal. Several other buildings survive of flourishing 13th–14th c town of Kesh.

SIMFEROPOL', Ukraine
406 **Art Gallery** Paintings by Repin, Shishkin, Aivazovskii, Venetsianov, etc.
407 **Neapol' Skifskii** Capital of a 3rd c BC Scythian state; excavations have revealed a wall with towers and a gate, necropolis, mausoleum and numerous buildings.

SMOLENSK, Russian Federation
408 **Art Gallery** Contains local and Western painting.
409 **Assembly of the Nobility** 1825, by Mel'nikov; the most notable of the 19th c buildings in Classical style.
410 **Cathedral of the Dormition** Started 1677–79, by A. Korolkov, continued 1732–40 by Schädel and completed in 1772.
411 **Church of St John Chrysostom** 1173–76.
412 **Church of St Peter and St Paul** 1146, with an 18th c extension.
413 **Fortified walls** A fine example of defensive architecture, built 1596–1602 by Kon.
414 **Museum** Contains an exhibition of Russian fine and decorative art of the 16th–17th c.
415 **Novodevichii Monastery** Cathedral 1524.
416 **Svirskaia Church** 1191–94.

SOCHI, Russian Federation
417 Several interesting buildings of 1930s and 1950s, including Institute of Rheumatology 1927–34 by Shchusev.

SOLOVKI, Russian Federation
418 **Monastic complex** Dating back to 16th c; impressive walls, numerous churches.

SOL'VYCHEGODSK, Russian Federation
419 **Art and History Museum** Russian icons.

STARAIA LADOGA, Russian Federation
420 **Church of St George** Mid 12th c with frescoes c.1167.

ST PETERSBURG see **LENINGRAD**

SUKHUMI, Georgia
421 **Bridge** 10th–11th c.

SUZDAL', Russian Federation
422 **Cathedral of the Annunciation** Recon-

structed 1222, a masterpiece of Vladimir-Suzdal'
architecture; fragments of frescoes of 1233,
mainly geometric and vegetable ornament.

423 **Church of the Dormition** 1695; with a
bell-tower.

424 **Kremlin** Cathedral of the Nativity 1222–
1528 with remarkable decorated 13th C golden
doors. Bell-tower 1636 and Bishop's Apartments
16th–17th C.

425 **Monastery of St Alexander** 1695; only
the doors remain.

426 **Monastery of St Basil** 17th C.

427 **Monastery of the Intercession** Founded
1364.

SVERDLOVSK, Russian Federation

428 **Regional Picture Gallery** Western,
Russian and Soviet paintings, and objects from
the Kishisk foundries.

TALLINN, Estonia

429 **Church of the Holy Spirit** Early 14th C,
strange minaret-belfry; Gothic altarpiece by
Berent Notken 1483; magnificent pulpit, and
17th C copper chandeliers.

430 **Church of St Michael** Reminiscent of
medieval secular architecture; Baroque icon
screen.

431 **Church of St Nicholas** About 1250; choir
reconstructed after 1433 fire. Fine altarpiece by
Rode, 1482.

432 **Church of St Olaf** Rebuilt after the 1433
fire; mainly 15th C, as is the altar. Highest spire
in the Baltic 1820.

433 **Citadel** 13th C, Danish architecture.
Splendid keep. Inside is the cathedral, of which
only the plan remains of the early 13th C
building, now restored to its original appearance, apart from the 15th C apse. Contains the
tomb of Admiral Grieg, in Neo-Classical style
by Martos, and Baroque pulpit.

434 **Estonian Theatre** 1913, massive but well
proportioned.

435 **Guildhall** (now the History Museum) 1410.
Heavy 17th C wooden doors, and door-knockers
of 1430. Fine gable of N German type.

436 **Kadriorg Palace** 1719–23, built under
Peter the Great. Typical of the architecture
fashionable in the early 18th C. The statuary and
fountains of the park are now at Peterhof.

437 **Medieval houses** Built in stone after 1428.
Very pointed roofs, narrow fronts and decorated gables.

438 **Ramparts** 14th–16th C.

439 **Tallinn State Art Museum** Three monumental altars of the 15th C by N European craftsmen. Small collection of 17th and 18th C works.

440 **Town Hall** Probably late 14th C.
Renaissance bell-tower of 1627. Old meeting hall, with
decorations including a carved wooden frieze.

TASHKENT, Uzbekistan

441 **Alisher Navoii Opera House** Built to the
design of Shchusev; six foyers in the individual
styles of various regions of Uzbekistan.

442 **Barak Khan Madrasah** (now the principal
mosque) Fully restored.

443 **Historical Museum.**

444 **Kukeldash Madrasah** 17th C; beautiful
ceramic decoration.

445 **Uzbek State Museum of Art** Rugs and
gold embroidery, wood carving and painting,
silk fabrics and jewellery. Also Western painting,
including Italian, Dutch, Flemish and French.

TBILISI (Tiflis) Georgia

446 **Church of Anchiskhati** 6th C, built under
Gorgasali Dachi. Restored 12th C.

447 **Georgian Museum of Fine Arts** Magnificent section of medieval Georgian architecture, cloisonné articles, metalwork, porcelain.
Major collection of ancient and contemporary
Georgian works of art and paintings by Russian
artists.

448 **Lurji Monastery** Contains 12th C church.

449 **Lenin Museum** 1937, by Shchusev,
sculptor I. Nikoladze.

450 **Metekhi Fort** 13th C, restored by the Turks
in 1576. Metekhi Church dates from the 5th C;
later restorations have left the plan intact.

451 **Narikala Fortress** In ruins.

452 **Paliashvili Opera** 1880–88, Oriental style
of architecture.

453 **Picture Gallery of the Georgian Artists'
Union** Mainly Soviet works; also a section of
Western painting, including early Italians.

454 **State Museum of Georgia** Ancient and
modern metalwork. Extensive collection of
antique Georgian items.

455 **Statue of Mother Georgia** Huge monument on a hill above the city, by E. Amashukeli
in grey granite.

456 **Statue of Ninoshvili** 1911, by I. Nikoladze.

457 **Underground** Started very recently,
stations are experimental in design, with vivid
colouring. Huge metal panels incorporating the
ancient Georgian techniques.

TERMEZ, Uzbekistan

458 Ruins of ancient town founded by Greco-
Bactrian king 2nd C BC and enlarged in antiquity and Middle Ages. Monuments include
monastery, palace, mosque, minaret also a
museum with collection of local antiquities.

THALIN, Armenia

459 **Two churches** 7th C, the smaller by Prince
Nerse Kamsarakan, cruciform with a very plain
exterior. The cupola of the larger church has
collapsed. Carving on the outside, remains of
paintings inside the apse.

THALISH, Armenia

460 **Church** 680–690, by Grigor Mamikon-
ianin, large and well preserved. Traces of 7th C
paintings in the apse.

TSAGHKADZOR VALLEY, Armenia

461 **Church of the Resurrection** 1220

462 **Kecharis Monastery** Typical 11th–13th C
ensemble. Church of St Gregory 1033; the
cupola has vanished, but it has a very fine
Classical interior, large 12th C narthex. Church
of Nshan 12th C. Cathedral 13th C; mouldings
on outside walls, cupola destroyed.

TSARITSINO, Russian Federation

463 **Palace** 18th C, intended for Catherine the
Great. Begun by Bazhenov in Gothic and
Moorish mixed style, continued by Kazakov.
Park with pavilions.

TSARSKOE SELO see PUSHKIN.

TULA, Russian Federation

464 **Kremlin** 16th C; now a sports ground.
Several fine 18th C houses in the town.

UGLICH, Russian Federation

465 **Museum of History and Art** Russian and
Soviet art.

UL'IANOVSK (formerly Simbirsk) Russian
Federation

466 **Museum of Art** Paintings from the collections of the local nobility and merchants. Mainly
17th C Western paintings, particularly Dutch,
with some Flemish and French. There are also
19th C works of the Belgian and Swedish
schools. Russian and Soviet art.

URGENCH, Turkmenistan

467 **Ancient town** Flourished 10th–14th C,
interesting monuments include several fine
mausolea, a minaret, decorated gates.

UZGEN, Kirgizia

468 **Ancient town** Architectural complex of
11th–12th C including a minaret and three
mausolea.

UZHGOROD, Ukraine

469 **Castle** 13th–14th C, resembling Western
defences rather than a kremlin; palace, 1598,
stands at the centre. It also contains the Picture
Gallery, with works by Aivazovskii, Shishkin,
Makovskii, Gué and Hungarian, Ruthenian,
Polish and Slovak artists.

VARAKSHA, Uzbekistan

470 **Fortifications** Pre-Islamic site.

VELIKII USTIUG, Russian Federation

471 **Museum of the Vologda Oblast'** Old
Russian icons.

VILNIUS (or Vilno) Lithuania

472 **Cathedral** 1777–1801, Gothic interior
retained when rebuilt in Classical style by L
Stuoka-Gutsevichius, all except St Casimir's
Chapel, 1636, by Tenkal.

473 **Church of St Anne** Beautiful late Gothic
style of the 16th C.

474 **Church of St Peter and St Paul** Rebuilt
1668–84 by Zaora; contains 2,000 pieces of
sculpture.

475 **Gedaminas' Castle** Mid 14th C, now in
ruins with one tower restored.

476 **Jesuit Academy** Late 16th C; earliest
example of the Renaissance style in Vilnius.

477 **Lithuanian State Museum of Art**
Lithuanian art, and work of Italian, German,
French and English artists.

478 **Palace** Built 1824–32 to a design by Stasov.

479 **Town Hall** (formerly the Fine Arts
Museum) 1783, a sober Doric building by
Stuoka-Gutsevichius.

VLADIMIR, Russian Federation

480 **Assembly of the Nobility** 1826, Classical
Russian style, influenced by past traditions.

481 **Cathedral of the Dormition** 12th C.
Originally square, with a single dome, it was
later enlarged, and arched openings made in the
original walls; there are now five domes. Stone
carving on the outside, fragments of 12th C
frescoes, and some outstanding frescoes of 1408
by Rublev and Chernyi. Baroque carved icon
screen.

482 **Cathedral of St Dimitrii** 1194–97, simple,
square building with one cupola, but unusual
because of the riot of carved decoration on the
outer walls, of various styles and motifs religious, pagan and secular. Some were replaced in
the 19th C. Inside, fragments of 12th C frescoes.

483 **Church of the Dormition** 1724.

484 **Church of the Dormition of the Virgin**
1649, unusual use of bricks.

485 **Golden Gate** 1164, rounded bastions and
gate chapel 18th C. The only remaining monument of 12th C Russian military arhitecture.

486 **Kniaginin Convent** (of the Princess)
Cathedral of the Dormition, original design of
1200 has disappeared. Notable late 17th C
frescoes.

487 **Monastery of the Nativity** Founded 12th
C, most of the surviving buildings date from the
18th C. Principal church reconstructed 19th C.

488 **Vladimir-Suzdal' Museum of History
and Art** Icons and other ecclesiastical treasures.

VOLGOGRAD (formerly Tsaritsyn, then
Stalingrad) Russian Federation

489 **Monument to the war heroes** Includes
various monumental sculptures, completed in
1967.

VOLOKOLAMSK, Russian Federation

490 **Monastery** Mainly 17th C.

VORONEZH, Russian Federation

491 **Museum of Fine Art** Russian and Western
painting, mainly from the 17th and 18th C.

492 **Potemkin Palace** 1760, Baroque.

493 **St Nicholas' Church** 18th C.

YALTA see IALTA

ZAGORSK, Russian Federation

494 **Monastery of the Trinity and St Sergii**
Founded mid 14th C. Fine Baroque belfry 1741–
67, by Rastrelli, 290 feet high. Cathedral of the
Assumption 1585, built in traditional style with
five enormous cupolas; inside are colourful
frescoes, and a sumptuous 17th C icon screen.
Church of the Holy Spirit 1554; built by craftsmen from Pskov. Cathedral of the Trinity 1422,
rich icon screen with its original priceless icons.
Fortifications 1540–50. Refectory Church 1469,
reconstructed 1686–92 in Baroque with a
multicoloured exterior. Large, bright interior
with frescoes and icons.

495 **Museum of History and Art** Religious
art, ecclesiastical robes and utensils. Also artisan
and peasant crafts, especially toys.

ZVARNOTS, Armenia

496 **Church of St Gregory** 641–661; its ruins
show circular groundplan, with cruciform
interior; the second and third storeys are
supported on pillars. Reconstruction at the local
museum.

ZVENIGOROD, Russian Federation

497 **Church of the Dormition** 1400, simple in
style, contains some fine old frescoes.

498 **Savvino-Storozhevsk Monastery** Includes the Church of the Nativity 1405, with
frescoes by the school of Rublev. Several 17th C
buildings: refectory with the Church of the
Transfiguration, bell tower and palaces of the
tsar and the tsarina.

Index

The numbers in Roman type refer to text and captions, the heavy type to illustrations, the italics to the Museums and Monuments index.

ACKNOWLEDGEMENTS

Numbers in heavy type refer to colour illustrations.

Photographs were provided by the following:

Artia, Prague (Karl Neubert) **half title, 55, 56, 57, 58,** 62, 70, **75,** 111, **112, 114, 123,** 126, **149, 150, 199, 200, 206, 207, 208, 217, 218, 219, 220, 221, 234, 236, 239, 248**; J. Blankoff, Brussels 59, 66, 77, 78, 79, 86, 130; Aurel Bongers, Recklinghausen **5, 14**; J. Bottin, Paris 136; E. Boudot-Lamotte, Paris **contents page,** 1, **4, 35,** 48, **49,** 88, 90, **143,** 154, 162, 163, 178, 194, **198,** 238, **243, 245**; British Museum, London 6; Camera Press, London 38, 104, 121, 124, 125; Cercle d'Art, Paris **32, 33, 44**; Courtauld Institute, London 119; Gerald Cubitt, South Africa 21, 23, **118**; Deutsche Fotothek, Dresden **142**; John Deverill, London **43**; Werner Forman, Prague 2, 7, 8; N. Gabo 229; Françoise Guerard, Paris **53, 74**; Sergei Hackel, Sussex 60, 85; Hamlyn Group Photo Library 182, 225; Hermitage Museum, Leningrad 3, 9, 10, 14–15, 17, 24, 25, 39; Milos Hrbas, Prague 26, 27, 37; John Innes **50**; Colin Jones, London 13, **146, 158, 159, 170,** 214; Victor Kennett, London **155, 156, 157, 160,** 165, **167, 168, 169, 172, 173, 174,** 180, 181, 186, 188, 195, **196, 197, 247**; Eric Lessing, Magnum Photos **201**; Louvre, Paris **94, 108, 128, 141, 183, 184, 246**; Bildarchiv Foto Marburg 38, 67; John Massey-Stewart, London 22, **36, 41, 42,** 122; Museum of Architecture, Moscow 82, 100, 105, 106, 213, 231; Novosti Press Agency, London 18, 40, 45, 46, 61, **64, 65,** 87, 101, 102, 109, **110, 115, 129,** 147, 151, 152, 153, 164, 176, 177, 179, 203, 209, **216,** 223, 230, **238**; Popperfoto, London **117**; Propylaen Verlag, Berlin 20; Pushkin Museum, Leningrad **242**; Realités, Paris **11, 12, 15**; John Sherman, London **171, 175**; Society for Cultural Relations with the USSR, London 6, 103, 107, 120, **127,** 132, 133, 134, 135, 187, 189, 190, 192, 193, 204, 205; John Stuart, London 68, 91, 92, **113, 116**; Fotochronika Tass **frontispiece, 16, 19, 28, 29, 30, 31, 34,** 47, **51,** 52, **54, 73, 93, 96, 98, 137, 138, 139, 140, 161, 185,** 191, **215, 222, 235, 237, 240, 241**; Tret'iakov Gallery, Moscow 202, 210, 211, 212, 226, 227; Unesco, Paris **63, 71, 72, 76, 95, 97, 244**; Weidenfeld & Nicolson, London 228.